S0-AHD-973

CARL A. RUDISILL LIBRARY
LENOIR-RHYNE COLLEGE

Persuasion and Influence in American Life

Gary C. Woodward
Trenton State College

Robert E. Denton, Jr.
Virginia Polytechnic Institute and State University

CARL A. RUDISILL LIBRARY
LENOIR-RHYNE COLLEGE

WAVELAND
PRESS, INC.
Prospect Heights, Illinois

For information about this book, write or call:

Waveland Press, Inc.
P.O. Box 400
Prospect Heights, Illinois 60070
(708) 634-0081

HM
258
.W66
1988
150430
Dr.1990

Copyright © 1988 by Waveland Press, Inc.

ISBN 0-88133-319-0

All rights reserved. No part of this book may be reproduced, stored in
a retrieval system, or transmitted in any form or by any means without
permission in writing from the publisher.

Printed in the United States of America

7   6   5   4   3

We dedicate this book to:

Allen and Nellie Woodward, who have always understood how to mix persuasion with compassion

and

To the memory of Robert Denton's grandparents, Margie and Bobbie Denton and Walter and Lillie Medlin, who were always grandteachers, grandsupporters, and grandpeople.

Table of Contents

Part 1   Origins of Persuasive Practice

2 The Advocate in an Open Society   25

3 The Advocate and the Manipulation of Symbols   49

Part 2   **Four Perspectives on the
                                     Nature of Persuasion**

4 Social Bases of Persuasion 69

5 Persuasion and Reasoning 99

6 The Psychology of Persuasion 129

7 Power, Credibility, and Authority   147

Part 3   Persuasion Industries

---

8 Advertising as Persuasion   187

9 Political Persuasion 215

Part 4   Practical Applications

10 Public and Mass Persuasion 251

11 The Construction and Presentation of Persuasive Messages 269

12 Interpersonal Persuasion 307

Acknowledgements

The authors would like to express special thanks to Charles Stewart and Carol Rowe for helping us find ways to say what we wanted to say and for encouraging us to communicate our thoughts with clarity. Gary Woodward would also like to thank Norman Heap and Harold Hogstrom for reading portions of the manuscript, and Jack McCullough for providing a schedule that left time for writing. Doris Shirk and Linda Strong helped photocopy chapter drafts as they evolved, and Dawn Biondo provided valuable feedback on chapters and exercises. The Trenton State College Faculty Research Committee also provided funds for xeroxing, and students in Dr. Woodward's Theories in Persuasion course demonstrated considerable patience in providing a forum for some of the ideas in this book. Robert Denton would like to thank his colleagues at Northern Illinois University for their continued support and motivation, and he thanks his students who have made the persuasion class a challenge and a joy. Dr. Denton is also indebted to his wife and sons who share in his every endeavor.

Preface

In his recent memoirs the accomplished author and economist, John Kenneth Galbraith, notes that the safest formula for putting together a textbook is to repeat the orthodoxies that have appeared in other texts. "The wisest course for the textbook writer is to say faithfully what has been said before with, as embellishment, some minor notes of novelty which the publisher can emphasize in his advertising."[1] Happily, Galbraith didn't follow this formula and instead produced a series of innovative studies on American economic life. His texts challenged his Harvard undergraduates, but they also changed the way thousands more viewed the old ideas of capitalism and socialism. This textbook on persuasion also rejects formulas, but for a more elementary reason. Even more than economics, persuasion is not a discipline unto itself. It is a hybrid study based on knowledge from many different fields. Because there are so many practical applications for persuasion in everyday life, it is unlikely that any two texts would offer the same mix of theories, concepts and ideas. To ask how persuasion works within human beings is to deal with an enormous diversity of activities: from selling products to religious conversion, from political discussion to private conversation between friends. The multitude of experts who have explored the vast persuasion terrain is impressive. Educators, managers, politicians, journalists, social scientists, and philosophers represent only a sampling of professional groups for whom persuading or being the objects of persuasion is all part of a day's work. The quantity of experts confronting so diverse a landscape precludes a simplistic theory. The wealth of information about the subject of persuasion offers tremendous opportunities to learn.

[1]*A Life In Our Times* (New York: Ballantine, 1981), 514.

Thus, this is only partially a "textbook." Our conclusions and observations are not stated in the textbook equivalent of carved marble tablets; we encourage you to consider a broad mixture of ideas and theories. The "open ended" nature of our subject is reflected in the way we have written this book. We have purposefully omitted most technical jargon, and in some sections we have raised as many questions as we have answered. In other places, we have deliberately offered competing explanations of how a particular type of persuasion works. Our goal is to encourage you to draw some of your own conclusions while you consider those that have already been put forth. Our pluralistic approach is reflected in the fact that this book includes theories, case studies, and applications. At times we urge you to be a shrewd analyst of the persuasion of others by using theories and case studies as tools of explanation; at other times we describe concrete skills that you can use to influence others. Our goal was not to define isolated concepts but rather to inspire a commitment to consider the intricate nature of persuasion.

1

Persuasion and Influence An Introduction

 OVERVIEW

To insist upon the importance of language may seem like battering at an open door. But there are times when it is necessary not to flinch from the obvious. In the society to which we belong, talking and listening, reading and writing, are so constantly present that familiarity blunts perception of the extraordinary character of such activities.[1]

The study of persuasion is intrinsically fascinating as well as truly essential. The process of influencing others has been perhaps the most studied and analyzed of all social activities. How do we change beliefs? What makes us susceptible to or immune from constant attempts to persuade us to accept ideas, products, and people? How do demagogues manipulate people to deny their beliefs and to accept an action that imposes personal hardship or violates their self interest? People have been asking such questions since the infancy of democratic government in ancient Greece. The study of the ebb and flow of influence reveals fundamental characteristics about human nature.

Communication is the lifeline of our existence. It is a medium unique to humans; it permits us to express the vital, invisible qualities of who we are and what we believe. In contrast to the rest of the living world, we make sense of our "place" by the way we define it and the ways others define us. However bravely the child repeats the age-old aphorism, "Sticks and stones may break my bones, but words can never hurt me," the reverse is closer to the truth. Words and symbols do hurt. We use them against our enemies and for our friends. We give language the awesome responsibility of carrying our judgments to others. Words convey praise, blame, guilt, and joy. Persuading others to see a corner of our world as we see it is a basic human need. The simple symbol of "F" on a student's final exam can inflict severe pain. We are rarely indifferent to the efforts of others to transform what we think and believe; we are never indifferent to our efforts to have others share our agenda of interests, concerns, and values. Persuasion is the process that constantly negotiates this give and take.

Persuasion occurs in contexts as diverse as simple exchanges of opinions with friends to elaborate, extended debates which may span several years. Efforts to manipulate attitudes may range from an audience of one or two persons to vast audiences interconnected by the mass media. A speaker from the Campaign for Nuclear Disarmament may try to win support from a small handful of listeners. The American Cancer Society, by contrast, may reach 40 million television viewers with one anti-smoking ad broadcast during a prime-time television show. Persuasion may originate within formal groups such as the National Organization for Women or the American Civil Liberties Union, or it may start with the efforts of individuals. The lonely advocate of an unpopular cause, a popular leader in politics and government, and a charismatic speaker from the world of business or religion all try to influence their audiences. Persuaders may be as well-financed as the Mobil Corporation or I.B.M., or as resource-poor as a small band of home-owners fighting the decisions of a local zoning board. The number of human contacts that require skillful persuasion is nearly endless. As citizens in an open society, we should not ignore the responsibility for organizing or participating in public persuasion. As individuals functioning in a web of personal relationships, we face the necessity of negotiating an enormous range of close relationships in the family, at work, and in groups. Life is filled with moments that call for persuasion, compromise, and agreement.

Influence and Attitudes: Four Introductory Cases

We begin our study of persuasion with an examination of four diverse persuasive circumstances.

Selling Beer

In 1982, the Miller Brewing Company faced a severe problem when its major product began to lose ground to Anheuser-Busch's Budweiser. Miller High Life was once the nation's second most popular beer. By 1984, it had fallen to third place. Anheuser-Busch moved into a controlling lead of the industry with a 35% share of the total market. Miller had slipped to a 20% share. If it failed to stem the falling sales of its major product, Miller would have to redefine itself as a smaller company—an unwelcome prospect for any enterprise. Miller's problems were compounded by a health-conscious America that was increasingly cautious about beer drinking. All brewers in the United States had to face the additional challenge of competing in an industry that was not expanding.[2]

Miller and its advertisers considered the problem to be public perception rather than product quality. Beer drinkers might argue over the relative merits of different brands, but most analysts within the brewing industry described Miller's problem in terms of image. Beer, like soap, exhibits little difference among the major brands. Advertising must sell more than the product's traits and merits; it must give buyers a reason to believe that the choice of a product speaks well for *the kind of person they are.* As one advertising executive noted, "People don't always drink the beer; they drink the advertising."[3]

In early 1985 the company committed 55 million dollars to change its image; the first step in the campaign was to replace its advertising agency with one of the biggest on Madison Avenue, J. Walter Thompson. Out went the old "Miller time" commercials which touted Miller beer as the reward for a hard-working day and in came new ads with the theme, "Made the American way." They were virtually hymns of praise for positive American values. "Typical" Americans were shown in representative American settings such as ballparks and friendly backyard barbecues. "Miller is one of the oldest breweries in America," noted J. Walter Thompson's Chairman, "and the man who founded it said a lot of things about quality, integrity, honesty, purity, and other things we see as part of the resurgence of American values. If we are correct, and we have a lot of research to back us up, there is a lot of confidence and pride in having those traditional characteristics..."[4] Beer is a way for the consumer to endorse feelings and values. "The man who drinks it," as the ad experts see it, "proclaims 'Here is my badge.'" Whether Miller's expensive ad campaign has been enough to rebuild loyalty in its product remains uncertain.

Advertising is a common and lucrative form of influence. Billions of dollars are spent on advertising each year in television, radio, newspapers, and magazines. It is high-stakes persuasion for merchandizers, even if most consumers treat it with far less urgency. Finding purchasers for America's wealth of goods and services is a never ending process. The advertising-based industries in the United States are the big consumer products companies, their advertising agencies, and the mass media that depend on the sale of space and time for their revenues. One thirty-second commercial on network prime-time television may cost five hundred thousand dollars. Such expenditures require that the most subtle aspects of ads (color, lighting, music, backgrounds) be carefully considered.

Although the financial stakes are staggering, the persuasive messages themselves may not be demanding, as the Miller campaign suggests. Advertising reflects us as we are. It usually does not try to shock us or to reshape our deepest values or basic beliefs. Advertising tries to affect our most superficial impulses: the decision to buy one brand over another. The cost of doing business in a massive consumer-oriented economy requires immense outlays of cash for corporate persuaders, but the final decisions we as consumers are asked to make are often of little personal consequence. The risks may be enormous for the producers, but the decisions are insignificant for consumers. Other forms of persuasion put greater demands on audiences and higher responsibilities on advocates.

Advocating a Dangerous Form of Religion

Persuasion affects our lives for good or ill. We rightly assume that most advocates have honorable intentions. When they do not and when their insensitivity is matched by their persuasive success, disaster may follow.

The remote South American nation of Guyana was the unlikely scene of an American tragedy in 1978. An American evangelist, driven by an intense sense of persecution, directed 912 followers to commit mass suicide. It as the final act of persuasion in what had been a long and increasingly desperate road for Jim Jones and his followers.

Jones was considered somewhat unorthodox in his California evangelist days but basically similar to other evangelists who mingled politics and religion. He was especially popular among the poor because his indignation toward "exploiters" and the rich struck a responsive chord. The mission he established attracted members through activities and services designed to make them feel special and different. Like Martin Luther King Jr., Jones was a powerful preacher. He used his pulpit to preach not only a religious doctrine but also a varied agenda which included social and political injustices. But where King persuaded, Jones manipulated. While the great civil-rights leader's goal was to foster peaceful change to end institutionalized segregation, Jones' goal was unfocused while he grew increasingly strident and isolated. He began to make every issue a personal one and every member a part of his own private crusade. He cultivated a following by cleverly mixing his gospel of social change with carefully orchestrated demonstrations of support. Members were required to give their money and personal allegiance to "The Father." King wanted the nation to live up to its expressed fundamental principles of fairness and justice, but Jones wanted his followers to substitute allegiance for thought. King's persuasion became an instrument for positive social change, and he never viewed himself as the reason for the movement that he led. In sharp contrast, Jim Jones became a Hitler, a man who thrived on a cult of personality.

With a number of People's Temples established in California, the ever-restless Jones decided to build an isolated town in the jungle of Guyana. He planned to take most of his devoted followers with him, using their willingness to go as a test of their religious faith. The remote village was to provide a new beginning free from the persecution he taught his followers to expect. "I am preparing a promised land for you in Jonestown," he said. "When you get there all of your tribulations will be over. There will be no need for discipline when you get away from the capitalistic society of America. There you will be able to love and be loved."[5]

According to one member of the People's Temple, Jones' "only source of pleasure was observing his follower's total devotion to him."[6] He became obsessed with his control over the inhabitants of the new village. Members were publicly beaten and humiliated. Bizarre marathon meetings were held in which he revealed his belief that he was the target of assassination plots. He began preaching with a gun at his side and erupting into tirades when a member tried to leave a meeting. These were ominous signs of his growing paranoia.

After hearing complaints from family members that relatives were being held against their wishes, California Congressman Leo Ryan decided to visit the Guyana village with several members of the press. His visit pushed Jones to a deadly state of rage. In poor health himself, he calmly planned the demise of his commune and everyone in it. After ordering the assassination of Ryan and several reporters, he persuaded and coaxed almost one thousand people to commit the ultimate act of self-destruction. Many willingly gave doses of a fruit drink laced with poison to themselves and to their children while others were murdered by Jones' bodyguards. A tape recorder that was left running preserved the bizarre final moments:

> So my opinion is that you be kind to children and be kind to seniors and take the potion like they used to take it in ancient Greece, and step over quietly, because we are not committing suicide. It's a revolutionary act. We can't go back, and they won't leave us alone. They're now going back to tell more lies, which means more congressmen. And there's no way, no way, we can survive.[7]

Jones' power to persuade his followers to commit suicide remains a partial mystery. The basic impulse to live should defeat even the most manipulative of persuaders, but we must not overlook the fact that the murder/suicide was only a last step in what had been an incremental process begun years earlier. From its start, the People's Temple had fostered the principle of personal obedience. Members of the church were more than followers of a set of religious beliefs. They were disciples of Jim Jones. Had he been a different person, they might have benefited from their identification with him because persuasion is both a social and rational process. The attraction to the idea of the People's Temple—a mission apart from society—became fatally tied to the magnetic personality of Jones. He had attracted supporters first to his ideas, then to his isolated mission, and finally to their deaths.

Jim Jones was the founder of the Jonestown settlement in
Guyana, headquarters for his controversial American religious sect.
Wide World Photos, Inc.

Persuasion and the Politics of Peace

Woodrow Wilson was one of America's most eloquent presidential orators. He built much of his long public career around his faith in the power of persuasion, but he overestimated even his considerable skills. His last attempt to shape public opinion left history with a fascinating case study of the clash between politics and principle.

Wilson reluctantly lead America into World War I against Germany in 1917. It was difficult to commit Americans to fight in a Europe that was splintered by age-old factions and disputes. The United States had been an island of peace preoccupied with its western expansion and new-found wealth; European quarrels seemed distant and petty. The 1915 attack and sinking of the liner *Lusitania* near the Irish coast pushed the Western Hemisphere closer to war. Nearly 1200 passengers perished, victims of new submarine technology and a willingness by the allies to mix civilians with military cargo. Eventually, German submarine attacks on other ships in the Atlantic forced Wilson to declare war.

World War I was a brutal and bitter conflict. The machine gun changed the technology of war, exposing long lines of soldiers to instant death on the desolate northern European plains. Army officers sent to the front to lead battalions of foot soldiers rarely returned alive. The possibility of an armistice began to emerge only after staggering losses developed on all sides. The world had never witnessed such concentrated fighting and killing; eight and one-half million soldiers and 28 million civilians were killed.

As early as 1918, Wilson began to grapple with the problem of finding a way to assure peace in Europe. The final form of the proposal was his "Fourteen Points" which contained a number of principles to be applied to a negotiated settlement. In a dramatic address before Congress, Wilson set out his plan that would save the world from future "force and selfish aggression." The principles included a call for no secret treaties, absolute freedom of the seas, the removal of Germans from Belgium and other countries, the removal of economic controls between nations, and evacuation of foreign troops from Russia. Wilson's highest goal was Point Fourteen: "a general association of nations must be formed under specific covenants for the purpose of affording natural guarantees of political independence and territorial integrity to great and small states alike."[8] His objective was to establish a world organization devoted to peace to be known as the League of Nations.

Germany was finally defeated, but the bitter fighting had exacted a heavy political cost. The German government soon accepted Wilson's Fourteen Points as a basis for an armistice, but the allies were reluctant to settle for anything less than enormous financial demands.

Britain and France did not want to see a prosperous neighbor re-emerge to their east. Leaders in both nations felt that the war had forced them to sacrifice the lives of the best and brightest of an entire generation. For his part, Wilson believed—probably naively—that a non-punitive American solution could be imposed on the European political landscape, but the rivalries were too deep and lasting.

Wilson faced two enormous dilemmas, both rooted in his need to change attitudes. One problem was how to win over the allies to accept a peace that did not further humiliate the defeated Germany. The other was how to get the American Senate to ratify the idea of a world organization dedicated to peace. In spite of his best efforts, Wilson failed on both counts. The allies forced Germany to pay a heavy price economically and geographically, and Wilson accepted far less than the original ideals embodied in the Fourteen Points. The ultimate irony, however, is that the resulting Treaty of Versailles probably assured a

A younger Woodrow Wilson accepting the Democratic Party's nomination for the Presidency, September 1916.

Arthur S. Link, ed., *The Papers of Woodrow Wilson, Volume 38: 1916.* Copyright © 1982 by Princeton University Press. Reprinted with permission of Princeton University Press.

future war. Germany's resentment made it ripe for a dangerous form of nationalism to develop under Adolph Hitler's Nazi Party.

Wilson's greatest political defeat was his failure to secure Senate ratification of the treaty establishing the League of Nations. He could not convince two thirds of the Senate to accept his plan and was unwilling to compromise and accept an amended proposal which would satisfy the opposition. Instead, he resorted to a classic presidential ploy. He was confident that he could override his opponents by a direct appeal to the American public. Wilson was sure he could persuade the American people that the League was essential and thereby force the Senate to ratify the proposal.

On September 3, 1919 he left Washington on a train that would take him eight-thousand miles in 22 days and permit him to deliver countless speeches in favor of the League. Radio was still too new to substitute for such an exhausting schedule. The grueling pace of the trip and Wilson's reluctance to work with the Senate leadership doomed him. After an impassioned speech in Colorado, he suffered a stroke and returned to Washington partially paralyzed and sensing defeat.[9]

His enemies in the senate—William Borah, Henry Cabot Lodge, and others—remained unmoved by pleas for American participation in the League of Nations. They argued that there could be no participation without compromise. The once energetic Wilson was felled by the stroke and by tenacious insistence on his vision which would allow no compromise. It was a sad end to a supremely proud man.

America did not join the League, and a true world organization never developed from the ruinous battles and treaties of World War One. The divisions that had created war remained, and Germany was forced against Wilson's wishes to accept harsh terms of peace. A line from one of Wilson's last speeches in favor of the League proved prophetic:

> I can predict with absolute certainty that within another generation there will be another world war if the nations of the world do not concert the method by which to prevent it [and in that struggle] not a few hundred thousand fine men from America will have to die, but as many millions as are necessary to accomplish the final freedom of the world.[10]

Persuasion in Everyday Life

The cases we have reviewed involve organizations or powerful institutions: the Presidency, a church, large advertising agencies and broadcasters. Undoubtedly, big organizations have the resources to affect large numbers of people with the same message; however, no overview of the process of persuasion would be complete without noting that everyday life is filled with attempts at influence. Sociologist Erving Goffman has a remarkable eye for locating influence in the daily actions of ordinary life. He notes "that when an individual appears before others he will have many motives for trying to control the impression they receive of the situation."[11] In routine exchanges with others, we want to be liked and to have our ideas accepted. We want others to show a regard for our feelings and for the values which serve as the anchors for our actions. As Goffman reminds us, children, teachers, parents, close friends, employees, employers, spouses, lovers, and co-workers all have strategies for projecting their interests to those with whom they come in contact. Since we perform many of these roles simultaneously, we are constantly faced with the need to make our actions and attitudes acceptable to others. In words, gestures, and small signs, we leave a trail of cues that are meant to guide the responses of our audiences. No moment in the routine events of the day is too small to be devoid of persuasion. Many instances of "impression management" collected by Goffman have become classic accounts of what could be called "micro-persuasion." His reference to George Orwell's account of the routine strategies of restaurant waiters is a favorite:

> It is an instructive sight to see a waiter going into a hotel dining-room. As he passes the door a sudden change comes over him. The set of his shoulders alters; all the dirt and hurry and irritation have dropped off in an instant. He glides over the carpet, with a solemn priest-like air. I remember our assistant maitre d'hotel, a fiery Italian, pausing at the dining room door to address his apprentice who had broken a bottle of wine.... "Tu me fais—Do you call yourself a waiter, you young bastard? You a waiter! You're not fit to scrub floors in the brothel your mother came from..."
>
> .   .   .   .
>
> Then he entered the dining-room and sailed across it dish in hand, graceful as a swan. Ten seconds later he was bowing reverently to a customer. And you could not help thinking, as you saw him bow and smile, with that benign smile of the trained waiter, that the customer was put to shame by having such an aristocrat to serve him.[12]

Life is full of such moments. Any novel or film could be studied for all the small but significant cues that are performed to elicit acceptance or approval. We "read" and perform such acts so routinely that we tend to forget how essential they are in oiling the machinery of everyday interaction. Consider, for example, how the following conventional situations invite the use of various persuasive strategies:

> A close friend and roommate decides to go home after her last Friday class and casually announces to friends over lunch that she will hitchhike the 45 mile stretch of lonely Interstate highway to reach her parents' house.
>
> A driver has been pulled over by a police officer for going a few miles over the posted speedlimit while passing a slow truck.

A friend has been in a deep depression for days. You would like the friend to see a counselor, but you don't want to "interfere".

You are broke. The prospect of eating oatmeal for dinner until the next paycheck arrives is too much to bear, but you do have some affluent friends...

You are an officer in a campus organization which needs new members, and you know where good prospective candidates are. It is just a matter of getting them to join.

A job interview is scheduled for the morning, and it could lead to a good career with an important company. The problem is how to make the "right" impression on the interviewer.

As a part-time salesperson, paid on commission, every sale increases the amount of your monthly paycheck. You attempt to locate a method for detecting serious buyers from more casual and time-consuming "browsers."

We could suggest an endless list of similar settings, some involving only brief segments of a busy day and others which are more structured and sustained. All represent instances that illustrate how the normal conversations of daily life require attempts to influence others. Moreover, in contrast to stereotypes of persuasion as a selfish act, attempts at influence are often generated by a selfless concern for the welfare of others.

What These Cases Show

We chose the cases in the first part of this chapter for their diversity. Even so, they share features that give recognizable form to attempts to change attitudes. All remind us that persuasion is a symbolic act that inevitably focuses on advocates as well as messages. In persuasion, *who* is communicating matters a great deal. Messages do not stand alone; consumers weigh both the quality of advocates as well as messages. Wilson felt that his presidential prestige could command a following sufficient to produce a constructive peace. With terrible efficiency, Jim Jones used his popularity to attract followers for his increasingly demented ideas.

These examples also remind us that the process of attempting to change attitudes is neither inherently good nor bad. Each case must be considered on its own merits. Miller's advertising campaign may leave us indifferent (unless we judge drinking to be morally wrong). The self-centered evangelism of Jim Jones surely repels us. Wilson's failed attempts reveal what *might* have been: *if* only he had been more flexible, *if* the Senate had been more supportive, *if* the allies had not given Germany justifications for revenge. Persuasion may spring from selfish motivations or from altruistic ones. We may gain money or prestige from our abilities to influence others, or—at the other extreme—we may act out of a genuine regard for the welfare of those we seek to influence. Although we may harshly judge much persuasion as "propaganda" or "manipulation," we could cite countless instances from personal experience where persuasion has served as a "therapeutic" form of communication, helping rather than exploiting.

Taken together, these cases also serve as a reminder of how difficult persuasion is. Advertising agencies consider the rebuilding of a product's reputation to be the toughest form of promotion. Huge advertising budgets may not be enough to return a brand name to its former popularity. The situation Woodrow Wilson faced was far more complex than Miller's, and the hindsight of history suggests that he hoped to do too much. He wanted to activate world opinion around his Fourteen Points, but even the finely tuned messages of an expert orator were no match for deep-seated attitudes and opinions. Ironically, the tragedy of Jonestown also points to the difficulty of changing attitudes. One reason the event stands out is *because* we find it difficult to believe that one person could engineer and manipulate so effective a form of persuasion. We assume that no amount of influence could create acceptance of mass suicide.

Finally, the first three cases should not distract us from the fact that persuasion is as much personal as it is institutional. We often dwell on dramatic, headline-making attempts because the publicized instances serve as obvious and interesting illustrations. Ultimately, the persuasive options that presidents, advertisers, and social activists face are very similar to the options the rest of us also face. Persuasion that organizations produce is not very different in form from the day to day communication we have with friends, co-workers, and family. Indeed, it is within the context of our own immediate contacts that the most significant attitudes are shaped. As Zimbardo, Ebbesen, and Maslach have noted,

> [I]t is impossible to overestimate the extent to which you are influenced daily to be the kind of person other people want you to be. "Tastes" in food, dress, art, music, friends, hobbies, and other things are acquired through subtle interpersonal influence processes.... The language you speak, your dialect, pronunciation, hand gestures, body semantics, and displays of affection or temper are all the products of how people communicated in your family, neighborhood, and cultural subgroup.[13]

Persuasion as a Subject for Study

The Love-Hate Relationship

The variety of cases we have cited—political, religious, commercial, and "therapeutic"—remind us that the study of persuasion attracts as well as repels. On the one hand, few questions are more intriguing than "What makes people change their minds or alter the ways they act?" We have a natural curiosity about the ways we manipulate and influence others and how others do the same to us. But through the ages, the subject has often exposed the darker side of human nature. Persuasion may succeed for all of the wrong reasons—as in the case of Jim Jones. It is an unpleasant fact that we sometimes succumb to efforts to exploit our fears and vanities. The victims of unethical persuasion often look like fools: too ready to agree and too willing to suspend critical judgment. Yet, as we will explore in the next chapter, a society that confronts the realities of persuasive practice provides its citizens with a valuable service. Analyzing the forms of influence which are common to modern life is the first step in acquiring an effective form of self-defense. Knowing when a good case has been made is as valuable as knowing when it has not. And knowing how to shape events is a critical step in gaining control over our lives. The Greek philosopher Aristotle was correct when he wrote:

> [I]t is absurd to hold a man ought to be ashamed of being unable to defend himself with his limbs, but not of being unable to defend himself with speech and reason, when the use of rational speech is more distinctive of a human being than the use of his limbs. And if it be objected that one who uses such power of speech unjustly might do great harm, *that* is the charge which may be made against the things that are most useful, as strength, health, wealth...[14]

Persuasion confers power, and by putting our knowledge of it to work, we force others to share this power. Knowledge of persuasive practice provides us with the opportunity to leave our imprint on events, both big and small. Indeed, granting the right to influence others may be the highest freedom a nation can allow its citizens.

The State of Our Knowledge

Persuasion is one of the oldest topics studied and taught in western civilization. Aristotle was among the first great teachers of the subject; he believed that advocacy should be a central concern in democratic societies. He wrote one of the earliest texts devoted exclusively to persuasion. *The Rhetoric* discusses the nature of attitudes, audiences, psychological appeals, and logical fallacies; it represents one of the initial attempts to outline the psychology of audiences. For example,

Aristotle noted that all messages should be constructed with the "character" of an audience in mind—their common traits and patterns of thought. To affect an audience of "young men," for instance, the persuader must understand their collective psychology, including some of the following traits:

> While they love honor, they love victory still more; for youth is eager for superiority over others, and victory is one form of this. They love both more than they love money, which indeed they love very little, not having yet learnt what it means to be without it.... They look at the good side rather than the bad, not having yet witnessed many instances of wickedness. They trust others readily, because they have not yet often been cheated.[15]

Aristotle wrote his text over 300 years before the birth of Christ. And yet, despite all of the effort that we have devoted to the subject over the last 2000 years, we still know little about the exact processes that govern attempts to influence others. We have theories but no "laws" of human persuasion. We can speculate that one type of appeal may affect particular audiences under specific circumstances, but we are far from a "science" that allows predictions with a high degree of certainty. Because human behavior is infinitely complex and varied, individuals do not react in consistent and predictable ways. Our knowledge of persuasion allows us only to note *tendencies* that may be observed in larger numbers. For example, we cannot predict whether a specific anti-smoking appeal will work on a particular individual, but we can estimate the appeal's probable effects on a national audience.

The study of persuasion requires us to look for causes and effects: to determine what *changes* people and to measure the extent of these changes. While the biologist can study a specimen of diseased tissue to know precisely what caused an infection, the student of persuasion deals with less quantifiable knowledge. The physical world may reveal its secrets willingly, but the mysteries of human thought are far more difficult to explore. We are at a stage where we know what questions to ask, but we are uncertain how to discover the answers. Even so, virtually all of the social sciences and professions have attempted to deal with how communication and persuasion affect their fields. Teachers talk about "behavior modification"; schools of business offer courses in "marketing" or selling; political scientists study campaigns; sociologists assess the effects of friendship and group membership; psychologists study the processes that accompany changes in attitude and behavior; mass media analysts track the ebb and flow of public opinion on an infinite variety of issues; and many of us participate in self-help groups designed to change aspects of our lives. Persuasion touches every part of our world, whether we seek money, support, friendship, conversion, or power.

Persuasion as a Form of Communication

We talk or write in order to accomplish something, even if our objective is not always fully conscious. It is useful, therefore, to classify forms of human interaction that imply different intentions.

Three "Pure" Types of Communication

A broad but useful distinction can be made among three types of communication: pure information-giving, pure expression, and pure persuasion. Although most messages contain elements of all three, their differences are revealing.

Information-giving involves the relating of facts, knowledge, or directions where the interest is primarily in the receiver's *understanding*. We want to be sure the receiver *heard* and comprehended the data that we cited. A stranger giving directions to a visitor from out of town, the Directory Assistance operator providing a phone number, and a Weather Service report are examples of pure information-giving. Communicators of pure information may not be interested in how we respond, beyond having us comprehend the message. From their stantpoint, we are free to accept or reject what they say.

Pure expression is characterized by a desire to speak one's mind rather than to influence others to agree or to disagree, to act or not to act. We may want to unload our anger, joy, anxieties, or fears merely for the sake of personal release. Cheering on the home team is an expressive statement as is denouncing the doctor in "General Hospital" who uses any pretext to cheat on his faithful wife. We feel better for having given our inward feelings some tangible outward form. Much of our talk serves this objective. What we say is not intended to elicit a reaction from someone else; instead, it has no purpose except to express a rapid succession of feelings.

Pure persuasion is different and more complex than information-giving and expression. It involves a new dimension: a concern with *how* a message affects someone else. The message is calculated to be believed, not merely understood. If a listener fails to adopt the view carried in a persuasive message, the persuader will feel that the attempt has been unsuccessful. If a listener says, "I understand what you are saying, but I do not accept it," the information-giver who has no personal stake in acceptance or rejection of a message may be satisfied. The persuader, however, wants a commitment. He or she seeks *acceptance* of the point of view expressed in the message, and perhaps personal acceptance as well.

How These Forms Merge

In reality these forms often overlap. For example, statistics on automobile seat belt use indicate that wearing belts saves lives. These numbers are—in a simple sense—pieces of information. However, we can imagine a persuader using them with the intention of gaining support for a state law requiring the wearing of seat belts. If a listener responds by saying that he understands the statistics, the persuader might ask impatiently, "Yes, but do you accept my conclusion?" Advocates want commitment as well as understanding. We often hear the expression, "Here are the facts, take them or leave them" from teachers, journalists, and others. That expression usually conceals the hope that we will not only "take" them, but will accept the larger visions of the world that they imply. A good deal of persuasion occurs under the pretext of information-giving. Most of us are not as indifferent as we may seem to how others accept our statements. As we will note in Chapter 4, all of us are motivated to find a place within the enormous maze of contacts that make up our lives. We want to be liked, so we seek approval for our feelings and frustrations. The urge to have others identify with our attitudes and values is very strong.

Does this mean that all communication is persuasive? Have the authors fallen into the trap of describing their subject as the inevitable center of the universe? To both questions we give a qualified "no."

Communication and persuasion are not interchangable terms. Not all communicators have as their goal the listener's acceptance of the legitimacy and importance of their messages. Even so, persuasion is a far more common process than may at first be evident. We frequently *do* want our messages to change the way others think, act and feel. It may be the exception rather than the rule when a communicator feels genuine indifference about how a message affects us. Even in the seemingly light-hearted world of prime-time television, we may examine the stated intention of producing pure entertainment and discover a deeper persuasive intent. We probably cannot enjoy a televised fantasy without also accepting some of the basic assumptions built into plots and characters. Two common underlying promises are that doctors are healers first and businessmen second and that police uphold rather than manipulate the law.

Persuasion Defined

Most definitions of persuasion are similar, although some emphasize the processes involved in wielding influence more than others. Erwin Bettinghaus begins his study of the subject by noting that a persuasive situation involves "a conscious attempt by one individual to change the attitudes, beliefs, or the behavior of another individual or group of individuals through the transmission of some message."[16] In another useful text Herbert Simons describes persuasion as "human communication designed to influence others by modifying their beliefs, values, or attitudes."[17] We would amend Simons' definition to include the important qualifier offered by Bettinghaus, that persuasion may affect *behavior* as well as attitudes and beliefs. A message may affect a person's feelings, behaviors, or both. We may induce someone to *act* differently (for example, to taste what seems like an awful kind of food), but not fundamentally affect the way they *feel.* Conversely, persuasion may create *internal changes* that are not seen in the way a person *acts.* Thus, internal attitudes and external acts are both important. They are different but equally valid outcomes of persuasive attempts. In addition, both definitions of persuasion should be expanded to include communication that has the effect of *maintaining* attitudes and actions rather than *changing* them. There can be little doubt that persuasion is never more apparent than when a transformation becomes apparent within an individual. However, an exclusive emphasis on change overlooks the important role communication performs in preventing the erosion of support. As most advertisers know, the most effective persuasive strategies are essentially defensive. It is easier to reassure a listener's faith in what is already accepted than to urge change to something new. There is a natural desire within individuals and groups to seek out order and stability rather than to change. An exclusive emphasis on persuasion as an offensive tool (i.e. against "old" attitudes) ignores the elaborate efforts of many persuaders to keep things as they are: to keep the lid on a simmering pot rather than encouraging it to boil over. For instance, many people who attend political rallies at election time *already believe* in the candidacy of the speakers; the rallies heighten positive feelings or make them less dormant and may guarantee continuity by providing reasons against changing attitudes. Like the advertisements we have heard thousands of times for McDonald's or Wendy's or Chevrolet, persuasion may keep feelings stable. The goal may be to hold a company's share of the market or to maintain the enthusiasm of political party members. The fact that positive feelings already exist does not relieve the persuader of the necessity to maintain them.

Thus, considering persuasion in its various phases, we define it as

1. the process of preparing and delivering
2. messages (through verbal and non-verbal symbols)
3. to individuals or groups
4. in order to alter, strengthen, or maintain
5. attitudes, beliefs, values or behaviors.

Our definition includes a range of desired outcomes from reinforcing or changing attitudes to affecting the ways people *think* as well as *act*. We also note that persuasion is directed to both individuals and groups. A single advocate, such as a Jim Jones or Adolph Hitler, can influence large numbers of people at one time. Although we often think of persuasion in terms of vast audiences, changes in the way we think and act must ultimately be understood in terms of the individual.

Finally, our definition places emphasis on the processes of planning as well as analyzing persuasive attempts. We think a complete understanding of persuasion necessarily includes a consideration of the art and technique of influence. In order to understand how the processes of influence work, it is necessary to apply theories of persuasion to practical problems. While it may be possible to appreciate music without being a musician, we doubt if it is possible to appreciate persuasion fully without actually understanding the use of practical strategies. Obviously, the study of this complex topic cannot be easy. It requires mental gymnastics to tackle a subject so varied and elusive as human thought.

Plan of the Book

This text is divided into twelve chapters within four broad sections. Part I addresses how persuasion serves democracy, and how human symbols are given shared meanings. Part II discusses four traditional approaches to the process of influence: sociological, philosophical, psychological, and character-centered. Part III is an examination of the many varieties of political and commercial persuasion that engulf us daily. Two chapters describe the most recognized applications of persuasion in modern life: advertising and politics. Part IV provides practical guidelines for presenting a speech, preparing an extended persuasive campaign, or considering the tactics of one-to-one persuasion. These final three chapters build on the theories and information offered in earlier parts of the book.

Each chapter concludes with questions for self-study which allow readers to determine if the ideas and concepts contained in the chapters have been understood. Intermixed with the questions are suggestions for putting ideas and strategies to work on specific projects. The projects may be adapted to the reader's needs and to course-related assignments. Each section of the book ends with a list of additional resources for readers wishing to explore more extensively the topics that have been discussed.

Notes

[1]Max Black, *The Labyrinth of Language* (New York: Mentor, 1969), 12.

[2]This case study is developed from Leslie Wayne, "How a Popular Beer Fell Out of Favor," *The New York Times*, 3 March 1985, F17. See also Scott Hume, "Beer Ads: Hurray for the Red, White, and Brew," *Advertising Age*, 11 February 1985, 84.

[3]Quoted in Wayne, F17.

[4]Quoted in Wayne, F17.

[5]Jones quoted in Jeannie Mills, *Six Years With God* (New York: A and W Publishers, 1979), 317.

[6]Mills, 319.

[7]Jones quoted in James Reston Jr., *Our Father Who Art in Hell* (New York: Times Books, 1981), 324.

[8]Wilson, "Address to Congress," 8 January 1918, in *The Politics of Woodrow Wilson*, ed. August Heckscher (New York: Harper, 1956), 306.

[9]Samuel and Dorothy Rosenman, *Presidential Style: Some Giants and a Pygmy in the White House* (New York: Harper and Row, 1976), 256-259.

[10]Wilson quoted in Rosenman and Rosenman, 258.

[11]Erving Goffman, *The Presentation of Self in Everyday Life* (New York: Anchor, 1959), 15.

[12]Quoted in Goffman, 121-122.

[13]Philip G. Zimbardo, Ebbe B. Ebbesen and Christina Maslach, *Influencing Attitudes and Changing Behavior*, Second Edition (Boston: Addison-Wesley, 1979), 1.

[14]Aristotle, *The Rhetoric*, trans. by W.R. Roberts in *The Basic Works of Aristotle*, ed. Richard McKeon (New York: Random House, 1941), 1328.

[15]Aristotle, *The Rhetoric*, in *Basic Works*, 1404.

[16]Erwin B. Bettinghaus, *Persuasive Communication*, Second Edition (New York: Holt, Rinehart, and Winston, 1973), 10.

[17]Herbert W. Simons, *Persuasion: Understanding and Practice* (Boston: Addison-Wesley, 1976), 21.

Questions and Projects for Further Study

1. As this chapter indicates, persuasion comes to us through many channels: advertising, face to face encounters, and news reports about issues and advocates. Try to audit your own exposure to these sources of persuasion in a single day. Keep a written log recording the number and types of advertisements you hear or see in newspapers, magazines, and broadcasts. Keep a record of the news and information sources you see and hear which contain bits and pieces of persuasive messages (for example, a film clip in a newscast in which a doctor warns viewers about the dangers of some product or activity). Note how frequently conversations with others contain requests for your agreement, time, or money.

2. Advertising such as that undertaken by the Miller Brewing Company may work in two basic ways. The *themes* of a new advertising campaign may strike responsive chords in the minds of potential buyers. Such themes may make the buyer feel differently about the product: associating Miller with patriotism, for example. On the other hand, any effort that features a product's name frequently enough will generate some sales. Some advertising, such as roadside billboards, does little more than create name recognition. Assuming increased sales for Miller Beer did result after the ad campaign, to which component would you attribute the greatest weight: the shift to new slogans and symbols or the renewed visibility of the Miller name in thousands of print and television ads? Explain your reasons.

3. Some analysts have suggested that Jim Jones was a more effective persuader in the remote jungle in Guyana than in the United States. What differences are evident in the two settings which might explain the increased allegiance of his followers in remote Jonestown? How do less dramatic changes in settings (such as moving from home to a college campus) affect individuals?

4. Woodrow Wilson's successors now go to their destinations on Air Force One rather than by train. What other technologies make the "Whistle stop" tour unnecessary or ineffective? Do listeners and viewers know as much about a President as those who only read printed remarks or, once or twice in a lifetime, see the Chief Executive in the flesh?

5. Look through a magazine, newspaper, or this text for statements that first appear to be informational but argue for a particular point of view. In the examples that you find, how is the persuasive intent hidden from the casual reader? How can persuasion be concealed as "information"?

6. As the Jonestown case suggests, strong leadership may bring misery upon those who succumb to it. Identify other examples of destructive persuasion. Identify positive cases that suggest persuasion can be a constructive process. Compare your examples with a colleague.

Additional Reading

Aristotle. *The Rhetoric.* Trans. W.R. Roberts in *The Basic Works* of *Aristotle.* Ed. Richard McKeon. New York: Random House, 1941.

Bettinghaus, Erwin P. *Persuasive Communication,* Second Edition. New York: Holt, Rinehart, and Winston, 1973.

Brown, J.A.C. *Techniques of Persuasion: From Propaganda to Brainwashing.* New York: Penguin, 1972.

Goffman, Erving. *The Presentation of Self in Everyday Life.* New York: Anchor, 1959.

Gordon, George N. *Persuasion: The Theory and Practice of Manipulative Communication.* New York: Hastings House, 1971.

Larson, Charles U. *Persuasion: Reception and Responsibility,* Third Edition. Belmont, Calif.: Wadsworth, 1983.

Simons, Herbert W. *Persuasion: Understanding, Practice, and Analysis.* Boston: Addison-Wesley, 1976.

Zimbardo, Philip G.; Ebbe B. Ebbesen; and Christina Maslach. *Influencing Attitudes and Changing Behavior,* Second Edition. Boston: Addison-Wesley, 1977.

PART 1

ORIGINS OF PERSUASIVE PRACTICE

Broadly speaking, persuasion in the United States is governed by a universal imperative shared by all human groups and by a cultural imperative shared by a more limited number of societies. Like all forms of communication, persuasion depends on the uniquely human attribute of symbol-using. The ability to influence others is based on the art of selecting the "right" symbols to guide thought and action. A universal feature of skillful persuaders of all nationalities is their sensitivity to the socially constructed meanings that are triggered by words and symbols. A complete view of persuasion, therefore, must review the basic materials at the disposal of each advocate in every kind of society. In order to understand how *American* persuasion works, we believe that it is necessary to emphasize the influence of several key western values on our culture-wide attitudes toward persuaders. In American society, persuasion is not simply grounded in the requirement to master language; it is also based on a shared conviction about constructive conflict and public debate. We begin this section in Chapter 2 with a look at some important but often neglected beliefs. In Chapter 3 we go on to review the vital role that symbol-using plays in all forms of persuasion.

The Advocate in
an Open Society

 OVERVIEW

We can never be sure that the opinion we are endeavoring to stifle is a false opinion; and if we were sure, stifling it would be an evil still.[1]

Persuasion is a universal feature of human life. In all societies, influence directed to co-workers, family members, and friends is pervasive in daily activities. Additional persuasive opportunities are available only to members of democratic societies; in these nations, major governmental and political decisions are subject to the approval of public opinion. The essential idea of democracy is that power is shared by a variety of citizens who are, at various times, both the initiators and the recipients of influence. This intimate tie between democracy and persuasion is the subject of this chapter.

Persuasion and Freedom:
Lessons Learned the Hard Way

Vladimir Ashkenazy and Arkady Shevchenko were both highly successful in their careers in the Soviet Union. As children, it probably never occurred to them that they would one day desert their families, friends, and homeland to begin new lives in the West. Such a grave decision is not lightly made, but both men eventually decided to leave. Starting over in a new culture was not easy. They had to cope with a language and patterns of living that were difficult to understand, and they were uncertain that they could support themselves in the West. Their experiences are relevant to this chapter's focus on persuasion as a vital manifestation of human freedom.

Vladimir Ashkenazy is comparatively young to have a world-wide reputation as a leading pianist and orchestra conductor. His musical reputation soared rapidly after winning Moscow's prestigious Tchaikovsky Competition in 1962. His records are sold everywhere, and he is in demand all over the world as a concert soloist — except in Russia. Along with his Icelandic wife, he defected to England in 1963 at the age of 26. As an emigre, he can never play again before Russian audiences, and Soviet authorities have forbidden other musicians from the U.S.S.R. to perform with him in concerts.

Ashkenazy's reasons for defecting are familiar to Westerners. He wanted more freedom. He hated spying on foreign students which the KGB (Soviet Security Police) asked him to do at the Moscow Conservatory, and he chafed against the idea that there is only one way of thinking, one way of acting, one acceptable point of view to be believed without question.

The pianist's first trip to America was in 1958. As is common with Soviet musicians traveling abroad, he came to New York under the watchful eye of a "companion," probably a KGB informant. The trip was very revealing. Ashkenazy made the mistake of giving an interview to the *New York Times* in which he said he enjoyed his tour and his American hosts. In fact, he was terribly homesick and unprepared for the long and arduous tour, but even his few diplomatic comments to an American writer were taken by the watchful companion as "un-Soviet" and "irresponsible."[2] Within a few years he had defected.

Figure 2.1

Ashkenazy with his Ministry of Culture "companion" in New York during his first American tour, 1958.

Jasper Parrot and Vladimir Ashkenazy, photo from *Beyond Frontiers.* Copyright © 1984 Jasper Parrot. Reproduced with the permission of Atheneum Publishers, Inc.

Ashkenazy recalls that he could not accept the view that history, culture, and politics were subjects which could be altered to please the state. Soviet citizens, he noted, had "lost the power to decide for themselves."[3] Choices about where to live, when to travel, what kind of music to play, and with whom to associate were dictated by the bureaucracy. The worst sin in the U.S.S.R. was to question publically the life that the state provided. Grateful though he was for the extensive musical training he had received, Ashkenazy wanted the freedom to exercise his talents in his own way.

In the field of international relations, Arkady Shevchenko experienced the same denial of personal choices. A brilliant Soviet diplomat with close ties to Foreign Minister Andrei Gromyko and other Kremlin leaders, he defected to the United States in 1978. To the great embarrassment of the Eastern bloc nations, the defector also held the prestigious position of Under Secretary General to the United Nations.

Just how "closed" his society was became apparent to Shevchenko on his first trip to the United States in 1958 (the same year as Ashkenazy's first North American concert tour). As a staff assistant to the Soviet United Nations delegation, Shevchenko was required to spend a great deal of time at the Long Island, New York mansion which housed Soviet officials. He vividly remembers his first impressions of life in the West, especially the first few times he was permitted to wander through the bustling streets of New York:

> Perhaps what struck me more than anything else was the wealth and volume of information of every imaginable kind in newspapers, magazines, books, television, and radio. I couldn't get accustomed to the incredible openness of American society. It was appealing and at the same time somehow frightening. I was like a starving man at a feast.
>
> I also discovered that I could buy *Pravda* and various other Soviet periodicals at newsstands that carried international publications. We had been told that the United States suppressed information about our country because it didn't want Americans to know about our better life in the Soviet Union.[4]

This sharp contrast between the open West and the suspicious East planted the first seeds of doubt that would eventually result in the diplomat's defection. Shevchenko realized that the freedom to disagree with an "official" view of events was exhilarating.

> At home in the U.S.S.R. everything was just the reverse of what I saw in the United States. All was under lock and key in the most literal sense—our mouths, newspapers, television, literature, our travel out of the country. We had to keep our own thoughts locked up if they differed with official opinion. [Then Soviet Premier] Khrushchev loosened the reins, yes, but in no way removed them.[5]

In a conversation with a high ranking KGB officer in a Moscow restaurant, Shevchenko made some critical comments about the Soviet government. Fortified by the wine and the atmosphere of the restaurant, he talked about how the country could be strengthened by more vigorous debate within the Communist Party. His companion's face froze in an icy stare. Finally, the official spoke. "Arkady, I was a great admirer of your father, so let me talk to you as a friend." The lesson was simple and plain. "Think what you want, but keep your tongue behind your teeth. That may annoy you, but it won't kill you. Speaking too freely...well, the consequences of that can be unpleasant."[6]

Silence or enforced agreement is the price of citizenship in a totalitarian system; freedom of thought and the power to persuade are the dividends that open societies pay to their members. As we shall see, each form of social life has its advocates and attributes, and each makes special demands on its citizens. Only the open democratic society allows its citizens to play an active role in the give and take of public debate and persuasion.

Freedom, Democracy and Persuasion: Early Debates

Mankind has long struggled with the question of how much choice should be left to the individual within society. Since humans are by nature social, and since living together requires common rules and procedures (i.e., whether to drive on the left or the right side of the road, whether criticizing others will be a crime, whether children shall be required to attend school), governments have always sought to impose rules that civilize daily life. A central issue that has been decided by those who establish or govern any state is *how much* public consent should be sought in the determination of common laws and rules.

From the first flowering of Western intellect in Greece about 800 years before the birth of Christ, there have been strong disagreements about the "best" forms of social organization. Teachers and philosophers in the earliest civilizations groped with questions about the degree to which people needed to be lead and guided by strong rulers. To what extent should the rules and choices that bind us to the community be self-imposed? Who should govern the activities of the individual in the culture: the individual or those who act in the name of the society and the state? These questions hold no great mystery for us today. We are nurtured from childhood in the values and attitudes of individualism, democracy, freedom of thought and speech. We assume that we have the right to influence others, just as they have the right to attempt to persuade us. We routinely believe that everyone has the freedom to make public claims on our loyalties: to sell us soap, to encourage us to vote for a candidate for Congress, to speak out against a foreign policy decision of our government, or to criticize the administration of a college in the campus newspaper. Collectively, these are rights of expression and action: rights to praise, criticize, and seek supporters. They are so familiar to us that we take them for granted.

Societies which tolerate a wide range of individual freedoms are the exception rather than the rule, however. Those who have argued against permitting dissent and vigorous public debate have had powerful allies. Indeed, as we shall see at the end of this chapter, the issue of how much individual freedom of expression is *too* much remains with us in contemporary America.

Plato and the Sophists:
The Feud Over the Value of Public Opinion

Most societies throughout history have opted for a limited role for individual choice. The great philosopher Plato was perhaps the most important opponent of democracy and self-government. A brief sketch of his attitudes and his opposition reveals several key ideas that still have credibility today.

Plato spent much of his adult life at his Academy on the edge of Athens arguing that democratic states were bound to fail. He thought ordinary people were incapable of making decisions about their communities because they lacked the intelligence and thorough training necessary for decision-making. One analyst summarizes his views this way: "Democrats are described as profligate and niggardly, as insolent, lawless, and shameless, as fierce and as terrible beasts of prey, as gratifying every whim, as living solely for pleasure, and for unnecessary and unclean desires."[7] Democracies were governed by mobs unable to separate rhetoric from reason. Few citizens were capable of discriminating between the thoughtful judgments of the well-trained leader—described in The Republic as the "philosopher king"—and the irrational "pandering" of the well-trained persuader. Because the democratic leader owed his power to the people, he would play to their fears and fantasies rather than to the more important needs of the nation. The leader chosen by popular will would substitute flattery of the "mob" in place of true wisdom. To Plato, leaders guided by public opinion were bound to be as misguided as teachers who let their pupils decide what should be taught.

Plato's view, however, did not go unchallenged. A bitter debate over the wisdom of democracy developed between Plato and other teachers who traveled through the city-democracies along the coasts of Greece,

Sicily, and Italy. Plato was among the few philosophers of his era to write down what his intellectual adversaries thought. He was deeply troubled and frustrated by the activities of independent tutors whom affluent parents hired to educate their male children. (The enlightenment of the Hellenic world excluded women, slaves, and the impoverished as full citizens, even in democratic Athens.) One of the tutors was Corax who taught public speaking skills to people who needed to learn how to speak before their peers in legal and political settings. Plato scorned these roving tutors, who were collectively known as Sophists. We suspect that he disliked them partly because they worked outside of the prestigious intellectual center of Athens and partly because they accepted fees on a pay-per-lesson basis. What really irked the great philosopher was that virtually all of these tutors taught the techniques of rhetoric or persuasion. His dislike of the Sophists was so strong that he named some of the weak-thinking characters in his dialogues after several of them. It is a tribute to Plato's prestige that the term "sophistic" survives as a label of scorn for people who play loosely with truth and fact.

The case of Gorgias is especially interesting. In a famous dialogue against the practice of teaching ordinary people the art of persuasion, Plato writes parts for his own honored teacher, Socrates, and his democratically-inclined opposite, Gorgias. In the dialogue, Gorgias is portrayed as a 5th Century B.C. version of a shady used-car salesman who is no match for Socrates' superior wisdom.[8] The real Gorgias was born in Sicily but taught and gave performances in many cities including Olympia, Delphi, and Athens.[9] Like all Sophists, he taught various subjects but always the art of persuasion. According to W.C. Guthrie, "a special feature of his displays was to invite miscellaneous questions from the audience and give impromptu replies." To his credit, "He saw the power of persuasion as paramount in every field, in the study of nature and other philosophical subjects no less than in the law-courts or the political arena."[10] And like many of his contemporaries, Gorgias believed that the freedom to speak in defense of opinions and beliefs required skill in knowing how to hold an audience's attention and how to shape their attitudes.

Plato disagreed with Gorgias and other Sophists on two important points. First, they disagreed about the certainty of truth. Plato believed that most issues that invited persuasion had a single best or "true" answer. Beauty, for example, was not in the eye of the beholder but closer or farther from the ideal of *perfect* beauty. Likewise, he felt that concepts such as justice were not relative to individual values or specific circumstances, but to "perfect" (and perhaps unknowable) forms. We might never discover the entirety of an idea, but the quest for better knowledge should be our primary goal. Considering opinions of others, he felt, was simply a wasted detour from the path of truth. Since there is perfect truth, perfect justice, and perfect beauty, the best life is spent working toward perfection rather than approval.

Second, Plato and the Sophists disagreed on the value of public opinion. The Sophists believed that many questions of public dispute were not solvable by application of rigorous academic reasoning but were better determined by appeals to public opinion. For instance, the question of who should be elected to lead a government could not be resolved by reference to one single standard. There may be no single "true" choice but a range of acceptable choices based on the specific interests and priorities of different people. One leader may be better for one group, but less beneficial to another. On policy issues, "good" solutions may change as public attitudes change. If we apply this principle to contemporary problems, we could argue that the 55 mile-per-hour national speed limit is a "good" law — whatever its merits in saving gasoline and lives — as long as it continues to enjoy public support. Given this view there is no way that individual facts or truths can substitute for how we collectively feel about an idea. As members of groups, we have values that lead us to certain kinds of preferences. But the pluralism that is built into complex societies leads us to recognize that others may have their own good reasons for disagreeing with us on topics as diverse as prayer in state-supported schools to the rights of mothers and fetuses affected by abortions. In democracies, public attitudes are and should be formed by reference to shared values and socially determined attitudes.

For the Sophists, and for democracies in general, public opinion is everything. Perhaps the clearest statement to that effect came from Protagorous, who offered a convenient declaration which could serve as a seven-word definition of democracy. He said "Man is the measure of all things...,"[11] not some absolute ideal privately determined by a philosopher. In matters that affect the collective welfare of a society, the people should be left with the power to judge what is just, true, and fair for them.

The concept that "man is the measure" is useful in two senses. First, it implies that many issues that spark public persuasion and controversy are about preferences rather than truths or ultimate answers. In a decision as trivial as which brand of soap to buy, or as important as a decision to speak against a colleague's proposal, the final choice is personal and unique to our situation. What we think and how we feel determines how we act. The Sophists felt that no eternal search for absolute truth could remove the responsibility of making choices from the democratic politician, the jury, or the electorate. Groups and constituencies have different answers and attitudes that may be addressed and changed by outsiders. They made the common sense observation that most answers to complex problems cannot be rendered totally "false" or useless for all people at all times. One side of a controversy will have some merits for some people some of the time.

Second, the idea that "man is the measure of all things" can serve as a refreshing reminder that, ultimately, the members of a democracy must have faith in the good sense of an audience to locate both the wisdom and the "puffery" within the debate that precedes a final decision. Plato's student, Aristotle, seemed to find the right middle ground. He opened his persuasion text by stating a belief in the ultimate soundness of public attitudes which have been exposed to the various sides of a dispute. Persuasion, he noted, "is useful because things that are true and things that are just have a natural tendency to prevail over their opposites..."[12] People, he felt, can judge for themselves. In closed societies where decisions are reserved for the few, there will be hostility to competition from others and the "unofficial" explanation of events. The totalitarian leader can be expected to claim that a variety of viewpoints will "confuse" and "bewilder" the ordinary public. The democrat, in contrast, shares the populist's faith that the public can find its own best answers in the give and take of public persuasion.

America Emerges: The Debate Renewed

Colonial America inherited a strong intellectual tradition in favor of the individual's right to engage in public persuasion. The French roots of the Englightenment, the ideas of British thinkers such as John Milton and John Locke, and the steady increase in the powers of Britain's Parliament all had their liberalizing effects. From these European origins, the colonists had inherited a belief in the "natural rights" of man; freedoms were given eloquent expression in the Bill of Rights and the Declaration of Independence. Underpinning these liberties was an undying faith in reason, and the freedom necessary to give human logic its rightful reign. The colonists believed that common sense was in ample supply within colonial society, and should not be ignored by a monarch and Parliament in distant Britain.

In addition to their philosophical reasons, citizens of the colonies had the more practical goal of establishing local democratic governments to replace the frequently indifferent colonial administrations. They wanted to be able to confront those who were legislating decisions, an impossibility with the seat of power in London. After the War of Independence, they designed autonomous states and adapted the basic principles and models of the governments which they had known in Europe. They attempted to secure for themselves what England had provided for its own citizens: local government and direct access to the legislative process. They also had pragmatic reasons for breaking with England. Many families had come to the new world as religious dissidents, most notably Baptists, Quakers, and Catholics. They brought different cultures, classes, and backgrounds and sought safety in their adopted land by creating governments that were tolerant of their differences. Liberty to speak out or to practice a religion different from one's neighbor was a kind of self-protection. By establishing a confederation of states to replace rule by a monarchy, the newly independent Americans attempted to assure that decisions affecting their lives would be subject to public discussion rather than private dictate.

The actual task of inventing a government in the late 1780s was not as easy as it might have seemed. The founders of the nation had to deal with one of the questions that divided Plato and the Sophists: how strong a role should persuasion and public opinion play?

Among the voices heard was Thomas Jefferson's. As the unofficial philosopher of American independence and writer of its Declaration, he expressed enormous faith in the ordinary citizen and favored local governments with direct ties to the "grass roots." Jefferson is remembered for his strong opposition to a centralized federal government, but his belief in the wisdom of the ordinary person and localized governance was not universally shared. Other founders of the nation such as James Madison and Alexander Hamilton had limited faith in how free citizens would ultimately exercise their liberty; they argued for the need to balance the dangers of "factions" against the ideal of broad individual liberties. They feared the "turbulence and contention" of pure democracies. "Factions"—their code word for angry citizens who could rise up and replace a ruling party or group by force or majority rule—had to be checked. "So strong is this propensity of mankind to fall into mutual animosities," noted Madison, "that where no substantial occasion presents itself the most frivolous and fanciful distinctions have been sufficient to kindle unfriendly passions."[13] Madison and other founders wanted to protect land and property owners from mob rule and unchecked public opinion. Jefferson wrote the Declaration's words, "all men are created equal," but few of his colleagues were willing to accept the idea that each should have an equal say in the society and its government. They wanted an orderly and stable society, something not necessarily guaranteed by one-man-one-vote democracies.

The colonists thus settled on a safer alternative which provided a layer of insulation between the hot tempers of ordinary citizens and the cooler reason of those who ran the government. They formed a republic, not strictly a government "of the people" but a government of representatives who would be elected by and act for the people. Even after the Constitution was adopted in 1789, only the members of Congress could vote for a President, and citizen voting was restricted to white male landowners. On the whole, the Constitution was intended as much to protect wealth and property as to insure the natural rights that were so much a part of the War of Independence against Britain.

Speaking for many others, Madison noted that "a pure democracy" was "no cure for the mischiefs of faction."[14] For him, a republic was a safe refuge from rapid changes in public opinion. Even to this day, the Senate of the United States functions as an institution of republican government. Senators are insulated from the public's wrath for six years at a time, and they are given an equal voice irrespective of the size of the states they represent. The House of Representatives is more democratic: members represent districts of roughly equal size, and must face voters every two years. Even in the most open of societies, there was suspicion of the power of the persuader. The fear that freedom of expression could combine with pure democracy to produce unwanted change was very real among the designers of American government. They believed in popular democracy and public persuasion, but only to a point. Most were less certain than Jefferson who wrote that "government degenerates when trusted to the rulers of the people alone. The people themselves are therefore its only safe depositories."[15]

The Nature of "Closed" and "Open" Societies

An open society encourages its citizens to take part in a wide range of personal and public decisions. The British philosopher Karl Popper noted that "the open society is one in which men have learned to be to some extent critical of taboos, and to base decisions on the authority of their own intelligence (after discussion)."[16] A society is open when it encourages discussion, criticism, and debate; argumentation and conflict are part of the normal functioning of its institutions. A society is closed when its leaders determine that differing viewpoints are unnecessary and dangerous. Open societies not only tolerate free expression, but they act upon the reverberations of public opinion. They guarantee the right to dissent on matters as diverse as religion, politics, and government policy. They sponsor genuine elections, frequently use juries rather than judges to decide cases, encourage competing voices in a variety of mass media, and foster competition among companies and products. Individuals are treated as free agents who may seek to change their status, improve their education, and exercise a range of liberties. Most importantly, people may organize into groups and use a wide variety of protected persuasive forms to seek changes in laws.

No society meets all of these standards. Only the most powerful Greeks had a say in public affairs. And Popper's own England—while providing the primary model for an open parliamentary democracy—was controlled by a self-selected, upper-class elite. The "old boy" network in government was largely populated by the children of the wealthy trained in upper-crust private schools and usually the products of Oxford or Cambridge. Openness is always a matter of degree. Even so, the practical differences between systems can be very real. For example, a national debate on the nature and limits of defense expenditures and weaponry has raged almost continually since John Kennedy campaigned against Richard Nixon in 1960. Kennedy charged that under the Eisenhower-Nixon administration, the U.S. had fallen behind in missile technology. More recently, the Reagan administration in its first four years fueled the debate by calling for larger expenditures on "Star Wars" strategic defense systems. Since Congress must approve all expenditures, the President must continually persuade Congress and the public of the validity of defense expenditures. By contrast, in the U.S.S.R. the public never participates in debates on the issue of "bread versus bullets." Soviet citizens are merely informed about the extent to which they must bear defense costs.

Public communication is the machine that drives an open society. A totalitarian system, on the other hand, sees decentralized public communication as a threat. To regulate the flow of information is to control the thoughts and ideas of citizens who might otherwise be enlightened by uncensored sources. Soviet managers regard the everyday photocopy machine and the video cassette recorder as potentially dangerous technologies. It is easy to see why. These devices make it possible to decentralize the flow of information. "Unofficial" points of view appear in print and on tape and can be duplicated without scrutiny for their "ideological correctness." Businessmen who used to work in the Soviet Union remember the periodic appearance of "the hammer man," a worker whose only job was to destroy photocopying machines ready for the junk pile. He always made certain that an old copier was rendered useless.[17] George Orwell's 1984 paints a similar picture of a society which sacrificed personal freedom for rigid certainty. The state outlawed public debate in favor of a centralized code of ideas and conduct from which there was no legitimate dissent. An efficiently-run "Ministry of Truth" kept citizens in a form of induced sleep.[18]

Indoctrination and the Denial of Free Expression

Persuasion is ultimately the tool of a free people. Being only one in a competing array of voices, a government is required to rule by consent rather than indoctrination. Giving citizens the right to speak, publish, and influence others liberates them from serving merely as cogs in the State's social wheel.

Several years ago, a Polish citizen was able to smuggle out hundreds of pages of official documents. These documents provide an excellent illustration of the differences between an open and closed society. The government papers contained citations that were withheld from newspapers, magazines, and literary journals by official censors; the opinions expressed were deemed unsuitable for general circulation. None of the documents dealt with state secrets. Most of the censored words and paragraphs merely stated points of view at odds with the official reality coming from the government. The censors deleted a lengthy passage from a magazine article written by a leading Catholic film critic, Stefan Kisielewski. Kisielewski's comparison of several films — two American and one Polish — says a good deal about the confidence and stamina of societies that have learned to tolerate a wide range of viewpoints.

> In Warsaw I saw an interesting American film with the para-phrased title *Defenseless Marigolds* [The Effect of Gamma Rays on Man-in-the-Moon Marigolds]. The film was preceded by a Polish short from the series celebrating the 30th Anniversary of the Polish People's Republic, this one devoted to Lodz. The short, a beautifully photographed, wide-screen color production, was bursting with joy, energy, and images of prosperity. Of course, it started off by show-ing a little bit of the ghetto ruins...but everything that followed was sweetness and light: construction, expansion, bright, spacious factory halls, smiling faces, good-looking, nicely dressed girls, color-ful streets, new theaters and new hotels. After this, the American film turned out to be a dreadfully sad experience...a stark contrast to the unrestrained joyfulness of Lodz....
>
> And in the same regard, I was struck by something else about this otherwise coincidental contrast. Here you have the world's most affluent great power showing us a film about its way of life that is embittered and self-doubting, and here we are whistling tunes about 'merry lads of Krakow,' marching off into a world without doubt and sadness. Someone will say that this is not the great power the United States, but rather film director Paul Newman, private citi-zen, describing his own observations and doubts. True, but he wanted to and was able to do this. Nobody was worried about creat-ing a bad impression or negative propaganda. I have also witnessed this sort of thing in an 'official' context. Warsaw recently played

host to an American gala: a screening of the film *The Sting*.... No
one was worried that the audience would generalize this view of life
in America, that the film would discredit the United States, deni-
grate it or present it in a bad light. Just imagine what a portrait of
sublime happiness, optimism and self confidence we would present
on this kind of occasion! And yet which approach is more
convincing?[19]

For Kisielewski, the film glorifying Poland's strengths was an ironic
sign of its own weakness. The forced optimism was intended to hide
reality. An American film showing life in less than ideal terms
demonstrated an unusual kind of strength, a tolerance for individual
expression and self-criticism. In a closed society, inflated propaganda
is a form of social control. In an open society, all the debate,
propaganda, selling, and counterclaims—the verbal battles of the
"factions" that James Madison needlessly feared—give the individual
a basis for countering the power that resides in institutions and
governments. For example, an editorial statement by the political
cartoonist, Tony Auth, makes a timely point by poking fun at a
President's ideas or actions. In a unique way, the political cartoon

Figure 2.2

Tolerance for criticism of public officials
is a positive sign of a nation's health.

Copyright © 1985 Universal Press Syndicate. Reprinted with permission. All rights reserved.

offers criticism of an official presidential view and contributes to the ongoing public dialogue about the wisdom of official statements or policies. The existence of differing views in many forums is evidence of a system's health.

The vitality of American life resides in tolerance of differences and· encouragement to express those differences. Supreme Court Justice Oliver Wendell Holmes noted in the trial of a socialist charged with distributing anti-government pamphlets that the "free trade of ideas" in "the competition of the market" is essential to a democracy. Perhaps no other figure has so clearly and succinctly summarized the necessity for freedom of expression:

> [W]hen men have realized that time has upset many fighting faiths, they may come to believe even more than they believe the very foundations of their own conduct *that the ultimate good desired is better reached by free trade in ideas—that the best test of truth is the power of the thought to get itself accepted in the competition of the market...*[20]

How "Open" is American Society?

The right to free speech—the right to persuade—is alive and well in America. However, we must conclude this discussion with some reminders of how imperfect the American marketplace of ideas has been.

Government Restrictions

The First and most important Amendment to the Constitution states that "Congress shall make no law...abridging the freedom of speech or of the press..." Recent history, however, is littered with examples of advocates who have been punished for the "crime" of speaking out. Since the First World War, thousands of American citizens have been jailed for distributing pamphlets against war, advocating the overthrow of the government, protesting against the military draft, marching against racial segregation, and joining unpopular political causes.[21] Authorities have used laws against libel (uttering "false" accusations), trespassing, spying, disturbing the peace, marching without a permit, and impeding a criminal investigation to stifle dissent. Here are just a few representative instances:

- In 1963, civil rights leader Martin Luther King and 3,300 other blacks were arrested in Birmingham, Alabama for parading without a permit. In Dr. King's words, "there is nothing wrong in having an ordinance which requires a

Figure 2.3

THE FIRST AMENDMENT

The United States Constitution was written in 1787. Many dele-
gates from the states wanted assurances that the new government
it established would preserve individual liberties. Ten Amendments,
also known as "The Bill of Rights," were finally adopted and took effect
in 1791. Even though the wording of the First Amendment is
straightforward and unequivocal, Congress, the courts, and public
agencies have all placed restrictions on where Americans may meet,
speak, and write.

> Amendment 1:   Congress shall make no law respecting an estab-
> lishment of religion, or prohibiting the free exercise thereof; or
> abridging the freedom of speech, or of the press; or the right of the
> people peaceably to assemble, and to petition the Government for a
> redress of grievances.

permit for a parade. But such an ordinance becomes unjust
when it is used to maintain segregation and to deny citizens
the First-Amendment privilege of peaceful assembly and
protest."[22]

- In 1968, David O'Brien spoke out against the Vietnam War
  and burned his draft card on the steps of a Boston court
  house. He was given a jail sentence with the agreement of
  the Supreme Court.[23] Although burning a draft card is clearly a form of symbolic expression, courts have ruled that it is
  not a "protected" form of speech.

- Several years ago the village of Orem, Utah served a criminal summons on the owner of the town's only bookstore.
  The shopkeeper's offense was selling four books: A Clock-
  work Orange, The Symbol, Last Tango in Paris, and The
  Idolators. Local Ordinance 210 established a "Commission
  of Decency" to seek out obscene books and any school teachers who assigned such materials.[24]

- In 1968, Washington, D.C. was the scene of a large but
  peaceful "Poor People's Campaign." The protest, made up
  mostly of the older working poor, resulted in the arrest of its
  leader, Ralph Abernathy, for demonstrating too close to the
  Capitol.[25]

- In 1976 *New York Times Reporter* Myron Farber began a jail term for refusing to turn over his private notes. He had interviewed several people about a number of unexplained deaths in a New Jersey nursing home. Farber's defenders argued that journalists should not be forced to act as extensions of the police. They put forth the view that valuable sources will talk to reporters only if anonymity is guaranteed.[26]

- Every year the State Department denies visas to scores of poets, writers, and politicians who want to visit the United States. For example, a visa application by the widow of Chile's former President Allende was refused undoubtedly because strong evidence existed to suggest that the United States helped rebels overthrow his government. Mrs. Allende would have said as much in her visit. Visas to travelers are not issued if it is the opinion of the State Department that the ideas a traveler might discuss would be "prejudicial to the public interest."

In many similar instances, courts and legislatures have weighed the ideal of free expression and freedom of the press against the desire for a peaceful and obedient society. Advocates of causes have often created problems such as traffic jams or angry crowds; such incidents can become a pretext for curtailing the right to persuade.

Access to Information

Not surprisingly, the flow of information from government to the public is another area where ideals and actualities clash. A society is open to the extent that information flows freely between government and the public. "We began our society," notes press critic Ben Begdikian, "on the principle that government exists legitimately only with the consent of the governed and that consent without significant information is meaningless."[27] Americans have more access to government sources than the citizens of most other nations. For example, anyone may write the F.B.I. and request a copy of any personal information that may be in its files.

Under the sweeping Freedom of Information Act, which in 1974 became a major tool for the press and the Congress to gain access to government files, federal agencies are obligated to handle requests for all kinds of information. Documents could be labeled "classified" only with good cause. The motive behind the act was the democratic idea that the public has a right to know what its government knows — with obvious exceptions such as the names of spies and certain military secrets. Over the years, the act has been eroded by presidents and the

Congress, sometimes with the apparent objective of concealing embarrassing information. For example, by 1984 Congress had denied public access to information

> submitted by manufacturers of hazardous products to the Consumer Product Safety Commission; unclassified information submitted to the Department of Energy about the production and transportation of nuclear materials; the records of professional review...organizations that review medical practices of institutions relying on medicaid funding...; and information about nuclear research...[28]

There have been enough cases in America's recent past—the Watergate Affair and the Pike Congressional report, to name just two—to raise questions about how willing government agencies are to share what they know. During the Watergate Affair, the Nixon Administration concealed information about the activities of several employees involved in spying on the Democratic Party's national headquarters. In 1976, the Pike Committee report detailed secret and often illegal activities conducted in other countries by the Central Intelligence Agency, activities that became known only because someone within the Congress violated congressional rules and "leaked" the material to the press.[29] Foreigners and diplomats sometimes express surprise that the U.S. does not try to enlarge the range of official secrets. Battles over government secrecy continue, primarily because large numbers of Americans have come to expect that popular government means open government.

The Growing Gap Between Free Speech and True Access

Today when we talk of "democracies" we mean something vastly different from what the early Greeks and the American colonists had in mind. The first Mediterranean democracies were frequently limited to individual cities. Aristotle said the ideal state is where "the land as well as the inhabitants...should be taken in at a single view."[30] He meant that popular government could work only if limited to a body of people which could meet in one place at one time. The designers of the American colonies thought in slightly bigger terms and located colonial Legislatures within easy reach of a state's citizens. With these limited spaces and populations in mind, the designers of the First Amendment in 1791 talked about freedom of speech and of the press in a literal way. The standard means of public communication then were simpler. Debate and discussion were largely conducted in local village newspapers and speeches delivered in courthouses, churches, and state legislatures. We wonder how the early Americans would react to electronic forums such as A.B.C.'s "Nightline" or the "Phil Donahue Show" that reach millions of viewers spread over an entire continent.

Any consideration of "freedom of speech" in the 20th Century must include the enormous changes that have occurred in the *way* Americans hear about major issues and events. The most influential mass media are no longer in the community; New York, Washington, D.C., and Los Angeles now serve as the centers for information dissemination. The unique needs and problems of one particular region have been supplanted by national concerns. The great persuaders of the 20th Century—the television networks, journalists, and opinion leading publications—are far removed from the areas where the Average American lives and works. The federal government and its hundreds of agencies have replaced local government in formulating many of the major policies by which we live. Corn prices in Iowa as well as water resources in California are allocated in financial and political centers hundreds of miles away. The television programs we see are determined by advertisers who pay the bills; they think in terms of national audiences rather than the needs of individual towns and communities.

In short, the forces of influence that act upon modern Americans are increasingly centered in national rather than local institutions. Because of these changes, many critics have asked if the First Amendment isn't itself in need of an amendment: a new right of access to the mass media which have replaced the town hall and the small-town newspaper as major opinion-leading sources of news. They argue that freedom of expression is only meaningful to the extent that citizens have access to significant numbers of listeners or readers. As First Amendment scholar Jerome Barron put it:

> In the contemporary life of ideas, the victories and defeats of politics and the fortunes of intensely important issues are resolved in the mass media.... Our constitutional guarantee of freedom of press is equipped to deal with direct and crude governmental assaults on Freedom of expression, but is incapable of responding to the more subtle challenge of securing admission for ideas to the dominant media.[31]

Barron's new definition of freedom of speech recognizes that the mass media have far greater impact than the face-to-face encounter. He and others suggest that the previous ideal of freedom of expression has been rendered impotent. There may be romance in the image of the ordinary citizen standing up for his convictions at a town council meeting, but the real battleground of public opinion has shifted to the broadcaster and the newspaper. The ideal freedom of speech, Barron and his colleagues argue, must include public access to audiences presently dominated by the television networks, major newspapers, and corporate advertisers.

Critics of this "access" ideal point out that it is unrealistic. They note that mass media must succeed first and foremost as businesses. In the United States, most of the mass media depend upon advertisers for their existence, and advertisers are reluctant to underwrite the kinds of persuasion that may provoke public debate. Enormous fees are paid to gain access to large audiences. One million dollars for 60 seconds in prime-time television is not unusual; for such high stakes, advertisers want to entertain and to reassure audiences rather than to inform and to provoke them. Few corporate sponsors are interested in subsidizing television programs that cast doubt on the audience's judgment or lifestyle. It is safer to sponsor entertainment that offers escape from the real world rather than public discussion of significant problems. For example, broadcast historian Erik Barnouw notes that a 1976 CBS documentary on gun control entitled "The Guns of Autumn" alarmed scheduled advertisers who feared that hunters might be offended. All but one of the hour-long program's sponsors cancelled their participation.[32]

Corporate sponsorship is thus a filter through which a large portion of ideas and issues must pass. To be sure, the best of the mass media can be remarkably independent of the pressures and views of advertisers, but the constant need for high ratings and large circulation numbers is always a factor in the ways ideas are distributed. The founding fathers had no forewarning that public information would be so heavily tied to information industries dominated by major publishing and broadcasting chains. Their goal for popular government was to disperse rather than to centralize influence.

Summary

Throughout history, people who have built nations or studied existing societies have disagreed about whether the power of persuasion—left in the care of ordinary people—can result in decisions that will show intelligence and civility. The choices we make as individuals and as citizens of a nation may never satisfy critics who dislike the power of public opinion and distrust its wisdom. But of this we are certain, the greater the diversity of choices within a nation, the more it needs vigorous public discussion. The role of the advocate in American society is basic. Few of us would risk giving up the franchise that allows us to attempt to influence others.

It is also important to note that the freedom to persuade implies special responsibilities in addition to special privileges. The American marketplace carries obligations for advocates as well as for the society to which they belong. Persuaders must use their protected rights of freedom of speech and freedom of the press judiciously. As we noted in Chapter 1, the abuse of an audience's openness can lead to disasters such as Jonestown, Guyana. Powerful leaders and the mass media should be willing to share their near-monopolies of the channels of communication with less powerful individuals and organizations. The freedom to persuade is rendered meaningless if it does not include the opportunity for ordinary citizens to have access to opinion leaders and audiences.

Notes

[1]John Stuart Mill, *On Liberty,* ed. Currin V. Shields (New York: Bobbs Merrill, 1956), 21.

[2]Jasper Parrott and Vladimir Ashkenazy, *Beyond Frontiers* (New York: Atheneum, 1985), 73.

[3]Parrott and Ashkenazy, 216.

[4]Arkady N. Shevchenko, *Breaking with Moscow* (New York: Knopf, 1985), 89.

[5]Shevchenko, 17.

[6]Shevchenko, 65.

[7]Karl R. Popper, *The Open Society and Its Enemies,* Vol. 1, Fifth Edition (Princeton, N.J.: Princeton University Press, 1966), 42.

[8]The dialogue is called *The Gorgias.* For an interesting modern analysis of Plato's attacks on Gorgias and the teaching of persuasion, see Robert M. Pirsig's best-selling biographical novel, *Zen and the Art of Motorcycle Maintenance* (New York: William Morrow, 1974), especially Part IV.

[9]W.C.K. Guthrie, *The Sophists* (Cambridge, England: Cambridge University Press, 1971), 270.

[10]Guthrie, 272.

[11]Guthrie, 183.

[12]Aristotle, *The Rhetoric* in *The Basic Works of Aristotle,* ed. Richard McKeon (New York: Random House, 1941), 1327.

[13]Alexander Hamilton, James Madison, and John Jay, *The Federalist Papers,* ed. by Clinton Rossiter (New York: Mentor Books, 1961), 79.

[14]Hamilton, Madison, and Jay, 81.

[15]Thomas Jefferson, quoted in Page Smith, *Jefferson: A Revealing Biography* (New York: American Heritage, 1976), 157.

[16]Popper, 202.

[17]Philip Taubman, "The Kremlin Worries That Too Many Know Too Much," *The New York Times,* 26 January 1986, 22E.

[18]George Orwell, *1984* (New York: New American Library, 1961), 5-7.

[19]Jane L. Curry, *The Black Book of Polish Censorship* (New York: Random House, 1984), 23.

[20]Holmes, quoted in Jerome A. Barron, *Freedom of the Press for Whom?* (Bloomington, Indiana: Indiana University Press, 1973), 320. The emphasis is ours.

[21]Howard Zinn, *Disobedience and Democracy: Nine Fallacies on Law and Order* (New York: Vintage, 1968), 67-87.

[22]Martin Luther King, Jr., "Letter From Birmingham Jail" in *The Rhetoric of No*, Second Edition, ed. Ray Fabrizio, Edith Karas, and Ruth Menmuir (New York: Holt, Rinehart and Winston, 1974), 301-302.

[23]Zinn, 77.

[24]Nat Hentoff, *The First Freedom* (New York: Delacorte Press, 1980), 296-297.

[25]Zinn, 4.

[26]Maurice R. Cullen, Jr., *Mass Media and the First Amendment* (Dubuque, Iowa: Wm. C. Brown, 1981), 215-216.

[27]Preface in Donna A. Demac, *Keeping America Uninformed: Government Secrecy in the 1980s* (New York: Pilgrim, 1984), ix.

[28]Demac, 77.

[29]For an interesting account of this incident, see news reporter Daniel Schorr's account in his *Clearing the Air* (New York: Berkley, 1978), 187-225.

[30]Aristotle, *The Rhetoric*, in *Basic Works*, 1284.

[31]Barron, 4.

[32]See Barnouw, *The Sponsor: Notes on a Modern Potentate* (New York: Oxford University, 1978), 136-137.

Questions and Projects for Further Study

1. One of the current battlegrounds over freedom of expression in the United States centers on shopping malls. Some state courts have denied advocates the right to distribute campaign and issue-centered materials at malls by noting that they are private property. Others have taken a more liberal view and have concluded that the shopping mall has become the new American main street. Contact the management of a mall near you and ask about its policy regarding distribution of materials. Alternatively, explore the question with a campus faculty member (in a law or criminal justice department) who is familiar with this issue.

2. The right to freedom of expression is easiest to defend when we consider the cause to be a "good" one, but free speech issues often develop from more unpopular roots. In 1977, for example, the American Nazi Party decided to hold a parade and make speeches in Skokie, Illinois. The northern suburb of Chicago has a large Jewish population, many of whom were survivors of Hitler's infamous World War II death camps. If you were the judge presented with Skokie's request to issue an injunction *against* the march, what would you decide? Try to defend your decision to another member of the class. Look at Nat Hentoff's book, *The First Freedom*, to find out what actually happened.

3. In *The Republic*, Book viii, beginning at section 554, Plato describes the problems in democratic governments. Read the pages of this section, consider his arguments, and prepare a short summary of his complaints against democracy. Use his analysis as the basis of a paper or a short oral summary presented to other members of your course.

4. How could a broadcaster or a newspaper implement a "public access" policy that would deal with the problems raised by Jerome Barron? What kinds of comments or programs might develop if stations or publishers set aside portions of space for public comments.?

5. Some large cable television companies operate "public access" channels. Contact a local station and ask if they allow access programing and facilities. Ask them to explain how it works and how it has been used in the past.

6. Students of the First Amendment have argued that some social innovations which eventually find their way into the American mainstream start out as part of a "radical" movement. Many ideas and policies we now take for granted, such as the progressive income tax, federal regulation of industries, and women's suffrage initially

came from "fringe" groups in the United States. Cite one or two recent examples of ideas or policies which needed First Amendment protections in order to gain acceptance.

7. In this chapter, Thomas Jefferson is described as a democratic hero, a strong believer in liberty and self-determination. Yet, Jefferson owned slaves. Explain this apparent irony (or hypocrisy). A good place to start is the chapter on Jefferson in Richard Hofstadter's popular book, *The American Political Tradition.*

8. Develop a questionnaire that can be completed by other students. In the questionnaire list various kinds of persuasive events such as a speech on campus against registering for the draft, the marching of Nazi Party members, the campus appearance of speakers representing an unusual religion, and so on. Design your questions so you can determine how much freedom of expression respondents are willing to tolerate. After asking a representative sample of people to respond to your questions, review the tabulated results.

Additional Reading

Barron, Jerome A. *Freedom of the Press for Whom?* Bloomington, Ind.: Indiana University Press, 1973.

Hentoff, Nat. *The First Freedom.* New York: Delacorte Press, 1980.

Hofstadter, Richard. *The American Political Tradition And the Men Who Made It.* New York: Knopf, 1973.

Klose, Kevin. *Russia and the Russians: Inside the Closed Society.* New York: Norton, 1984.

Orwell, George. *1984.* New York: New American Library, 1961.

Pirsig, Robert M. *Zen and the Art of Motorcycle Maintenance.* New York: William Morrow, 1974.

Plato. *The Republic.* Book VIII. Trans. W.H.D. Rouse in *Great Dialogues of Plato.* Ed. Eric Warmington and Philip Rouse. New York : Mentor, 1956.

Popper, Karl R. *The Open Society and Its Enemies.* Vol. 1. Fifth Edition. Princeton, N.J.: Princeton University Press, 1966.

Tedford, Thomas L. *Freedom of Speech in the United States.* New York: Random House, 1985.

The Advocate and the Manipulation of Symbols

 OVERVIEW

And however important to us is the tiny sliver of reality each of us has experienced firsthand, the whole overall "picture" is but a construct of our symbol systems.[1]

The presidential campaign of 1976 was one of the most unique and exciting campaigns of recent history. Within the shadows of Watergate, the presidential election provided a classic electoral contest. Gerald Ford, the "unelected" incumbant ran against an "overnight" newcomer and former governor of Georgia, Jimmy Carter. The primaries were intense, and presidential debates were revived. The general election was close, intriguing, and historic.

One of the most interesting rhetorical events of the campaign was Jimmy Carter's interview in *Playboy* magazine.[2] The November, 1976 article was the result of five hours of interviewing by Robert Scheer generated over a three month period. Carter was questioned on such substantive topics as Vietnam, Chile, civil rights, homosexuality, taxes, prayer, and the possibility of his own assassination. None of his answers on those issues created a stir.

What did stimulate controversy was Carter's use of the words "screw" and "shack up" while revealing that he too, like other humans, has "looked on a lot of women with lust," thus having "... committed adultery in [his] heart many times."[3] Why were Carter's statements and language shocking? There are several explanations. First, society avoids open and public discussion about sexual behavior. Second, the statements contrasted with the "moral," "Christian," "born again" image Carter had created. Thus, his statements were characterized as shocking, vulgar, and full of lockerroom language. Third, an appearance in *Playboy* magazine was problematic. Many Americans felt that the medium was inappropriate for a presidential candidate. Aspirants to this office, while allowed to campaign as one of "us," must be above the petty attitudes and behavior of the "common man." With the release of Nixon's White House transcripts, for example, many Americans were upset that the President of the United States would use, even in private, such profane language.

It appears, then, that Carter misjudged the audience. The medium and word usage were counter to the public's norms and values. His rhetorical choices seemed inappropriate. But were they? Liberal Democrats were skeptical and cautious about Carter. What better medium than *Playboy* to express to this audience that he would not impose his "born-again" beliefs upon them? Clearly, Carter adapted to his immediate audience. In addition to using a recognizable medium, the words "screw" and "shack up" were in line with the readers' language. More formal expressions would have been inconsistent with the audience, medium, or stated purpose of the interview. Finally, Carter's admission to lusting in his heart portrayed him as "normal," not "holier than thou" or morally superior. From this perspective, Carter's rhetorical choices appear to be appropriate. Thus, for some individuals, Carter's language was offensive; for others it was appropriate. For some individuals, his language contradicted the principles of Christianity while for others he showed wisdom and capitalized on an opportunity to expound the virtues of love and forgiveness. The words and language of Carter were the same but their perceived meanings and interpretations varied greatly.

Human language is a marvelous and powerful tool. In this chapter, we are going to investigate the nature of language, to identify the elements of language and meaning, to consider how language allows us to create the realities upon which we act, and to consider political uses of language.

The Nature of Language

Most of our early education in language emphasizes the meaning of words, their proper usage and placement in sentences, and how sentences form paragraphs. For those who attended school in the 1960's, language education consisted primarily of lessons on diagraming sentences and proper punctuation. Language, however, is more than a collection of words. Language is the instrument and vehicle for human action and expression. How important language is to us can perhaps best be illustrated by contrasting the "extentional world" with the "intentional world." The extentional world is the world of our senses, the world we know through firsthand experiences. You know the room you are sitting in because you are there: the precise color of the walls, the texture of the carpet, the comfort of the chair. The intentional world, however, is the world of language, words, and symbols, the world we know by received impressions. Perhaps you have never been to Europe, but you could describe many European things, people, and places because of what you have read or have been told by others. We know a great deal about the Civil War (the culture, the issues, the battles) not because of firsthand experience but because of what we have read. The point is obvious. For most of us, the world we know and understand is based upon knowledge which does not depend upon actual experience.

Signs

For purposes of discussion, it is useful to distinguish between signs and symbols. Signs have a one-to-one relationship to things signified. For example, thunder is a sign of a storm; fever is a sign of an illness; the tapping of a beaver's tail is a sign of danger. Signs have a fixed and concrete meaning regardless of context or audience. From this characterization, signs appear to be a function of natural elements beyond human manipulation. While this is largely true, signs can also be innate or learned. In America, a red octagon sign on the right side of a highway *always* means to stop an automobile. Because of the degree of international travel, signs are being introduced that pictorially provide universally agreed upon instructions for automobile driving.

Symbols

Symbols, in contrast to signs, may have many relationships to the thing signified. Basically, a symbol is that which stands for something else. The names of things, people, and events are symbols. Your name is a symbol that stands for or represents you. A minister is a symbol and stands for or represents a specific set of beliefs, values, and modes of conduct. Words are symbols that are conventionally agreed upon to represent certain things. Words, as symbols, are convenient. They simplify the amount of information needed to communicate about something. We need only say "chair" and we know that it is an item upon which we sit. We do not need to describe and explain that a "chair" is an item with a seat, back, and legs that supports one's weight. In addition, words enable us to communicate about things not physically present. They enable us to go beyond the limited world of our firsthand experiences; we can talk about past events and future endeavors. Symbols, therefore, are contextually flexible, arbitrary, and culturally learned.

Meaning

The relationship between a symbol or word and the thing it represents is what we call meaning. There is not a one-to-one relationship between words and meanings. Meanings are responses to symbolic stimuli grounded in commonality or experience. Ogden and Richards, in a simple diagram, clearly articulate the relationship of the symbol, object, and meaning.[4]

Figure 3.1

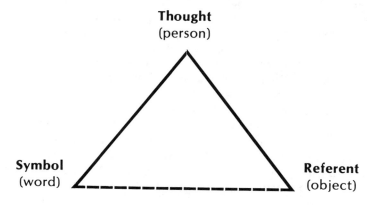

The relationships among symbols, thoughts, and objects.

The symbol is an approximation of the real thing. Words are, by definition, incomplete descriptions of objects. What if you are refering to abstract concepts such as freedom, equality, or liberty? Human communication is really a "stirring-up" process rather than a "transmitting" process. Words, as symbols, are arbitrary; they are created by humans and have significance only when two or more people agree to some general interpretation of the symbol. Everyone assumes the meaning of "chair" is clear. When the authors, with their academic backgrounds, think of a "chair," they may think of a leather, winged-back chair. Perhaps your mother thinks of a Queen Anne chair, or your father thinks of a big, comfortable recliner. Thus, words and symbols, even ordinary ones, have multiple meanings. In fact, the 500 most frequently used words in the English language have more than 14,000 meanings assigned to them.[5] The relationships between our symbols and what they represent are elusive, arbitrary, conventional, and ever changing.

There are two types of meanings. *Denotative meanings* refer to formal, dictionary, agreed upon meanings for words. The relationship between the word and its meaning is generally universal, informative, and describes essential properties of the referent. In this context, the word "chair" denotes an object upon which one sits. But it is the *connotative meanings* of words that provide positive or negative overtones. In this sense, the relationship between the word and the object are individual, personal, and subject to interpretation. If we say that an individual "sits in the chair of power," we mean more than the object upon which the person sits. For us, the eagle means more than a bird, the flag more than a piece of cloth, and a cross more than a piece of wood. As a result, words can have positive and negative meanings simultaneously. For some people, abortion is murder. For others, it is a constitutional right. The meaning of words change over time. A "bad" suit for your parents may imply an ugly, ill-fitting suit. To your peers, however, it may mean a sharp, good-looking suit. It should not surprise us, therefore, that Jimmy Carter's word choice in the *Playboy* interview shocked some people and reassured others.

There are several conclusions we can generate based upon the unique relationship between symbols and the things symbolized.

1. Meanings are in people and not in words. Words evoke different meanings in different people. They are relative and are based upon shared experiences and common culture. As Dan Rothwell asserts, "When we treat words as things, it is tantamount to eating the menu rather than the food."[6]

2. Words have more than one meaning. There may be as many meanings for a word as there are people who hear it.

3. As society and culture changes, so do common meanings of words and their acceptable usages. The words "colored," "Negro," "nigger," "black," and "Afro-American" have referred to the same race of people during the past half-century and each word has varied in degree of acceptability.

4. No word is inherently "good" or "bad." Society sanctions our morality, and language is used to justify it. Thus, the morality of words is culturally determined.

5. Words never tell everything there is to know about a person, event, or thing.

6. Words have no authority, people do.

We will further explore each of these implications as we continue our discussion of language.

Language

Language is an organized, agreed upon, and yet arbitrary system of symbols for communication. Each culture selects the sounds, symbols, and syntax that it uses as components of its language. Language is also experience-bound. We associate our daily experiences with symbols or names for our actions or behaviors. Soon it is difficult to separate the symbol from the act. In fact, some scholars believe that language acquisition is simply stimulation from communication transactions with others.

Language serves four basic functions. First, language is the vehicle for social interaction, a practical tool for getting things done. Each language system allows us to share information and to express desires. It allows us to function as a unit—to build, to create, and to destroy.

Language is our primary means of relating to the environment and to others, and language habits reflect our personality and emotional states. Through language, then, we organize reality and seek security and information.

Second, language facilitates thought and creativity. An interesting question is whether our behavior is a function of the language we speak. According to Benjamin Lee Whorf, the linguistic system a people uses shapes their ideas and guides mental activity.[7] Unique needs and precise responses to the environment require the development of inventive modes of thinking. For example, Eskimos have many words to describe the numerous kinds and conditions of snow while we have only a few. Aztecs have only one word for our "cold," "ice," and "snow." The limits and boundaries of our world are the limits and boundaries of our language; language facilitates creative and reflective thought.

Language is also based upon human experience. It is a way to "name" experiences and to establish categories that differentiate our experiences. At one extreme, we may argue that each word is simply a name of a category of experience because most languages do share thousands of common categories. For example, the English word "horse" is the French word "cheval" and the German word "pferd." Some categories of language, however, are untranslatable. The reasons may be grammatical, semantical, or experiential. Is a person's behavior a function of the language the person speaks? The argument is that each language system provides special ways of communicating about experiences and these particular communication methods create specific needs, responses, ways of thinking and, ultimately, behavior.

Third, language is a form of social behavior. If we are, as Aristotle proclaimed, "social animals," then language allows us to be so. Through language, we define social roles and rules of behavior, and our behavior is regulated more by words than by physical force. S.I. Hayakawa has noted that language has the same relationship to experience as a map does to an area of land.[8] A map is a pictorial representation of the territory and, to be useful, must be accurate and current. If not, we might get confused, lost, or even injured. Thus, it is important that a map reflect precisely the physical territory it represents. This is also true for language. Our language system must reflect accurately the extentional, empirical world. If our language is not precise, others may be confused or hurt. Misunderstanding may escalate to violence. There have been times in American history when the symbols of "liberty," "equality," and "equal opportunity" did not reflect the real world experience of some citizens. When Frederick Douglass, an ex-slave, was invited to commemorate the signing of the

Declaration of Independence in Rochester, New York in 1852, he began
by asking,

> Fellow citizens, pardon me, allow me to ask, why am I called upon
> to speak here today?... Are the great principles of political freedom
> and of natural justice, embodied in that Declaration of Indepen-
> dence, extended to us?... The blessings in which you, this day,
> rejoice are not enjoyed in common."

Confusion and violence occurred. Hitler described a world
unacceptable to other nations and war followed. Patrick Henry
articulated the importance of liberty for people that resulted in a
commitment to arms. In each case, language was the vehicle for social,
collective action. As communicators, the lesson is obvious and the
responsibility is clear.

Finally, language links the past with the present and makes
civilization possible. We can record our ideas, thoughts, plans, and
discoveries for future generations. We can then build upon our
knowledge and experiences. Isolated, alone and unable to
communicate through words, we would have to rediscover again and
again the making of fire, the use of tools, the treatment of disease, and
so on. We are, therefore, a product of all who have preceded us.
Human knowledge grows because we can record and transmit past
knowledge. We do not need to start our education again each day
because we can benefit from centuries of knowledge and experience.
Thus, language is vital to the growth and continuation of human
civilization.

With this broad overview of the importance and functions of
language to social life, let's now consider in greater detail how
language aids in the creation of self, reality, and society.

Language, Interaction, and Reality

The Creation of Reality Through Interaction

Why do students take so many classes? For some, the classes are
requirements. For others, class selections are electives. For most
students, however, classes are the means for obtaining a degree. Why
are so many different classes offered from so many different
departments? Most academic endeavors are overt attempts to
understand the nature and social behavior of human beings. We live in
relationships with others; formal education is a process of presenting a
variety of perspectives from which to study or view reality. Sociology,
psychology, history, science, politics, humanities, to name only a few,
represent perspectives that individuals may adopt to create and guide

their perceptions and interpretations of the world. Of course, no one perspective or discipline can account for all social phenomena. Thus, the exposure to different courses of study helps us to understand better the world in which we live.

Communication courses assume that people live in both a symbolic and physical environment. We, as well as elements of nature, are part of a physical reality. Our bodies are comprised of atoms, chemicals, etc. Since humans can learn and use symbols, we can interact with others to solve problems and influence our physical environment. Symbolic reality is an interpretation of physical reality. A tree in nature certainly has a physical reality. If, however, we were to paint a picture of it or attempt to describe it, our interpretation would be a reflection of reality. Further, if we were to seek the tree's shade or use it to make furniture, we have transformed its essence because it has become an object of selection, interpretation, and transformation.

People are constantly undergoing change through interaction. Thus, society is also constantly changing through interaction. Interaction among people creates our reality which is largely symbolic—that is, we *construct* meanings, *define* situations, and *provide* justifications for behavior. Hence, communication and interaction with others give "meaning" to the world and create the reality toward which we respond and act. We alone can create, manipulate, and use symbols to control our behavior and the behavior of others.

Language is the "vehicle" for shared meanings and interpretations. Our behavior is a by-product of interaction. Before a response to a situation can be formulated, the situation must first be defined and interpreted to ensure an appropriate response. Meanings of symbols are derived from interaction in rather specific social contexts. New interaction experiences may result in new symbols or new meanings for previous symbols. Consequently, one's understanding of the world may change. In the 1960's when black Americans were challenging years of white domination and discrimination, language played an important role in transforming perceptions of society. A "brother" was a fellow black person and "black power" represented group identity, pride, and self-awareness. The movement redefined the heritage of "Negro" into "Afro-American," reinforced a positive self-concept of "Black is Beautiful," and declared a new political activism.

Our view of the world may change as our symbol system is modified through interaction. This notion suggests that our social reality consists of symbolic systems and that reality is a social product arising from interaction or communication. Our reality is limited, specific, and circumscribed, but we can use social interaction to extend or limit our reality. Communication is the primary means for constructing and maintaining our social relationships. The world, as we know it, is simply a complex network of relationships.

"Self" as a Product of Interaction with Others

Who are you? What are you? Why do you like and dislike certain things? Why do you believe the things you believe and take the positions on issues you take? The answer lies in your personality as a social product that grows out of communicating with others. From birth we send out signals for others to confirm, deny, or modify. We interpret the signals sent back by people hoping to determine who we are and where we fit in. We gradually discern our status, our strengths and our weaknesses. Through communicating with others we become "somebody" and have opportunities to change ourselves.

The "self" actually becomes a social object that we share with others in communication. We come to "know" self in interaction with others. Throughout our lives we isolate, interpret, and define ourselves. The self literally becomes a separate entity to be modified, evaluated, and reinforced resulting from interaction with others.

Interacting with others thus provides a better understanding of ourselves. We discover who we are, what we are, and what we want to become. Our perception of the world, how the world perceives us, and how we perceive ourselves depends upon our contacts with other people.

Society as a Product of Interaction with Others

Since the most significant characteristic of the human race is its ability to communicate, it may be impossible to exaggerate the importance of speech in human society. We may define society as individuals in interaction, individuals acting in relation to each other, individuals engaging in cooperative action, and individuals communicating with self and others. People are constantly interacting, developing, and shaping society. As individuals communicate and interact, new situations are constantly arising requiring modification or reinforcement of existing rules of society.

Self-control is inseparable from social-control. The interrelationship between social-control and self-control is the result of commitment to various groups which produce self-fulfillment, self-expression, and self-identity. Social-control is not, therefore, a matter of formal governmental agencies, laws, rules, and regulations but a direct result of citizens identifying and internalizing the values of a group. Thus, values become essential to our self-esteem and act to support the social order. Adherence to the rules of society, therefore, becomes a fair price to pay for membership in a society. Communication joins all people.

Language, of course, provides the major framework for dictating ways of interpreting society and is more than a vehicle of thought.

Figure 3.2

Society usually teaches us "proper" responses to social situations. But for Lucy, words were not sufficient.

© 1972 United Feature Syndicate, Inc.

Language is thought and regulates our behavior by allowing a norm or value to supercede other symbols. For example, when you think aren't you actually "talking to yourself?" Don't you think in words and symbols? Aren't you aware of "bad" thoughts when you consider certain actions or behaviors? The point is that even in our private thoughts, we impose learned value judgments. Thus, in addition to creating expectations of behavior, symbols create social sanctions (i.e. war as God's will) or function as master symbols or "god terms" (i.e. to die for freedom). People are much more enclosed within symbolic systems than by the physical restraints of space and time. Our nation sent troops to Vietnam to ensure "freedom" for the Vietnamese people and to stop the spread of "communism." We are told that MX Missiles are the "peacekeepers" of the future. When followers, through socialization, have been taught "significant" symbols which uphold social order, they require leaders to "play" defined roles. Leaders and superiors must create and use symbols that unite and transcend individual and collective differences. Leaders articulate positions of superiority, inferiority, and equality; they persuade us through symbols of power, majesty, and authority.

Throughout our interactions, therefore, we learn what is good or bad, right or wrong. In discovering self, we identify, isolate, and assume socially defined roles. Society, then, is a product of a multitude of interactions that legitimize and sanction various roles which, subsequently, affect individual behavior.

We have certainly drawn a rather large circle in our discussion. We started with the role of language in defining and discovering ourselves and concluded with demonstrating how language maintains social order. Although in unit three of the book we are going to consider persuasion in specific contexts such as advertising, politics, and social movements, it is useful to examine further how language structures our social relationships and how those who rule over us use language.

Political Uses of Language

Language is not reserved for the good, honorable, or skilled. This human tool is available to all — the good and bad, the kind and cruel, the generous and selfish. It is, therefore, open to abuse as freely as it is to proper usage.

What makes language political is not the particular vocabulary or linguistic form but the substance of the information the language conveys, the setting in which the interaction occurs, and the explicit or implicit functions the language performs. Political language is often designed to evoke *reaction,* not thoughtful response. Political consciousness results from a symbolic interpretation of sociopolitical experience. To control, manipulate, or structure the interpretation is the primary goal of politics in general. A successful politician, then, will use rather specific linguistic devices that reinforce popular beliefs, attitudes, and values. Politicians actually must seek to avoid careful critique or analysis of complex issues, positions, or arguments.

Doris Graber identifies five major functions of political language: information dissemination, agenda-setting, interpretation and linkage, projection for the future and the past, and action stimulation.[9] Information is shared in many ways with the public in political messages. The most obvious, of course, is the sharing of explicit information about the state of the nation. Such dissemination of information is vital to the public's understanding and support of the political system. This is especially true in democratic nations where the public expects open access to the legislative debates and decision making of government officials. But the public, being sensitized to uses of language, can obtain information from what is *not* stated, *how* something is stated, or *when* something is stated. Often, especially in messages between nations, the public must read between the lines of official statements to ascertain proper meanings and significance of statements. Such inferences are useful in gauging security, flexibility, and sincerity. Sometimes the connotations of words communicate more truth than the actual statements. Are our relations with the Soviet Union "open," "guarded," or "friendly?" There are times, especially in tragedy that the very *act* of speaking by an official can communicate support, sympathy, or strength. Thus, the act of speaking rather than the words spoken conveys the meaning of the rhetorical event.

The topics politicians choose to discuss channel the public's attention and focus on issues to be discussed. This agenda-setting function of political language occurs in two ways. First, before "something" can become an issue, some prominent politician must articulate a problem and hence bring the issue to public attention. The issue can be rather obvious (poverty), in need of highlighting (status of American education), or created (The Great Society). Political language establishes a national agenda by controlling the information disseminated to the public. Within this realm there is always a great deal of competition because only a limited number of issues can maintain public interest and attention. While certain self-serving topics may be favored by a person, party, faction, or group; the same topics may be perceived as meaningless or even harmful to other factions, persons, or groups. While President Nixon wanted to limit discussion of the Watergate break-ins and tapes, rival groups wanted public debates and revelations to continue.

The act of calling the public's attention to an issue defines, interprets, and manipulates the public's perception of the issue. Causal explanations are often freely given but may be suspect. Control over the definition of a situation is essential in creating and preserving political realities. Participants in election primaries, for example, all proclaim victory regardless of the number of votes received. The top vote-getter becomes the "front runner." The second-place winner becomes "the underdog" candidate in an "up-hill battle." The third-place candidate becomes a "credible" candidate and an alternative for those "frustrated" or "dissatisfied" with the "same old party favorites." Political language defines and interprets reality and provides a rationale for future collective action.

A great deal of political language deals with predicting the future and reflecting upon the past. Candidates present idealized futures under their leadership and predict success if their policies are followed. Some predictions and projections are formalized in party platforms or in major addresses such as inaugurals or state of the unions. Nearly all such statements involve promises — promises of a brighter future if followed or Armageddon if rejected. Past memories and associations are evoked to stimulate a sense of security, better times, and romantic longings. An important function of political language, therefore, is to link us to past glories and to predict a successful future in order to reduce uncertainty in an increasingly complex world.

Finally, and perhaps most importantly, political language mobilizes society and stimulates social action. Language serves as the stimulus, means, or rationale for social action. Words can evoke, persuade, implore, command, label, praise, and condemn. Although political language is similar to other uses of language, it also articulates, shapes, and stimulates public discussion and behavior about the allocation of public resources, authority, and sanctions.

Common Political Language Devices

It should be obvious by now that the connotative, personal, interpretive meanings of words are potentially the most dangerous and easily abused. Words can be both descriptive and evaluative. As a result, a specific reality is constructed toward which we act and react. It is useful for us to identify some of the more common ways language is used to evoke specific responses in people.

Labeling. Defining and labeling stimuli and elements in our environment makes life easier. Labels tell us what is important about an object and what to expect; socialization prescribes how we should act or interact with the object defined. Labeling also forces us to make judgments and evaluations. The potential for abuse is expanded by the use of labels. It is easier to kill a "gook" or "jap" than a human being. Labeling an action as communistic or "socialistic" produces negative connotations in America. How should we characterize the government's "bail-out" of the Chrysler Corporation? What is government's role in terms of subsidies to the poor or Social Security? Are these examples of socialism? The point is obvious. Although we value the concepts of capitalism, free enterprise, and democracy, none of these concepts exist in a pure form. If governmental officials had described the saving of Chrysler as a socialistic solution, the legislation probably would have failed. Labeling works because it renders judgment by making positive or negative associations. How we act toward and perceive an individual differs greatly if we are told the person is inquisitive or nosey, cool or frigid, reflective or moody, thorough or picky, forgetful or senile.

Doublespeak. Doublespeak is saying one thing but meaning something else. It confuses or hides the true meaning or intent of the communicator. For example, there is a very different reality and interpretation created by calling a concentration camp a "pacification center," a military retreat a "tactical withdrawal," tax increases a "revenue enhancement," or MX missiles a system of "peacekeepers." Such uses of language may con us into accepting unreasonable arguments or policies.

Jargon. Specialized terms tend to mystify and lend an air of credibility to topics. As with other language uses, jargon can also confuse or hide the truth. The need to conduct a "needs assessment" (a survey) in order to develop an adequate "evaluation tool" (a test) for those who will manage a "transportation component" (a bus) certainly sounds like a complex and expensive project. Legal documents are full of specialized jargon. Such documents require "special" interpretations which make us dependent upon attorneys for help, advice, and action. The medical profession also relys heavily upon specialized jargon to communicate. Notice how the use of technical language reduces interference from those outside the inner circle and acts as an inhibitor to full, open discussion in Figure 3.3.

Figure 3.3

> ### A Letter from the U.S. Tariff Commission to the Administrative Conference of the U.S.
>
> This is in reply to your letter concerning the "data-gathering and processing systems of this agency having to do with administrative proceedings."
>
> The problems and considerations therein presented, together with ancillary ramifications, have been carefully analyzed in conjunction with manipulative and non-manipulative factors relative to administrative equilibrium. Our conclusions, while tentative and perhaps unsuited to peripheral institutionalization, suggest in marked degree a sub-marginal coefficient of applicability vis-a-vis the activities of the Commission, and have thus been deemed an appropriate basis for non-actional orientation toward the questionnaire accompanying your letter.
>
> Please advise us if further information is needed.

Slanting.   Slanting is a form of outright misrepresentation where a particular implication is suggested by omitting certain crucial information. For example, a politician may proclaim that more people are employed today than ever before in our nation's history while the percentage of people employed might well be lower than ever before. Thus, without lying, the information presented could create a different impression than the facts warrant.

Summary

We began this chapter by considering the impact of Jimmy Carter's words "screw" and "shack-up" in his presidential campaign of 1976. For some, these words challenged his sincerity, credibility, and integrity. For others, it showed he was human and non-judgmental.

Symbols are human inventions. They have meaning or significance only when, through experience or agreement, we interpret them. Through language we construct reality which influences our behavior. Through interaction with others we come to know who we are, how we fit in, and what we are supposed to do.

Finally, we investigated the nature of political language. We saw how language can be used to control us, to confuse us, and to hide information from us. Human communication can never fully capture reality because it is fundamentally a process of selection, interpretation, and symbolism. All communication is, however, purposeful. Thus, we must not only focus on the structure of arguments or the evidence provided but also on the language used to define or describe our "reality."

Notes

[1]Kenneth Burke, *Language as Symbolic Action* (Los Angeles: University of California Press, 1966), 5.

[2]Robert Scheer, "*Playboy* Interview: Jimmy Carter," *Playboy* (November 1976), 63-86.

[3]Scheer, 86.

[4]C. Ogden and I.A. Richards, *The Meaning of Meaning* (New York: Harcourt Brace Jovanovich, 1923).

[5]Dan Rothwell, *Telling It Like It Isn't* (Englewood Cliffs, NJ: A Spectrum Book, 1982), 13.

[6]Rothwell, 48.

[7]See "The Function of Language Classification in Behavior" by John Carroll and Joseph Casagrande in Alfred Smith, *Communication and Culture* (New York: Holt, Rinehart & Winston, 1966), 491.

[8]S.I. Hayakawa, *Language in Thought and Action*, Third Edition (New York: Harcourt Brace Jovanovich, 1972), 27-30.

[9]Doris Graber, "Political Languages," in *Handbook of Political Communication*, ed. Dan Nimmo and Keith Sanders (Beverly Hills, CA: Sage Publications, 1981), 195-224.

Questions and Projects for Further Study

1. Does it matter if we say a glass is half full or half empty? Why?
2. Think of words or expressions for which the meanings are clear to you but may not be clear to your parents? Can you explain why?
3. What is your greatest strength? How do you know?
4. What is your greatest weakness? How do you know?
5. Give an example of how you define "self" through an interaction you've had with another or others.
6. Do you stop at a stop sign even if no one is around? Why?
7. What does the term "freedom" mean to you? What does the term "equality" mean to you?

Additional Reading

Adler, Ronald; and George Rodman. *Understanding Human Communication*. New York: Holt, Rinehart, and Winston, 1985.

Blumer, Herbert. *Symbolic Interactionism: Perspective and Method*. Englewood Cliffs, NJ: Prentice Hall, 1969.

Denton, Robert E., Jr.; and Gary Woodward, *Political Communication in America*. New York: Praeger, 1985.

DeVito, Joseph. *Human Communication*. Third Edition. New York: Harper and Row, 1985.

Duncan, Hugh. *Symbols in Society*. New York: Oxford University Press, 1968.

Goodall, Lloyd. *Human Communication: Creating Reality*. Dubuque, IA: Wm. C. Brown, 1983.

PART 2

FOUR PERSPECTIVES ON THE NATURE OF PERSUASION

In this section we look at four different ways to explore the nature of influence and attitude change. As rhetorical theorist Trevor Melia has noted, every field of knowledge provides a different means of understanding the same human events. Like four peaks surrounding a valley, each of the perspectives in this section offers a unique point of view on the varied terrain of persuasion. All four perspectives can be used to examine messages; however, each chapter provides a singular vantage point from which the careful observer may analyze particular aspects of messages. In many ways the traditions overlap, but each also offers distinct and sometimes contradictory conclusions about certain persuasion processes.

Chapter 4 begins with a brief comparison of the two social science traditions in the study of persuasion: the social and psychological. It then focuses on the social perspective that accounts for the formation of attitudes within groups and the society. Chapter 5 examines persuasion from a logical point of view with emphasis on the invaluable criteria that help us determine when assertions are worthy of belief. Chapter 6 explores the internal or psychological processes which occur when attitudes are challenged and changed. It describes several extremely useful models that account for what happens "inside" the receiver. The final chapter in this section concludes with an exploration of the important roles that leadership and authority play in winning converts.

4

Social Bases
of Persuasion

 OVERVIEW

[A] man's opinions depend not so much on his own character, as on his social environment, on the people he associates with and lives among.[1]

Explanations of persuasion generally operate along two perspectives. The psychological perspective is concerned with the internal processes within the individual that accompany persuasive attempts. The social perspective focuses primarily on how group beliefs and values affect the construction of messages. After exploring the differences between these two approaches, this chapter looks at the social view with special emphasis on how public opinion affects the ways we act and think.

Social and Psychological Perspectives Contrasted

A knowledgeable mechanic looks at a new car differently than the salesperson who must sell it. While the mechanic understands the car in terms of its internal systems, the salesperson sees it as one of many products competing for attention in the marketplace. The salesperson knows that advertisements for automobiles have more to do with desirable images and lifestyles than pure mechanical facts. For instance, advertisers would have us believe that cars, and presumably the people who buy them, are "elegant," "fast," "sporty" or "awesome." A car is not only transportation; it becomes a status symbol for the buyers who are attracted to it.[2]

The differences between the social and psychological explanations of how persuasive processes work are similar to the differences between the mechanic and the salesperson. Psychological explanations of persuasion (discussed more completely in Chapter 6) account for the internal processes which occur when individuals are confronted with messages that reinforce or challenge existing attitudes. For the psychologist, the ultimate subject is the individual, and the primary medium of study is the individual's behavior. Like mechanics, psychologists of persuasion want to know what is going on "inside." Unlike mechanics, they must resort to models or formulas which give form to the unseen thoughts guiding behavior. Examples of areas for psychological research might be: how do people react to a persuasive appeal encouraging consumption of fried grasshoppers?;[3] what does the detailed charting of a magazine reader's eye movement tell us about the way people respond to the layout of graphics and text in a print ad?;[4] or what attitudes do children develop as a result of watching hundreds of hours of television news shows portraying the social chaos of crime, corruption, and human tragedy?[5]

By contrast, theories of persuasion which have their roots in *social* explanations assume that the personalities of specific individuals are reflections of the society in which they live. Like salespersons who learn to work with an automobile's socially-generated image, social theorists look at the power of culture to shape values and beliefs. They start with the premise that we are largely what our contact with others has made us. As soon as we enter the world, we begin to acquire attitudes from a maze of interactions which give our lives meaning and purpose. This socialization process begins with the family, but it is soon joined by a variety of forces including church, school, work, and the casual associations of daily life. Our world becomes governed by networks of obligations and memberships through which we acquire and share common attitudes.

A complete understanding of persuasion depends upon combining all possible perspectives. Communication is both an individualistic and group-centered process. The use of one approach does not exclude the other because each focuses on a different level of explanation. Persuasion involves some degree of *internal* transformation of attitudes, beliefs, opinions, and behaviors.[6] At the same time, what we believe is largely socially determined.[7] The presence of formal and informal groups within a culture accounts for how we acquire and hold attitudes.[8] We may exercise our choices on many decisions, but we first acquire an awareness of our choices through the dominating presence of our associations. As one of the early founders of Sociology, Emile Durkheim, put it:

> Sentiments born and developed in the group have a greater energy than purely individual sentiments. A man who experiences such sentiments feels himself dominated by outside forces that lead him and pervade his milieu. He feels himself in a world quite distinct from his own private existence.... Following the collectivity, the individual forgets himself for the common end and his conduct is oriented in terms of a standard outside himself.[9]

The familiar claim that we are "social" animals is thus basic to the study of persuasion. By nature, we are learners and imitators. For persuasion theorists these patterns are analyzed in *audiences* made up of people with similar beliefs or characteristics who have access to the same persuasive messages.

Auditioning Messages:
Identification and the Audience Analysis Process

Persuasion is different from other forms of communication because it is primarily directed to an audience beyond oneself. The test of the practical effectivensss of persuasion rests in determining whether specific messages will produce desired responses from audiences. Experienced persuaders usually "try out" their messages prior to presentation. This auditioning may be informal. For example, we often attempt to predict the probable reactions our friends will have to an opinion before we actually express our ideas. The audition may also be formal. Elaborate and expensive audience analysis studies are used by broadcasters and advertisers. In either case, the goal is the same: to locate points of identification that will "bridge" the gulf separating persuaders from those they want to influence.

Auditioning Messages, Hollywood Style

Preview House is a 400-seat theater in Hollywood used by advertisers and the television industry to audition new programs and commercials.[10] Ordinary people are given free tickets to screenings. The participants begin their roles as audience members by completing questionnaires about their television-viewing and product-purchasing habits. They are then seated in the comfortable theater where each seat contains a control knob which can be turned to settings reflecting the opinion of the audience member: very good, good, normal, dull, and very dull. Each seat is connected to a computer which registers the audience's collective reaction to whatever is on the screen. The equivalent of a spirited television game show host guides the audience through the evening's viewing. One recent and wary participant recalls his experiences:

> He shows us an ancient Mr. Magoo cartoon so we can practice rating what we see.
> On comes the [television] pilot for "Owl and the Pussycat." My pointer settles into the dull range. Upstairs in the control booth, computers are recording all our responses and logging them for later analysis.
>
> . . . .
>
> On comes a series of dreadful spot commercials.... There's one for a mouthwash, a pain reliever, a savings and loan, etc. Our pointers are busy.

Once the commercials are over, we fill out more papers. They want
to know what we remember about the commercials. Translation:
Did they brand the brand name into our brains.

Then comes Preview House White Lie No. 1: They're sorry, but one
of the sheets we filled out was missing a product category. Would
we mind filling it out again. This is a phony ploy to see if we like
Excedrin better after seeing the commercial than we did before.
Most everybody falls for it.

. . . .

Finally they want us to see a short animated film.... The film turns
out to be the award-winning Ernest Pintoff-Mel Brooks short subject, The Critic, a guaranteed laugh riot. This is the control study: If
we won't laugh at this, we have no sense of humor and our group
attitude toward "Owl and the Pussycat" is invalid.[11]

Preview House involves an elaborate kind of auditioning, but it
follows patterns common to every form of persuasive communication.
Perhaps advertisers and the networks are more anxious than other
persuaders to follow rather than to lead opinion; but like all of us, they
know that audience judgments are important.

The Principle of Identification

Not all communicators are persuaders; that is, some communication
is not intended to win over audiences. For example, poets or musicians
may work to please only themselves or to achieve a private aesthetic
goal. The act of self-expression may be its own reward. Although most
art *is* rhetorical (meaning artists seek receptive audiences), it is
plausible for a defiant writer or composer to say, "I like it, and that is
all that's important." Persuaders, however, must always go further;
they must construct messages which narrow the gap between their
attitudes and those of their audiences. In ways not demanded of
artists, they must reconcile their differences with those whom they
seek to influence. "You persuade a man," notes theorist Kenneth
Burke, "only insofar as you can talk his language by speech, gesture,
tonality, order, image, attitude, idea, *identifying* your ways with his."[12]
Reaching an audience is rooted in a persuader's ability to understand
what its members believe, what they like and dislike, what they take
for granted, and what they will challenge. Persuasion may be
described as a process which uses the familiar to gain acceptance for
the unfamiliar.

The principle of identification may be the most universal of all the
rules of persuasion. St. Augustine noted that a person is persuaded if
he "embraces what you commend, regrets whatever you built up as
regrettable, rejoices at what you say is cause for rejoicing," in short,
when the person thinks as you do.[13] This classical idea can be seen at

work in the mind of a masterful creator of modern radio and television commercials, Tony Schwartz. Schwartz believes that the most effective persuasion acts as a stimulus to trigger experiences and feelings *already contained* within a person. A persuader, he notes, "must deeply understand the kinds of information and experiences stored in his audience, the patterning of this information, and the interactive...process whereby stimuli evoke this stored information."[14] Identification is the sharing of experiences and values; it is achieved when listeners and readers sense that what is being said expresses their feelings.

We can establish identification on many different levels. Our manner of dress and style of delivery can communicate physical similarity, while the expressions and examples we use can reassure an audience that we share similar experiences. In examining two speeches by civil rights activist Stokely Carmichael, for example, analysts have confirmed that Carmichael changed considerably when speaking to different audiences:

> He gave one of the speeches to a predominantly black audience in Detroit on July 30, 1966 and the other to a predominantly white audience in Whitewater, Wisconsin on February 6, 1967. The addresses were surprisingly similar in content and examples, but they differed greatly in style and persuasive appeals. For the black audience, Carmichael personified the ideology he was advancing— in delivery, style, attitude, while for the white audience, he dwelt mainly on the explanation of ideology.... He advocated violent resistance in the Detroit speech, but in the Whitewater address he used milder references to violence and used them in a context of self defense.... Clearly Carmichael "identified" with each of his audiences.[15]

Identification Through Norms and Commonplaces

The word communicate has its origins in the Latin word, *communicare:* meaning "to make common to many." The Latin definition is a perfect reminder that communication is fundamentally about the process of locating ideas that audiences can recognize as their own.

Universal Commonplaces. Widely shared cultural beliefs are sometimes called *commonplaces.* They represent the core values and beliefs which characterize a particular society. As basic expressions of shared values, commonplaces are frequently unstated but important assumptions behind everyday thought. According to the French social theorist Jacques Ellul, a basic commonplace may be taken for granted as part of the fabric of ideas governing everyday life:

It serves everyone as a touchstone, an instrument of recognition. It is rarely quoted, but it is constantly present; it is behind thought and speech; it is behind conversation. It is the common standard that enables people to understand one another when they discuss politics or civilization.[16]

Some of the most faithful compilers of commonplaces have been anthropologists and sociologists determined to "map" out the ideological landscape of a tribe, nation, or culture. W. Lloyd Warner's classic five volume "Yankee City" series, for example, studied the "typical" American city of Boston with the same intensity and objectivity that a visiting team of anthropologists might employ in looking at an unknown tribe on a Pacific island. Warner examined political speeches, advertisements, sermons, cemetery markers, and even floats in a Memorial Day parade to discover what they revealed about the beliefs and values of Boston's social life.[17] In 1935, researchers Robert and Helen Lynd studied an American city dubbed "Middletown" with a similar interest in the attitudes commonly held in large sections of the community. They catalogued the essential commonplaces of the city, "the things that one does and feels and says so naturally that mentioning them in Middletown implies an 'of course.'"[18] A sampling from their list of attitudes on the general subject of "the proper roles for government" points out the durability of many American commonplaces. The Lynds recorded some of the following government-related commonplaces held by the citizens of Middletown:

That the American democratic form of government is the final and ideal form of government.

That the Constitution should not be fundamentally changed.

That Americans are the freest people in the world.

That America will always be the land of opportunity and the greatest and richest country in the world.

That England is the finest country in Europe.

That Washington and Lincoln were the greatest Americans....

That the voters, in the main, really control the operation of the American government.

That newspapers give citizens "the facts."

That the two-party system is the "American way."

That it does not pay to throw away one's vote on a minority party.

That government ownership is inefficient and more costly than private ownership.

That the government should leave things to private initiative.

"More business in government and less government in business."[19]

Not every individual would accept all of these fundamental starting points, nor do they remain unchanged from generation to generation.[20]

They are, however, "universal" because they reflect mainstream public opinion at a specific time. We can isolate them as the building blocks of persuasion because they are readily accepted by so many within a culture. Awareness of key commonplaces makes it easier to initiate a sequence of persuasive appeals.

Tracking Two Commonplaces from the Lynd's Study.   Almost any persuasive message can be shown to have broad-based commonplaces as key starting points. Presidents, for example, frequently employ two of the last three commonplaces cited by the Lynds:

> That government ownership is inefficient and more costly than private enterprise.
>
> That the government should leave things to private initiative.

In his 1982 State of the Union Address Ronald Reagan stated these as keystones of his political agenda.

> We must cut out more nonessential Government spending and root out more waste, and we will continue our efforts to reduce the number of employees in the Federal work force by 75,000.[21]

He also pledged to turn over more governmental functions to private groups using wording which paraphrased the Lynds' commonplace. He said,

> Our private sector initiatives task force is seeking out successful community models of school, church, business, union, foundation and civic programs that help community needs. Such groups are almost invariably far more efficient than government in running social programs."[22]

Both statements reflected specific policy objectives that the Reagan administration advocated to Congress and the American people, and both were aided by long-standing American suspicions about the ability of governments to perform efficiently.

Consider two additional examples from the 1976 Presidential campaign that pitted incumbent Gerald Ford against Jimmy Carter. Each of the candidates ran television commercials featuring the theme of governmental size. Carter's commercials emphasized his business background as a peanut grower and his cost-cutting work as Governor of Georgia. One of the commercials began:

> CARTER: (talking to the camera) When I was elected governor, I went into office not as a politician but as an engineer, a farmer, a businessman, a planter. We had 300 agencies and departments in the government. We abolished 278 of them.... That saved a lot of money.... With a new budgeting technique called zero-based budgeting we eliminated all the old obsolescent programs. [We] put into

effect long-range goals, planning, and cut administrative costs by 50 percent, and shifted that money and that service ... toward giving better government services to our people.[23]

A Ford commercial countered with references to the same embedded commonplaces about the evils of big government:

ANNOUNCER: [Jimmy Carter's] ads say that he will do the same thing as president that he did as governor of Georgia. (Pictures of Georgia map with % increased numbers superimposed) Then you should know that during one term as governor, government spending increased 58 percent. Government employees went up 25 percent. Georgia went over 20 percent into debt. Don't let Jimmy Carter give us more big government. (Picture of Gerald Ford) Keep President Ford.[24]

Both ads explored the same themes by glorifying the efficiency of American business practices and casting suspicion on the dangers of "big government." Irrespective of party, most Presidents seek common ground from which to make their appeals. In the words of one White House insider, "Everything here is built on the idea that the President's success depends on grass roots support."[25]

Audience-Specific Norms.   Some topics require persuasion that uses more specific and more controversial starting points. Audience specific norms differ from universal commonplaces by appealing to a limited number of groups within a society. Divisive subjects such as abortion rights for women, controls on the sale of firearms, mandatory requirements to wear seat belts, prayer in schools, the death penalty, and farm subsidies for tobacco growers have passionate supporters on both sides. As issues become more specific, individuals become more selective in the values and attitudes they accept. American society consists of thousands of organizations and coalitions: some formal and some informal. All of us are in the mainstream of opinion on some topics and in the minority on others. Our membership in a complex society frequently makes us "floaters" moving with the tide of public opinion sometimes and swimming against the prevailing current at other times.

As public discussion of controversial issues becomes more specific, differences emerge that cannot be resolved by persuasion based on universal commonplaces. The presence of controversy makes audience-specific norms important. These "in group" ideas are not universally accepted by a society, but are sustained by specific groups. Most controversies displayed in headlines encourage persuasion directed to various constituencies with specialized priorities or norms. Examples range from Action for Children's Television against the major television networks, the organization "Green Peace" against

Figure 4.1

A word to smokers
(about working together)

Whether you're a billboard painter or just, as you obviously are, a reader of magazines, you've discovered that there's a difference between *non*smokers and *anti*-smokers.

We all work with nonsmokers — and they work with us. Roughly 60% of the people around us are nonsmokers, and 40% of them are smokers — so we *have* to work together. And, like our sign painters, we do.

Anti-smokers are a breed apart. They don't want us to work together with nonsmokers. And they go to some extreme lengths to see that we don't.

Two examples:

1. A nationally known TV and film star was prevented from performing by a band of anti-smokers threatening violence because the star frequently smoked on stage. The occasion was a benefit to raise funds for handicapped children.

2. The executive director of one anti-smoking group announced plans to build an "army" of 2,000,000 anti-smoking militants who would go about "zapping" smokers in the face with spray from aerosol cans.

"You don't know what a rewarding feeling it is," he is quoted as saying, "the first time you spray a smoker in the face. It's hard to work yourself up to the first spray. It takes guts. But once you've broken the ice, it's easy. And you feel exhilarated."

Such people clearly do *not* represent the nonsmokers we all know and work with. They would not last long in any working environment where people must cooperate to get the job done. And we doubt very much that the "zappers" will find 2,000,000 others to go along with them. Americans just don't think that way.

Such anti-smokers are not only anti-smoking. They're giving themselves the reputation of being anti-individualism, anti-freedom of choice, anti-everything that does not agree with their special prejudices. And in that they're as much a threat to nonsmokers as they are to smokers.

THE TOBACCO INSTITUTE
1776 K St. N.W. Washington, D.C. 20006
Freedom of choice
is the best choice.

Warning: The Surgeon General Has Determined That Cigarette Smoking Is Dangerous to Your Health.

An ad using universal commonplaces.
Used by permission of The Tobacco Institute.

A word to nonsmokers
(about working together)

Wherever you work — even if you're a billboard painter — you work with smokers, and always have.

There's nothing remarkable about that. Forty percent of the people around you are smokers, and 60% are nonsmokers. Still, we work, live, and enjoy ourselves together.

Lately, however, we've all become super-sensitive to each other and to each other's privileges and obligations. And that's not a bad thing.

We agree on many things. There are places (crowded elevators, to take the simplest example) where smoking is not appropriate. In closed and private places, the ancient courtesy of "Do you mind if I smoke?" is still the best rule. Smokers, we believe, have become more generally conscious of that courtesy. The occasional careless smoker, waving a lighted cigarette or cigar, should, in our opinion, be as quickly reminded of others' preferences by a thoughtful smoker as by a nonsmoker.

Nevertheless there *are* some people— anti-smokers rather than nonsmokers — who will never be satisfied with our sensible accommodations to each other. They don't want us to work together at all. Instead they want to segregate us by law — literally to build walls between us — at considerable expense to both smokers and nonsmokers — in places where we work, shop, eat or just go to amuse ourselves.

We know that such anti-smokers do not represent the great majority of nonsmokers. And the anti-smokers know it, too. But there is a danger that others will think they do.

"When I went to the legislature," says one anti-smoking lobbyist, "they thought I had about 10,000 people behind me. That was a laugh. It was just me. I had the law passed by myself."

If it is a "laugh" for the anti-smoker, it is no joke for the rest of us for we must all, smokers and nonsmokers alike, pay the cost of such foolish laws. All of us are losers when any one of us is denied freedom of choice.

We don't think that, over the long run, that's going to happen. We think that, like our billboard painters, we'll go on working together until we get the job done.

THE TOBACCO INSTITUTE
1776 K St. N.W. Washington, D.C. 20006
Freedom of choice
is the best choice.

industrial polluters and whaling nations, the National Rifle Association against the National Association of Chiefs of Police, to Mothers Against Drunk Driving against state legislatures and the courts. It is vital to remember that some groups have very different ideas about what is "good," "just," "fair," and "important."

Consider the diverse audiences the American tobacco industry must address, especially in light of widely reported research on the harmful health consequences of cigarette smoking. The industry's public relations arm, The Tobacco Institute, is active on several fronts: preparing ads to counter publicity on the negative health effects of smoking, lobbying against restrictive policies on smoking in public areas, defending tobacco farming and agricultural subsidies, and dealing with non-smokers over the disputed effects of "secondary smoke." In its ads to general audiences in magazines and newspapers, The Tobacco Institute usually invokes the most universal commonplaces such as ideals of fair play and freedom of choice. In the ad reprinted in Figure 4.1 they note that some "anti-smokers are not only anti-smoking. They're giving themselves the reputation of being anti-individualism, anti-freedom of choice, anti-everything that does not agree with their special prejudice." Appeals that evoke the familiar commonplaces of individualism and freedom are meant to define smoking as an activity that falls within the universally accepted rights of individual choice and liberty.

In addition to general audiences, the tobacco industry also wants to reach more specific groups, especially opinion leaders in the mass media. The industry regularly advertises in *Broadcasting*, a slick weekly magazine read by many news producers and broadcast journalists. Ads like the one reprinted in Figure 4.2 remind broadcasters that it is possible to "spark a lot of interest" and "get people involved" by using tobacco industry spokespersons on programs where smoking issues are debated. The tobacco companies adapted their techniques to fit the new audience. They appealed to the broadcasters' desire to enhance ratings by implying that tobacco industry advocates provoke controversy. In short, the industry uses universal commonplaces for general audiences, and audience-specific norms to reach specialized groups such as television producers.

Audiences Considered:
Traditional Methods for Judging Attitudes and Beliefs

The thoughtful persuader can discern many of the attitudes of an audience without much difficulty. It takes no extensive study to predict that an advocate for higher tuition is going to meet predictable opposition on a college campus. The process of audience analysis is not always so precise. Generalizations about what a collection of people

Figure 4.2

WHERE THERE'S SMOKE, THERE'S CONTROVERSY.

People feel strongly about smoking. You can spark a lot of interest by exposing them to both sides of issues involving cigarettes.
Walker Merryman can help. His job is giving straight answers to tough questions about cigarettes. In person or on the phone.
Get the other side too. And you'll get people involved.

CALL TOLL-FREE **(800) 424-9876**
THE TOBACCO INSTITUTE.

An ad using an audience-specific norm.

Used by permission of The Tobacco Institute.

"think" are reliable only if individuals in the group are similar in basic and important ways.

There are two ways to learn about audience characteristics. One is to make generalizations about what the audience *thinks* based on the kind of people they *are*. Certain attributes such as age, occupation, and religious affiliation can predict attitudes. The second method is to test for attitudes by systematically polling a representative sample of the audience. In actual practice, both of these methods are used together, but it is useful to consider their differences.

Inferring Audience Attitudes   Every audience can be profiled by certain traditional measures: age, sex, income level, educational level, geographical location, and membership in formal associations. These are standard "demographic" categories. Demographics means, literally, "measurement of the people." Since most groups show greater similarities than differences in at least some of these traits, it is possible to make cautious generalizations about group attitudes. Radio stations and their advertisers, for example, generally find that preferences for musical formats correlate with particular kinds of listeners: teens, older adults, suburban adults, men, and so on. As Figure 4.3 shows, the major television networks, including NBC, attempt to show prospective advertisers that their programs reach

Figure 4.3

NBC

OUR INVESTMENT IN QUALITY PRIMETIME PROGRAMS IS PAYING DIVIDENDS.

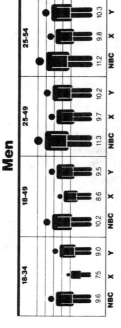

Adults

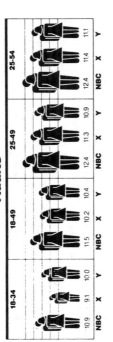

Women

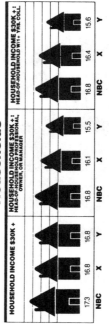

Men

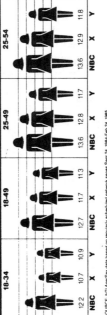

Households

SOURCE: NTI Age/Sex data based on regularly scheduled network series Sept 24, 1984–Feb 24, 1985. Household income data NAD Network Prime Time average Oct, Nov, Dec 1984. Audience and related data subject to qualifications available on request.

For broadcasters, favorable demographics are crucial in attracting advertisers.

Copyright © 1984 National Broadcasting Co., Inc. All Rights Reserved.

commercially lucrative segments of the population such as high income households and adult women who make a high percentage of family purchases.

Inference-making is partly a matter of guesswork. It involves using known facts to arrive at conclusions about unknown facts. Although such inferences are inexact, it is advantageous to make assumptions about the attitudes of people based on what is known about their personal and social situations. Audiences with heavy concentrations of farmers should be treated differently than audiences of bankers, retirees, union members, or college seniors. Persuaders addressing these groups would work backwards from general traits to an estimate of probable attitudes and values each group could be expected to endorse or to condemn. The famous trial lawyer Clarence Darrow routinely employed this process to find the most elusive of audiences: 12 people who might be sympathetic to a person charged with a crime. Before a trial begins, lawyers screen prospective jurors on a wide range of criteria. Darrow thought certain demographic features were reliable indicators of probable juror sympathies. He wrote:

> The main work of a trial lawyer is to make a jury like his client, or at least, to feel sympathy for him; facts regarding the crime are relatively unimportant. I try to get a jury with little education but with much human sympathy. The Irish are always the best jurymen for the defense. I don't want a Scotchman, for he has too little human feelings; I don't want a Scandanavian, for he has too strong a respect for the law as law. In general I don't want a religious person, for he believes in sin and punishment. The defendant should avoid rich men who have a high regard for law, as they make it and use it .... The man who is down on his luck, who has trouble, who is more or less a failure, is much kinder to the poor and unfortunate than are the rich and selfish.[26]

Darrow's simple hunches may seem crude and inexact. Yet, generalizations from broad demographic categories frequently require second-guessing—sometimes with enormous success. For instance, when the multi-million dollar gambling industry in Atlantic City sought to increase traffic through the lucrative gaming halls, the casino operators wanted to know what kinds of people were potential visitors and spenders. The demographic profile they arrived at was far different from the movie image of the "high roller." The average gambler was married, frequently elderly, often retired, and living within 150 miles of Atlantic City.[27] This information made it possible for casinos to adapt to the needs of their customers. Among other things, "free" one day bus trips were offered to pensioners living in the Northeast.

Surveying Audience Attitudes   Inference-making is useful but
risky. Concluding that "older Americans" think in a certain way
because they are older involves a good deal of simplistic stereotyping.
Age (sex, income level, education level, and so on) by itself is no
guarantee that someone will think or act in a certain way. In addition,
large and demographically diverse audiences cannot be easily
targeted for specific and unique sets of attitudes.

Direct measurement of attitudes usually gives more reliable
information about an audience than an inferred assessment. Survey
research is more expensive and time consuming than simple
demographic analysis, but it will reveal more than who the audience *is*;
it will measure what they *think*. Access to a representative sample of a
target group in face-to-face interviews (or in settings such as Preview
House) makes it possible to determine the values and beliefs that may
present opportunities for or obstacles to persuasion.

Persuaders such as advertisers and political campaigners use many
different survey research techniques. Among them are "in depth"
interviews with sample audience members and questionnaires which
use scales to measure responses to key concepts or evocative words.
As the attitude scale in Figure 4.4 demonstrates, it is relatively easy to
determine specific attitudes individuals may have toward one concept
such as the proposal that television advertising of beer and wine be
banned. Understanding why negative or positive feelings are triggered
by certain words can help determine how a controversial subject
should be approached. Regardless of the system used, the goal of
attitude surveys is to learn as much as possible about the priorities,
feelings, and judgments of those who will be the focus of appeals.
Although survey research is now common for professional persuaders,
it is prohibitively expensive. For most of us, an unfamiliar audience
must still be understood by generalizing from who they are to what
they think.

An Audience-Based Model for Auditioning Ideas

Persuasion, in its simplest form, can be reduced to three important
variables. For persuasion to occur, there must be an *advocate*
(someone or group with a viewpoint to express), a *message* (the point of
view the advocate wants listeners to accept), and an *audience*
(listeners, viewers, or readers). Removal of any variable makes
communication impossible. Our three-sided model of this process
presented in Figure 4.5 is based on the work of researchers attempting
to look at how people maintain and change their attitudes.[28] What the
model reveals about six possible types of persuasive encounters is the

Figure 4.4

For the past several years, Congress has been considering whether television advertising for beer and wine produces harmful effects. The
following Attitude Rating Scale might be used by advocates on this issue
(the wine and beer industry, and other groups) to determine audience
attitudes. Respondents are asked to mark a place on the scale that comes
closest to their own feelings about a specific topic. In this case:

Television and Radio Commercials for Beer and Wine
(Mark the scale at the point closest to your own feelings.)

Helpful						Useless
Unwise						Wise
Fun						Dangerous
Silly						Clever
Exciting						Dull
Truthful						Untruthful
Useless						Useful
Informative						False
Safe						Dangerous

subject of the remainder of this chapter.

This simple guide illustrates the fact that advocates, audiences, and
messages directly interact with each other in six different
configurations. It implies that two key questions should be asked about
any persuasive encounter: 1. Does the audience like the advocate?
and 2. Does the audience share the advocate's point of view?

Here is how these important questions are answered. Imagine that
for any persuasive setting it is reasonable to estimate relationships
between the three variables as positive (+) or negative (−). A positive
sign indicates approval; a negative sign indicates disapproval. For
example, the most difficult form of persuasion is diagrammed in 4.5f.

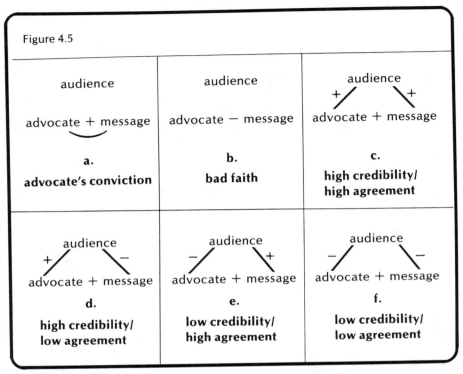

Six possible persuader-audience relationships.

This is a case where—as we would expect—the persuader has a positive regard for his ideas, but it is also a setting where the audience has negative feelings toward both the persuader and his ideas. Before turning to this and other variations, however, we begin our analysis with a look at the only relationship that *should be* (but is not always) constant: the advocate's positive faith in the rightness of his ideas.

The Unchanging Relationship: The Advocate's Conviction

Figure 4.5a diagrams a normal expectation built into all communication. Although what an audience thinks about a topic may range from approval to disapproval, the audience assumes that the persuader's faith in what is advocated is unshakable. Assuming no coercion, people would be unlikely to construct a message that argues in favor of a rejected point of view. Such "bad faith" communication is diagrammed in Figure 4.5b. An ethical presumption underlying all forms of persuasion is that advocates believe in what they want others to accept. Not surprisingly, however, there are times when people are required to "front" for viewpoints they personally do not accept, as when a Presidential press spokesman defends an official policy with which he privately disagrees. In the remainder of this section, we will assume that this positive relationship between advocate and idea is the only one that remains relatively fixed and invariable, even as advocates and audiences change.

High Credibility/High Agreement: The Ultimate Positive Relationship

The ideal communication environment is one in which the audience is positive about both the message *and* its presenter. In this case, they agree with the persuader's message and have a positive attitude about the persuader's character. Figure 4.5c represents situations in which enthusiastic supporters gather to hear a popular leader recite esteemed beliefs. Republican campaign speeches given to Republican audiences and Methodist sermons given to Methodist congregations are two examples of "preaching to the converted." Audiences attentive to a candidate appearing on television or face-to-face are heavily populated by people who already appreciate the source and the message.[29] Basic persuasion research teaches that "people pay attention primarily to content that already interests them and that is congenial to their point of view."[30]

High credibility/high agreement persuasion may seem unnecessary, but there is a need for "reinforcing" communication. Rhetoric which fits in with an existing attitude is extremely satisfying; it fulfills our need for membership in associations and it involves practically no risk. This is more rewarding and less threatening than facing down an audience at odds with us. Reinforcement may seem ritualistic, but organizations and movements must periodically remind believers of the tenets basic to their faith. Speeches, messages, rallies, and leaflets prolong the enthusiasm of members who need occasional renewal.[31]

Persuasion for reinforcement also benefits from mass media exposure which allows it to reach the *unconverted*. A message which *seems* to be intended for people who are already true believers may actually be designed to use the enthusiasm generated to infect a larger and previously indifferent mass media audience. The audience's support becomes part of the persuasive message. The planners of political conventions exploit this dual audience arrangement. They know that potential voters watching television may be influenced by the zeal of the convention floor. A familiar sight is a presidential candidate addressing like-minded party members who can be counted on to provide bursts of approval. The activity of the supporters is a perfect backdrop against which to address the undecided five or six percent who could make the difference between electoral success and failure.

High Credibility/Low Agreement Persuasion

In 1984 the most popular television commercial to appear before the public was yet another skirmish in "the cola wars." Few people have deep loyalties to items as ordinary as soft-drink brands because objective differences between simple products are minimal. Since the 1930s, the two largest cola makers have enlisted the help of celebrities to combat this built-in inertia. In 1984, Pepsi spent 40 million dollars on an ad campaign featuring popular singers to influence buyers. Ten million dollars was spent on two commercials featuring pop singer Michael Jackson.[32] One of these ads became a media event because it was first aired during the Grammy television show and because Jackson was accidently burned during its filming. News of the accident raised the "hype" for the commercial to a level that circus tycoon P.T. Barnum would have admired.

Also in 1984, Ronald Reagan took to the hustings and the airwaves on behalf of increased military spending and increased research efforts for the Strategic Defense Initiative (S.D.I.) dubbed "Star Wars." S.D.I. provoked controversy because opponents of increased spending had partially succeeded in pointing out that the federal budget was spending less on "people" and more on military "machines." The brand of cola we consume has no lasting personal consequence, but our willingness to support military programs does. Even so, these dissimilar events have one common feature. They both illustrate a persuasive situation in which a very popular advocate took on a less popular cause. This setting is diagrammed in Figure 4.5d. Pepsi's ad campaign featuring Jackson was a countermove to Coca Cola's pretigious endorser, Bill Cosby. Likewise, the Reagan administration hoped that the President's high personal credibility would be enough to win widespread support for military spending and increased funding for controversial programs. The High-credibility/low-agreement setting is the classic persuasion case. The advocate has earned the goodwill of the audience, but must discover a way to use that goodwill to establish the merit of unpopular ideas.

Two very different strategies seem well suited to the high-credibility/low-agreement setting. One is to intensify audience identification with the favorable public image of the advocate ("If such a terrific person believes this, perhaps my own view is wrong"). With this approach, time is spent intensifying the advocate's association with the proposal but downplaying the ideas associated with it. Most celebrity endorsements of products function in this way. Very little is said in behalf of the product other than the fact that it is associated with a person we admire. A second strategy—and one which has far greater merit—is to make the best case possible in defense of the idea to which the audience is indifferent or hostile. The advocate's reputation is sufficient to guarantee that an audience will listen to a reasoned presentation. Pepsi used the first strategy because there is not much to say about a product consisting of sugar, water, and flavoring. The Reagan administration had no choice but to explore the second high-credibility/low-agreement strategy since the Strategic Defense Initiative needed a concrete explanation and defense.

A high-credibility/low-agreement setting is not without risks. Since a well-liked person is affirming a position that many do not accept, it is possible that the personal prestige of the advocate will suffer. In 1968, Robert Kennedy toured college campuses arguing in behalf of his pro-civil rights and anti-Vietnam War attitudes. Kennedy had decided to challenge his party's Vietnam policy; later, he went even further by opposing President Johnson's hand-picked successor, Vice President Hubert Humphrey. It was the most bitter Presidential primary campaign in modern American history. The softspoken Robert Kennedy was a microcosm of the ironies and dilemmas of the age. He denounced the Vietnam war, but he also stunned his draft-age audiences by urging that the draft-deferments that kept many college students out of the war should be ended. Facing both friendly and hostile Indiana medical students, for example, Kennedy pushed his message for equality uncomfortably close to home:

> Part of civilized society is to let people go to medical schools who come from ghettos. I don't see many black faces who will become doctors .... You are the privileged ones here. It's easy to sit back and say it's the fault of the Federal Government. But it's our responsibility, too. It's our society too, not our government, that spends twice as much on pets as on the poverty program. It's the poor who carry the major burden of the struggle in Vietnam. You sit here as white medical students, while black people carry the burden of the fighting in Vietnam.[33]

Kennedy's views cost him some supporters, but his youthful image also won at least a willingness to consider his political agenda. The positive support an audience has for a persuader can be the basis for urging consideration of an unpopular idea. Tragically, Kennedy never finished the campaign. He was assassinated in a hotel hallway minutes after giving a victory speech to supporters who helped him win the California Primary.

Low Credibility/High Agreement Persuasion

The situation represented in Figure 4.5e represents an arrangement that is just the reverse of the previous case. Unlike the well-liked persuader outlining what an audience does not want to hear, the audience in this situation fundamentally *agrees* with the ideas being expressed but has *low regard* for the advocate.

A persuader might analyze this situation and conclude, "Why bother? I'm content if the audience agrees with me. There's no need to attempt to persuade if my presence might be counterproductive and might risk a loss of support for the very attitude that I want them to support." Fear of alienating an audience in this way is based on what is called the "boomerang effect." A persuasive attempt "boomerangs" when receivers of a message respond in ways that are just the reverse of what we want. The humor created by a number of characters in television situation comedies works on this principle. "All in the Family's" Archie Bunker often attempted to reshape the political views of his daughter Gloria and son-in-law (the "Meathead") Mike. But Archie's outlandish observations inevitably alienated them even further.

The clever advocate can find at least one major reason for using low credibility/high agreement persuasion: it offers the opportunity to increase the persuader's personal credibility. By exploiting the audience's agreement on an issue, a persuader may reverse previous negative impressions. Like the chameleon that blends in with the colors of a landscape, the advocate may gain protection against an audience's hostility by carefully using their ideas as a vindication of his own suspect character. The mythical Senator Claghorn of modern political folklore thus clothes himself in whatever he thinks his constituents want to hear.[34] As a windbag in constant search of votes for the next election, he represents the politician we love to stereotype: supporting farm subsidies in agricultural communities, tax breaks for homeowners in the suburbs, free food for the inner-city poor, and "less government" for audiences who are ineligible for federal handouts. It does not matter that the combined proposals of countless speeches are ultimately contradictory. Each individual speech before a distinct audience serves as a way to reduce suspicions about his competence; he uses ideas as membership cards for easy access to groups. The trick for the Claghorns of the world is to keep audiences isolated.

Surprisingly, there are probably fewer Claghorns in modern politics than we think. The mass media have broken down at least some of the walls that had traditionally separated different audiences. Politicians must be more consistent in their verbalized beliefs than private citizens whose activities are not the subject of press reports and analysis. Politicians do more of their work in the public eye and are, therefore, less able to change attitudes without detection. There is a sense, however, in which all of us need to be Claghorns. It is human and understandable to use ideas as keys to open doors of approval from others. Far more than we recognize, important decisions in personal and professional lives are based on the natural human tendency to "fit in" to a new social setting. The ideas we voice can be phoney, but they can also be legitimate reflections of changed circumstances. We often think carefully about how our behaviors will please or alienate listeners. Contrary to the stereotypes of the opportunist, we may not be less "genuine" for having "adapted ideas to people and people to ideas."[35]

When Mark Twain parodies the "proper" etiquette for funerals, for example, he reminds us of the importance of the ways we *act* as evidence of who we really *are*. The advice may be humorous, but it suggests that if we wish to secure our place in groups we must behave in ways appropriate to routine expectations:

> Where a blood relation sobs an intimate friend should choke up, a distant acquaintance should sigh, a stranger should merely fumble sympathetically with his handkerchief. Where the occasion is military, the emotions should be graded according to military rank, the highest officer present taking precedence in emotional violence, and the rest modifying their feelings according to their position in the service.
>
> Do not bring your dog.[36]

In sum, we are not only spokespersons for positions, but we are also advocates attempting to cultivate our personal credibility as well. As we note in more detail in Chapter 7, the question of what makes a source "credible" has produced different and sometimes conflicting answers. It is evident here that credibility can be sought by taking public positions that will be embraced by an approving audience.

Low Credibility/Low Agreement Persuasion

Figure 4.5f suggests the persuasive situation which carries the heaviest burdens. It indicates a lack of audience support for *both* the persuader *and* his or her ideas. Not unexpectedly, this is not an arrangement that most would willingly tackle. Indeed, more than a few students have suggested that a persuader should come to this setting only with bodyguards and a familiarity with possible escape routes. Reality is usually less ominous.

Films and novels occasionally suggest that a single-minded persuader may reverse the tide of hostility built into the low credibility/ low agreement double-dilemma. This theme is built into Sidney Lumet courtroom dramas such as: *Twelve Angry Men* with Henry Fonda and *The Verdict* with Paul Newman. Actual results are less dramatic than our imaginations or Hollywood suggest. Audiences are rarely won over by such attempts, but they are usually less hostile than the model might suggest. Liberal Senator Ted Kennedy, for example, has often spoken in hostile settings such as conservative Jerry Falwell's Liberty Baptist College. Kennedy, as one writer aptly put it, tested Falwell's and the "Moral Majorities belief in forgiveness."[37] And yet he has come away from such encounters with his dignity intact, even if his audience's attitudes on abortion, school prayer, and the Equal Rights Amendment were probably unchanged. Likewise, during a visit to the U.S.S.R. in 1959, Vice President Richard Nixon gave a television address to the Soviet people despite his reputation as an avid anti-communist. It would be unrealistic to expect that the address changed the feelings of his listeners, but he gamely made an attempt to suggest that the Soviet and American peoples had many similarities.[38] While many people feel the burdens are more than they would want to undertake, others have guaranteed themselves some respect by facing down hostile audiences and noisy hecklers. New York Mayor Ed Koch once noted, "I like the give-and-take of the crowd and the heckler .... You can really make great points when there are hecklers in the audience."[39]

Summary

The central theme of this chapter has been that successful persuasion must be measured against the necessity to adapt to specific audiences. Built into this theme is what many consider the troubling question of when adaptation goes too far. Plato called excessive adaptation to audience beliefs "pandering," and claimed that it was a common feature of persuasion. "Isn't it highly likely," modern counterparts to Plato might argue, "that audience-based persuasion forces the persuader to sacrifice personal beliefs as the price for winning audience approval? Doesn't the presence of the audience and its norms put enormous burdens on a persuader, even though his or her personal vision may be superior to that of the group whose support is sought?"

These are good questions, but they pose several false dilemmas. They presuppose that many forms of communication are not audience based. In truth, the reactions of others are factors in almost every context. The admonishments to "be ourselves" and "not to worry about what others think" sound good but are almost impossible to obey. Unless we are entirely self-sufficient economically and socially, we must confront audience demands daily. The process of considering how our words affect others does not preclude asserting ourselves. There is ample room for us to learn how to be rhetorically accommodating without "selling out." Much of the activity of daily life is a constant process of mediation between our own and other people's beliefs. We are fit company for others largely because of our willingness to engage in this accommodation. We heap a great deal of praise on personalities who show the courage to "do and say what they think without regard for what others may say." Henry Fonda, Clint Eastwood and Sean Penn have played their share of independent-thinking heroes, perhaps serving as surrogates for the rest of us who like the fantasies of the defiant "outsider" better than the reality. There is very little evidence to suggest that people are happier and better adjusted when they are able to ignore the ideological constraints around them. For better or for worse, the wards of mental hospitals are filled with people who are unable to adjust their attitudes to the differing views of others. To be sure, not all attempts to "fit in" are necessarily healthy, but successful accommodation to audiences is not by itself an intellectual crime.

The ethical line is crossed when adaptation extends beyond the natural process of mediation and reaches into the betrayal of our true convictions. The persuader who deliberately ignores beliefs for the sake of performance has violated the acceptable threshold of accommodation. It is reasonable and shrewd to determine and to exploit audience values which coincide with a deeply held personal belief. It is, however, unethical to sacrifice personal feelings for the sake of simply winning over others. A former Presidential Press Secretary, Jerald terHorst, faced this ethical issue squarely when he was asked to defend a decision he abhorred. The action was President Ford's sudden and total pardon of Richard Nixon in September of 1974, granting the former Chief Executive immunity from prosecution for covering up information during the Watergate Affair. The newsman-turned-Presidential-spokesman served only thirteen days before realizing that he could not be an advocate for policies with which he strongly disagreed.[40]

Finally, remember that it is the *audience* which is asked to do most of the "giving" in many persuasive situations. The persuader's intention to transform a group of people implicitly says "give me both your attention and the benefit of your agreement." The audience rather than the persuader is expected to risk giving up old attitudes for new ones. Under those circumstances, it is reasonable to view audience adaptation as a kind of "dialogue" between the advocate and audience. The persuader who seeks change from a group but is unwilling to give the group's ideas serious consideration is perhaps more unreasonable than the person who is accused of "pandering" too much.

Notes

[1]Chaim Perelman and L. Olbrechts-Tyteca, *The New Rhetoric: A Treatise on Argumentation,* trans. John Wilkinson and Purcell Weaver (Notre Dame, IN: Notre Dame University Press, 1969), 20.

[2]See, for example, "Our Autos, Ourselves," *Consumer Reports*, June, 1985, 375.

[3]Philip G. Zimbardo, Ebbe B. Ebbesen, and Christina Maslach, *Influencing Attitudes and Changing Behavior*, Second Edition (Reading, MA: Addison-Wesley, 1977), 105-107.

[4]Arthur T. Turnbull and Russell W. Baird, *The Graphics of Communication*, Fourth Edition (New York: Holt, Rinehart and Winston, 1980), 85.

[5]Richard Flaste, "Survey Finds That Most Children are Happy at Home but Fear World," *The New York Times*, 2 March 1977, A12.

[6]In this chapter, we use these terms interchangably, although other analysts have attempted to differentiate between them. See, for example, George N. Gordon, *Persuasion: The Theory and Practice of Manipulative Communication* (New York: Hastings House, 1971), 244-250.

[7]This provocative thesis has been at the heart of the Sociology of Knowledge, which informs persuasion studies by linking what we *say* with what we *know*. See, for example, Peter L. Berger and Thomas Luchmann, *The Social Construction of Reality* (New York: Anchor, 1969), 1-17; and Karl Mannheim, *Ideology and Utopia* (New York: Harvest, 1936), 1-5.

[8]For an interesting comparison of the social and psychological perspectives, see Solomon E. Asch, *Social Psychology* (New York: Prentice Hall, 1952), 3-38.

[9]Emile Durkheim quoted in Hugh Dalziel Duncan, *Symbols and Social Theory* (New York: Oxford, 1969), 152-153.

[10]This summary is drawn from Todd Gitlin, *Inside Prime Time* (New York: Pantheon, 1983), 36-40; and Ron Miller, "At Preview House, Viewers are the Guinea Pigs," *Philadelphia Inquirer*, 16 August 1983, 6E.

[11]Miller, 6E.

[12]Kenneth Burke, *A Rhetoric of Motives* (Berkeley, CA: University of California, 1969), 55.

[13]Augustine quoted in Burke, 50.

[14]Tony Schwartz, *The Responsive Chord* (New York: Anchor, 1974), 25.

[15]Charles Stewart, Craig Smith and Robert E. Denton Jr., *Persuasion and Social Movements* (Prospect Heights, IL: Waveland Press, 1984), 91-92.

[16]Jacques Ellul, *A Critique of the New Commonplaces*, trans. Helen Weaver (New York: Knopf, 1968), 13.

[17]W. Lloyd Warner, *The Living and the Dead: A Study of the Symbolic Life of Americans* (New Haven, CT: Yale University, 1959), Parts I-III.

[18]Robert S. Lynd and Helen Merrell Lynd, *Middletown in Transition: A Study in Cultural Conflicts* (New York: Harvest, 1937), 402.

[19]Lynd and Lynd, 413-414.

[20]Some commonplaces in the Lynd's study have largely become antiques. For example: "That a married woman's place is first of all in the home, and any other activities should be secondary to 'making a good home for her husband and children," and "That married people owe it to society to have children." 410.

[21]Ronald Reagan, State of the Union Address, 26 January 1982, in *American Rhetoric from Roosevelt to Reagan*, ed. Halford Ross Ryan (Prospect Heights, IL: Waveland Press, 1983), 282.

[22]Reagan quoted in Ryan, 283.

[23]Quoted in Robert Spero, *The Duping of the American Voter* (New York: Lippincott and Crowell, 1980), 154.

[24]Quoted in Spero, 157.

[25]Sidney Blumenthal, "Marketing the President," *The New York Times Magazine*, 13 September 1981, 110.

[26]Quoted in Martin Maloney, "Clarence Darrow," in *A History and Criticism of American Public Address*, Volume 3, ed. Marie Hochmuth (New York: Russell and Russell, 1965), 296.

[27]George Sternlieb and James W. Hughes, *The Atlantic City Gamble* (Cambridge, MA: Harvard, 1983), 13 and 108.

[28]This model is adapted from one originally proposed by psychologist Fritz Heider. For a review of his model and other variations on it, see Charles A. Kiesler, Barry E. Collins, and Norman Miller, *Attitude Change: A Critical Analysis of Theoretical Approaches* (New York: John Wiley, 1968), 155-178. Also see Chapter 6.

[29]Thomas E. Patterson and Robert D. McClure, *The Unseeing Eye: The Myth of Television Power in National Politics* (New York: G.P. Putnam, 1976), 121.

[30]Kurt Lang and Gladys Engle Lang, *Politics and Television* (New York: Quadrangle, 1968), 16.

[31]To cite studies of just two types of messages, see Arthur M. Schlesinger, Jr., "Annual Messages of the Presidents: Major Themes of American History," in *The State of the Union Messages, 1790-1860*, Volume 1, ed. Fred L. Israel (New York: Chelsea House/Robert Hector, 1966), xiii-xli; and Donald Wolfarth, "John F. Kennedy in the Tradition of Inaugural Speeches," *Quarterly Journal of Speech*, April 1961, 124-132.

[32]John J. O'Connor, "New Pepsi Ads Turn to Humor," *Advertising Age*, 27 February 1984, 1 and 78.

[33]Quoted in Jack Newfield, *Robert Kennedy: A Memoir* (New York: E.P. Dutton, 1969), 256.

[34]"Senator Beauregard Claghorn" was a character created with some affection by radio humorist Fred Allen. See Arthur Frank Wertheim, *Radio Comedy* (New York: Oxford, 1979), 335-342.

[35]A persuasive case for the absolute necessity to perform different roles at different times is made by Erving Goffman in *The Presentation of Self in Everyday Life* (New York: Anchor, 1959), Chapters 1 and 3.

[36]Mark Twain, *Letters From the Earth*, ed. Bernard DeVoto (New York: Fawcett, 1962), 152.

[37]Phil Gailey, "Kennedy Tells Falwell Group of Tolerance," *The New York Times*, 4 October 1983, A17.

[38]The speech is reprinted in Richard M. Nixon, *Six Crises* (New York: Pyramid, 1968), 472-480.

[39]Edward I. Koch and William Rauch, *Mayor: An Autobiography* (New York: Warner, 1984), 5.

[40]Robert T. Hartmann, *Palace Politics: An Inside Account of the Ford Years* (New York: McGraw-Hill, 1980), 265.

Questions and Projects for Further Study

1. How do commonplaces differ from audience-specific norms? Look for key commonplaces within an article in a mass-market magazine, such as *Reader's Digest*. Locate more specialized norms in a magazine with a narrower audience, such as *Ms. Magazine* or *Soldier of Fortune*.

2. In your own words, summarize the difference between audience analysis based on demographics and analysis based on survey research. Apply your discussion to the example of Preview House cited in the chapter.

3. *Broadcasting* magazine and *Advertising Age* are filled with discussions of audiences and their characteristics. *Broadcasting*, for example, contains numerous ads for syndicated programs that stations may rent, programs which already attract certain kinds of desirable audiences. *Advertising Age* contains articles describing the plans of companies for reaching certain audiences. Prepare a written or oral summary of the audience that one advertiser or program producer wants to reach.

4. In spite of the fact that we believe that we are responsible for our own commitments, a major theme in this chapter is that we acquire most of our attitudes through our associations with others. What contacts or associations can you identify that have influenced your beliefs and attitudes?

5. At one point in the chapter, the authors note that "an ethical presumption that goes with all forms of persuasion is that persuaders should believe in what they want others to accept." Publicly arguing for a position in which one does *not* personally believe is sometimes called "fronting." Cite an instance of "fronting" that involved you or cite some situations where fronting is common and perhaps necessary. Do any of these situations suggest that fronting may be ethical?

6. Using examples from television, films, or recent news events, illustrate what is meant by the following terms:
   Boomerang Effect
   Low Credibility/Low Agreement Persuasion
   Audience-Specific Norms
   Pandering

7. Most libraries have copies of *Vital Speeches of the Day* which reprints speeches given in a wide variety of fields and indicates the nature of the audiences. Using the scheme presented in Figure 4.5, look through several recent issues and diagram three different

kinds of communication settings (such as 4.5c, d, and e).

8. Pick an issue or position on which you hold strong views. Given your position on the particular question chosen (i.e., defending a politician, a controversial policy, a group, or controversial decision), identify an organization that would hold contrary or different attitudes. Imagine that you were invited by this organization to explain your convictions. After giving your "invitation" some thought, explain your case to a friend. Describe the norms and commonplaces you think the hypothetical audience holds, and how you would "build bridges" to increase their support or understanding of your point of view. Ask your partner how his or her approach to this audience might be similar or different.

Additional Reading

Gitlin, Todd. *Inside Prime Time*. New York: Pantheon, 1983.

Goffman, Erving. *The Presentation of Self in Everyday Life*. New York: Anchor, 1959.

Gordon, George. *Persuasion: The Theory and Practice of Manipulative Communication*. New York: Hastings House, 1971.

Johannesen, Richard L. *Ethics in Human Communication*. Second Edition. Prospect Heights, IL: Waveland Press, 1983.

Kiesler, Charles; Barry E. Collins; and Norman Miller. *Attitude Change: A Critical Analysis of Theoretical Approaches*. New York: John Wiley, 1968.

Lynd, Robert S.; and Helen Merrell Lynd. *Middletown in Transition: A Study in Cultural Conflicts*. New York: Harvest, 1937.

Perelman, Chaim; and L. Olbrechts-Tyteca. *The New Rhetoric: A Treatise on Argumentation*. Trans. John Wilkinson and Purcell Weaver. Notre Dame, IN: Notre Dame, 1969.

Ross, Raymond S. *Understanding Persuasion: Foundations and Practice*. Second Edition. Englewood Cliffs, NJ: Prentice Hall, 1985.

Safire, William. "The All Purpose Political Speech." in *The Rhetoric of Our Americans*. New Haven, CT: Yale University, 1959.

Warner, W. Lloyd. *The Living and the Dead: A Study of the Symbolic Life of Americans*. New Haven, CT: Yale University, 1959.

5

Persuasion and Reasoning

 OVERVIEW

Plato said that the worst fate that can befall a man is to become a misologist, a hater of reason; for him it was clear that since man is essentially reasonable, when he ceases to reason he ceases to be a man. I happen to believe this unfashionable doctrine.... I also believe that when any society loses its capacity to debate its ends and means rationally, it ceases to be a society of men at all and becomes instead a mob, a pack, or a herd of creatures rather less noble than most animals.[1]

Are the processes through which we try to influence others always "rational," or is successful persuasion frequently empty of good reasons? This chapter explores some of the advantages and disadvantages of utilizing models of logical reasoning as models for persuasion. Aristotle believed that a special kind of "practical reasoning" can serve the needs of persuaders. Our purpose in this section is to explain several key observations about argumentative persuasion and to point out the need for persuaders to consider the *kinds* of claims they are supporting. Persuaders who fail to recognize the degree to which an assertion can logically be supported are usually doomed to failure.

We begin with a modern case study that shows how important the ability to analyze reasoning patterns can be. This extended example is followed by an overview of basic types of reasoning, common logical mistakes, and a discussion of why reasoning is only one component of persuasion.

Who Made the Better Case?:
Sorting Out What Happened in Chicago

In late August 1968, the Democratic Party held its national political convention in Chicago. Its task was Herculean at best. How would the party heal the wounds created by a year of disastrous events? The Vietnam war was raging and required 200,000 more soldiers;

widespread rioting engulfed cities like Los Angeles and Detroit, and the nation was reeling from the assassinations of Robert Kennedy and Martin Luther King. America had not experienced such confusion and political turmoil since the Civil War.

Planners were forewarned that a wide variety of protesters intended to use the convention as a forum to express their dissatisfaction on numerous issues and to lobby for political change. As a condition for holding the convention in Chicago, Mayor Richard Daley assured the Party that he was willing to use his considerable control over city services to do what was necessary to keep the convention "orderly." No one anticipated the tumult that ensued. "All of Chicago seemed to have come unglued," Dan Rather later recalled.[2] *Newsweek* magazine described the week's events under the front-cover headline, "The Battle of Chicago." Violence between police and demonstrators repeatedly flared up in front of the candidates' headquarters at the Hilton and Blackstone Hotels, in Grant Park across the street, and in countless scuffles on the streets of the city. Twelve thousand policemen and National Guard troops patrolled the Loop using clubs, tear gas, and bayonets affixed to rifles to disperse the protesters.

Norman Mailer proclaimed the strife "the seige of Chicago."[3] Every ugly disturbance and retaliation was transmitted to millions of viewers by the three major television networks. No one escaped the brutality. Dan Rather and Mike Wallace were shoved and pummeled along with thousands of demonstrators, tourists and other reporters. The bloody skirmishes were called the "Chicago Police Riot" by the press. A normally "orderly" political process had become disturbingly savage and violent. What went wrong? Had the five days in Chicago proved that lawless mobs were bent on violent confrontation or were the incidents caused by a city unwilling to permit peaceful protest?

Two separate reports were commissioned to explain the events in Chicago. The version prepared by city lawyer Raymond Simon defended the decisions of the Daley administration.[4] The National Commission on the Causes and Prevention of Violence prepared the second report under the leadership of Chicago Crime Commission lawyer Daniel Walker.[5] Although both reports attempted to document what happened, they arrived at diametrically opposed conclusions. Each analyzed the same evidence to arrive at very different conclusions about the behavior of the demonstrators, the press, and the police.

How many serious incidents of violence occurred during the convention? The city report claimed that 62 incidents had occurred; the national commission documented over 300, and noted that there were probably more.[6] Did the city of Chicago give the dissenters a fair

CARL A. RUDISILL LIBRARY
LENOIR-RHYNE COLLEGE

Jeers greet Chicago police as they attempt to disperse demonstrators outside the Conrad Hilton hotel on Wednesday, August 29, 1968.

Wide World Photos, Inc.

chance to protest peacefully? The city claimed that it "sought to protect [the] constitutional rights of freedom of assembly and freedom of speech."[7] The Federal Commission stated that the Daley Administration "attempted to discourage an inundation of demonstrators by not granting permits for marches and rallies..."[8] And who were the demonstrators? "An overwhelming majority of the persons arrested," according to the city's Simon Report, "were not youngsters, were not students, and were not Chicagoans. They were adult troublemakers."[9] The National Commission's Walker Report reached the opposite conclusion: "The majority of those arrested *were* under 26 years of age, male, residents of metropolitan Chicago, and had no previous record."[10]

These two reports asked the same questions yet arrived at contrasting answers. Rational persuasion calls for careful analysis of how assertions are developed and supported. In the remainder of this chapter, we will look at how reasoning processes occur in persuasion, and we will come back to these two reports for further examples.

Understanding Practical Arguments: Basic Terms

Reasoning notes Stephen Toulmin, Richard Rieke, and Allan Janik, "is a collective and continuing human transaction, in which we present ideas or claims to particular sets of people within particular situations or contexts and offer the appropriate kinds of 'reasons' in their support."[11] When we reason with others, we attempt to establish connections that link our claims with ideas or evidence that will secure a favorable reception. *Claims* are the assertions that we want others to accept which may be challenged. Some claims are never stated in public because we feel we do not have the rational means to defend them. We may privately believe prejudices like "the French are lazy," or the "Irish drink too much," but when we *publicly* express our conclusions we enter the realm of reasoning. Our claims must be able to withstand the critical scrutiny of others. Phrases such as "I know...," "It's true that...," "I believe...," and "It would be difficult to doubt...," all carry a tone of certainty that implies we can provide evidence to defend the assertions that follow. Statements that support claims are called *premises*.

Aristotle was among the first to put practical reasoning at the center of persuasion theory. An overview of reasoning processes should recognize his pathfinding efforts to show that practical logic is natural to human communication. He criticized other teachers of persuasion in ancient Greece for presenting "but a small portion of the art," neglecting the important role that practical reasoning plays in winning converts. "Persuasion," he noted, "is clearly a sort of demonstration" that depends on a sequence of logically related statements or arguments. "A statement is persuasive and credible either because it is directly self-evident or because it appears to be proved from other statements that are so." Aristotle called these arguments containing facts or judgments acceptable to an audience "enthymemes" and noted that they "are the substance of rhetorical persuasion."[12] We will discuss the special nature of enthymemes shortly, but first we should highlight several key differences between "formal" arguments used by logicians and the more ordinary "practical" arguments used in persuasion.

Reasoning Processes: Some Useful Distinctions

Implied and Stated Components of Arguments

Many times logical relationships that lead to assertions hardly need to be explored at all, as when we make passing comments about the weather. The claim that "It is too hot today" is usually accompanied by obvious evidence (temperature, bright sun, high humidity, etc.) which makes it unnecessary to provide supporting reasons. If pressed, however, we could make the reasoning explicit by writing down all relevant claims and premises including those that are assumed but unstated. Our complete argument about the weather might include a *factual premise* ("The thermometer reads 92 degrees") and a *judgmental premise* that "interprets" the significance of the facts ("92 degrees is, by definition, too hot"). This argument diagrammed as an enthymeme would be:

Factual Premise: "The thermometer reads 92 degrees."
Judgmental Premise: (implied but not stated) "A temperature of over 92 is too hot."
(Therefore...)
Claim: "It is too hot today."

Persuasion, of course, is neither so formal nor so simple. We rarely "argue" about the weather. In addition, arguments from everyday life often have *many* judgmental and factual premises which require proof. As in our simple example, it is often unnecessary to make all of the premises (and sometimes even claims) explicit. Aristotle reminds us that we can count on our listeners to supply parts of the reasoning sequence because speakers and listeners frequently share similar assumptions about what evidence implies. When the Walker Commission argued that the "police violence was a fact of convention week'' in Chicago, for example, it presented an argument containing specific evidence, but the premise linking the evidence to the claim was only implied, not actually stated. Readers could be counted on to fill in the reasoning sequence:

Claim: "[P]olice action was not confined to necessary force, even in clearing the park."

(because...)

Factual Premise: "A young man and his girlfriend were both grabbed by officers. He screamed, 'We're going, we're going,' but they threw him into the pond. The officers grabbed the girl, knocked her to the ground, dragged her along the embankment and hit her with their batons on her head, arms, back, and legs. The boy tried to scramble up the embankment to her, but police shoved him back in the water at least twice. He finally got to her and tried to pull her in the water, away from the police. He was clubbed on the head five or six times. An officer shouted, 'Let's get the fucking bastards!' but the boy pulled her in the water and the police left."[13]

Judgmental Premise: (Implied but not stated) (Such police behavior is a case of unnecessary force.)

Similarly, an argument used by the Simon Report to argue that the anti-war demonstrators "taunted" the police also used a key but unstated premise to show that evidence was relevant to their conclusion:

Claim: The demonstrators "used guerrilla and psychological warfare tactics."[14]

Factual Premises: "The mob which was about 1500 in number at this time began to throw some rocks and pieces of building tile at the police. Firecrackers were going off after being thrown toward the police. The crowd was chanting 'Hell no, we won't go' and 'Kill the pigs.' (It should be noted that in the taunts and chants the word 'pigs' was the demonstrator's vernacular for the words, 'police' and 'policemen.') The crowd was now lining the set edge of Clark Street opposite the park screaming invective at the police. 'Kill the pigs'..."[15]

Judgmental Premise: (Any reasonable definition of taunting includes physical and verbal assaults.)

This argument, in turn, became a premise for the broader claim in the Simon Report arguing that "In the heat of emotion and riot some policeman may have over-reacted but to judge the entire police force by the alleged action of a few would be... unfair..."[16]

Analytic Arguments and Practical Enthymemes

The reasoning of "formal" logic is very different from the enthymemes of ordinary life. Formal logic starts with the ideal of the *analytic argument* where claims *necessarily follow* from a series of premises. An argument is "analytic" when its conclusion is "contained in" (or absolutely follows from) the premises.[17] In this kind of ironclad reasoning sequence the conclusion is "necessary" rather than "probable." Acceptance of the premises dictates acceptance of the conclusion. Although the circumstances of real life rarely allow us to construct valid and true analytic arguments, the reasoning model is useful to persuaders.

Mathematics provides the easiest language for the writing of analytic arguments because mathematical symbols are unambiguous. The expression

$$2 + 5 = 7$$

is analytic because it's conclusion (7) necessarily follows from its premises (universally accepted definitions of what "2," "5" and " + " mean). Similarly, the equation

$$(3 \times 6^2 \div 4) - 25 + 8 = 10$$

uses a rigid logic that leads to an unchallengable conclusion. A mathematically competent person (whether a Socialist, or a Capitalist, a Catholic, and so on) could be expected to reach the same correct conclusion by applying universally accepted rules and premises to find the answer. We can also use letters rather than numbers to represent analytic arguments. For example:

1. If A then B.
2. A.
   Therefore,
   B.

In this argument (sometimes called "deductive" or "syllogistic"), the relationship defined in the first premise ("If A is present then B is present") sets up a reasoning sequence that leads to the claim. Since the second premise specifies that A is present, the claim *has to be* that B is present as well. An effort to substitute ordinary language in place of letters or numbers could take the following form:

1. If George's wife votes for Senator Smithers, then George will too.
2. George's wife says she will vote for Smithers.
Therefore,
George will also vote for Smithers.

The most interesting characteristic of valid analytic arguments is that there is no way to deny the validity of their claims *if* you accept the soundness of their premises. This built-in certainty has attracted philosophers and scientists for hundreds of years. The promise of asserting statements of fact or judgment which cannot be refuted is extremely alluring. Many important philosophers from Descartes to Bentham hoped that mankind would benefit from a logic that used known premises to reach lofty conclusions. They were intrigued by the possibility that people could move beyond the "fictions," "falsehoods" and exceptions common to ordinary discussion. As "a system of necessary propositions which will impose itself on every rational being," the idea of the valid analytic argument promises timelessness and absolute truth.[18] To them this was more than an idle, scholarly pipedream; a logic as universal as the logic of mathematics might provide a way to end disagreements and enable mankind to live in harmony.

The potent force of analytic arguments has intrigued persuaders for similar reasons. Just as we do not argue about the answers to basic math problems (an answer is either "right" or "wrong"), analytic arguments used in actual persuasive situations would make the conversion of listeners or readers a simple matter of explaining ironclad relationships. It is hardly surprising, therefore, that in many persuasive statements we see the general form of analytic arguments. For example, to paraphrase an argument made by Ronald Reagan in 1984:

Any nation that does not honor human rights is evil
The Soviet Union violates human rights.
Therefore...
The Soviet Union is evil.

Or consider the unstated claim (indicated by parentheses) implied by this "A is B" premise once used as a slogan in advertisements for microwave ovens:
"Only Amana sells the Radarange microwave oven."
(If you want a microwave oven,)
Therefore...
(You must buy an Amana.)
While these examples have a superficial certainty that makes them seem like analytic arguments, the premises themselves are not

necessarily true. For example, many arguably decent countries such as the United States and Great Britain have drawn criticism for human rights violations by international groups who monitor civil rights activities. It is probably too simplistic to define a country as "evil" by only one vaguely defined standard. Similarly, the advertising slogan for microwave ovens offers a calculated ambiguity. Someone seeing the ad may have drawn the unwarranted conclusion that only Amana made microwave ovens. The slogan has far less impact when it is accurately interpreted as claiming that only Amana sells ovens with the registered brand name "Radarange."

The problems with these cases are symptomatic of two difficulties in developing analytic arguments on persuasive topics. First, because ordinary language is such an important carrier of personal and cultural values, its use makes unanimous agreement difficult to achieve. The farther we move away from purely denotative languages such as mathematics, the greater the difficulty in locating valid analytic arguments that deal with the complexities of the real world. Language is less precise than numbers. The symbols "2", or "%," for example, have single stipulated meanings. By contrast, words like "too much," "evil" or "gay," have a wide range of meanings. The definitions of numbers or signs with invariant meanings, such as in computer languages like BASIC or Fortran, are in the symbols. As we noted in Chapter 3, the meanings of expressive words reside within us as well. Language carries our values and evokes personal feelings. In certain contexts we may feel good or bad, angry or pleased about subjects represented with words like "cops," "dogs," "business executives," "teachers," or "professional athletes." We would find it extremely odd to hear that a friend "liked" "7" better than "2," or grew angry at the sight of "%," but it does not surprise us that humans have failed throughout history to produce agreement about what constitutes "justice," "beauty," or even "truth."[19]

A second reason why it is difficult to make "airtight" analytic arguments is that most persuasive statements do not apply to *all* cases. The claim "all As are Bs" is easy to state (and manipulate) as an abstract expression, but it is much more difficult to make comparable categorical assertions that would help settle real human differences. People, groups, and cultures are rarely *all* of anything. In the realm of human affairs, the only statements that can be made without citing important exceptions are either obvious ("Water is necessary to sustain life.") or trivial ("All children have parents"). Aristotle shrewdly noted that the enthymeme was "sort of" analytic, because ordinary persuasion finds its premises in the "probably" existing opinions of audiences rather than the categorical truths (the "alls" and "if-thens") of formal logic.[20] He noted that the conclusions of enthymemes are *contingent* on audience acceptance; they are not certain. Because enthymemes spell out logical relationships based on generally accepted opinions,[21] they must be at least partially judged by how well the persuader has used audience beliefs as premises for persuasion. Here, for example, is an enthymeme that Aristotle used to show how to argue from generally accepted beliefs to persuasive claims:

> Thus it may be argued that if even the gods are not omniscient, certainly human beings are not. The principle here is that, if a quality does not in fact exist where it is *more* likely to exist, it clearly does not exist where it is *less* likely.[22]

Or, in a simpler diagrammatic form:

Premise: Even the gods are not perfect.
Premise: (Since the gods are better than people,)
  Claim: Certainly human beings are hardly perfect.

Note that the premise "the gods are not omniscient" is a statement of social belief, not (at least for us) a truth for which there could be universal agreement. Even so, the reasoning sequence in this practical argument "makes sense" *if* the premises are accepted.

Demonstration and Argumentation

Aristotle noted what many current teachers of reasoning have rediscovered: the reasoning of analytic arguments is a form of *demonstration* and everyday persuasion requires *argumentation*. The differences between the two are useful to keep in mind. A mathematics problem is a "demonstration" because its final sum is self-evidently true. The transformation of the various operations into a conclusion is "beyond discussion." No one "deliberates" claims that are self-evident by definition or by direct observation. In contrast, *argumentation* is not so much concerned with Truth as with the possible agreement of readers or listeners. We may argue a point to a hostile audience using a wide variety of reasoning skills, but we know that we cannot sweep away all of their doubts in the same way that we can correct an incorrect math problem. As Aristotle noted, practical reasoning works from "opinions that are generally accepted." Demonstrations work from basic premises where it would be "improper to ask any further for the why and wherefore of them."[23] There probably are no universal procedures for "demonstrating" conclusions such as "the United States is the most open society on earth." We may *argue* this point successfully before many audiences, but there is no way to make claims premised on opinions and values immune from potential disagreement. Practical persuasion is thus always subject to the acceptance of a particular audience. In locating persuasive ideas to build arguments we meet our audiences "on the ground... of their own convictions."[24]

Reasoning to Discover and to Defend

It follows from what we have said that reasoning is used to "rationalize" ideas as well as to discover them. We can employ the processes of logical demonstration to *discover* what we did not know; for example, the numbers in our checkbook may reveal that we are overdrawn at the bank. Similarly, computers use advanced programs and vast amounts of information to calculate everything from shifts in the earth's crust to the movements of hurricanes. When we learn how to program a computer or to use existing "software," we harness elaborate reasoning sequences (computer codes and logic) to extend our knowledge beyond its present limits. The reasoning of argumentation, however, more commonly defends what is *already* known or believed. As a persuader on a given topic, your view is more or less fixed; what you hope to alter is the attitude of your listeners. This form of practical reasoning, notes Toulmin and his colleagues, is "not a way of *arriving at ideas* but rather a way of *testing ideas critically.*"

Argumentative reasoning

> is concerned less with how people think than with how they share their ideas and thoughts in situations that raise the question of whether those ideas are *worth* sharing. It is a collective and continuing human transaction, in which we present ideas or claims to particular sets of people with particular situations or contexts and offer the appropriate kinds of "reasons" in their support.[25]

We should add an important qualification to the idea that reasoning is often "rationalization." The quality of persuasion cannot be very good if, at some point, reasoning is not also employed as a tool of discovery. Aristotle's teacher, Plato, noted that elaborate efforts at persuasion without equally intense efforts to discover the "best" or "true" will result in the exploitation rather than the enlightenment of an audience.[26] When we wonder if celebrities actually use the services they endorse in advertisements, we are using this principle. An endorsement is justifiably suspect if a celebrity asks others to use products or services known to be dangerous or poorly made. Returning to the Walker and Simon reports, it seems evident that the Simon Report was part of a public relations campaign to improve the tarnished image of the Mayor and police. The report was so one-sided, "like a primer of the propagandist's art," according to some journalists, that Simon's vindication of the city seemed to surpass his interest in the discovery of the truth.[27] For example, Simon scarcely mentioned what the Walker Report conclusively documented: that injuries to demonstrators included many head wounds. Instead, Simon dwelled at length on the many injuries to hands and fingers sustained by the police. These facts led Chicago's well-known columnist, Mike Royko, to the irreverent observation that "a lot of dastardly citizens must have been going round smashing policemen's knuckles with their faces."[28]

Factual and Judgmental Claims: The Differences Between Truths and Preferences

Claims differ significantly in their subject matter. Earlier we noted that the supporting premises in an argument may include factual and judgmental statements. When trying to persuade others, we must pay particular attention to the distinctions between the two. We frequently confuse judgmental with factual claims. Thus, we overestimate how much "proof" we need to provide and underestimate how much disagreement can be expected. The word "is" in a claim is sometimes the culprit. "Is" and other indicative verb forms (i.e., "was" and "were") have an aura of finality that makes judgmental claims sometimes seem as provable and timeless as known "facts." For instance, the statement "Gerald Ford was a *better* President than Jimmy Carter" is not a statement of fact. As applied to the Presidency, "better" can be legitimately defined in different ways. One person may rank a President's foreign policy decisions higher than his domestic policies; someone else may reverse these priorities. By contrast, factual claims are statements that are demonstrable as true or false, regardless of your own beliefs.[29] Here are some examples:

> Water at sea level boils at 210 degrees F.
>
> Sirhan Sirhan killed Senator Robert Kennedy in 1968.
>
> Bob Hope spent most of his broadcasting career with NBC.
>
> Smoking increases a person's chances of contracting lung cancer.
>
> Germany was the first nation to develop rockets with lethal payloads.
>
> Crime is a major result of poverty.
>
> General Motors is the largest American automaker.
>
> On March 24, 1979, Willie Hollingsworth walked 18 and one half miles with a pint of milk on his head.[30]

All of these statements share the possibility of being verified as right or wrong. We say "possibility" because the available evidence is sometimes insufficient to discover the truth about actual events. For example, we know (it is an unchallenged fact) that the baby of aviation hero Charles Lindburgh mysteriously disappeared from his family's Hopewell, New Jersey home. We also know that a carpenter, Bruno Richard Hauptmann, was convicted of kidnapping the baby and was later electrocuted. However, there are still serious doubts that Hauptmann committed the crime.[31] Persuasion frequently involves factual claims in widely varying situations: the courtroom ("Hauptmann was probably innocent."), the physical sciences ("Some deep sea plants do not need sunlight to flourish."), and social issues that attribute specific effects to specific causes ("Children watching violent television programs imitate the violence they see.").

The most common claims are judgmental.[32] These cannot be proved or settled by citing supporting facts, nor can they be known in the same way that we "know" the truth of a statement such as "Texas was once part of Mexico." A judgmental claim involves the assignment of personal preferences to persons, objects, or laws. The words we use in these claims indicate how we feel about what we are describing. The object of our attention is "good," "bad," "worthwhile," "dangerous," or "desirable," reflecting our (and often our culture's) preferences about what is "right" or "wrong," "decent" or "indecent," "moral" or "immoral," "important" or "insignificant." Consider these samples:

> Sean Connery was a better "James Bond" than Roger Moore.
>
> Deaf grade school students should be required to learn hand signs.
>
> Catholicism is superior to other forms of Christianity.
>
> The Republicans have done a better job than the Democrats in keeping us out of foreign wars.
>
> Lee Iacocca would make a good President.
>
> College students should be required to spend a year in some sort of national service.
>
> Insurance companies unfairly discriminate against young car drivers.
>
> Many supposedly "serious" television dramas are little more than "cartoons."
>
> California's northern coast is ideal for camping.

Note that in every statement certain words are used to give a judgmental "spin" to the claim. Words such as "better," "should," "good," "unfairly," "cartoons," and "ideal" express feelings about the qualities of ideas or objects. While we can "prove" to the satisfaction of most reasoning people that "smoking increases a person's chances of contracting lung cancer"—a valid cause and effect factual claim with ample proof to support it—we cannot with the same certainty "prove" that "Catholicism is a superior form of Christianity."

The old axiom that "you can't argue about religion and politics" is not necessarily correct. We inevitably argue about our preferences with others; preferences are the basis of most of the laws and codes we live by. Yet, it is unreasonable to expect that reasoned argumentation will put all contrary positions to rest in the way that a piece of evidence may "prove" that a defendant in a trial is guilty beyond any reasonable doubt. Communicators frequently forget that "differences of opinion" are not necessarily resolved by appealing to "the facts." Determinations of what is best or worst occur because people are different. As Kenneth Burke has noted, the temptation may be great, "but we cannot call a man illogical for acting on the basis of what he feels to be true."[33]

Finding "Good Reasons" for Claims

One of the most practical guidelines for persuaders searching for a method of clear reasoning is also one of the easiest to understand: locate "good reasons" for your claims. We have described "reasoned" persuasion as the support of "claims" with relevant premises, stated or implied. A useful guide for judging whether a premise "works" is to consider whether it is a "good reason" for supporting a claim. According to Karl Wallace, "Good reasons are a number of statements, consistent with each other, in support of an *ought* proposition or a value-judgment."[34] They provide explanations for controversial judgments which the persuader judges will probably elicit widespread agreement from an audience. The anticipated agreement is based on the fact that they frequently state what members of a society already accept as true or "right." Here are two samples of judgmental claims and their "good reason" premises:

Claim: Companies that direct advertising to very young (under 5) children are engaged in unethical conduct.

Reason: Young children lack sufficient sophistication to "discount" for the "puffery" in advertising.

Reason: Ethical persuaders do not exploit gullible audiences who lack the ability to weigh the motives of communicators.

Claim: It would be better to depend on coal rather than nuclear power for our electricity needs.

Reason: Although coal has some safety problems associated with mining and air pollution, existing technology makes coal safer and cleaner than nuclear fuel.

Reason: As the 1986 Soviet Chernobyl nuclear reactor accident
                proved, radiation effects can produce a bewildering degree
                of lethal contamination.

You may disagree with these arguments, or find fault with one or more of the good reasons. There are times when one person's "common sense" is another's irrationality. Even so, you can usually sense when you have located reasons that will hold up under public scrutiny. Your impression of whether a statement will gain acceptance is an inexact but invaluable guide in determining the strongest defenses that can be made for claims.

Practical reasoning frequently boils down to "common sense." The mental processes that allow us to make quick and amazingly shrewd determinations of "what reasonably follows what" are still largely unknown. Common sense remains a remarkable guide to locating good reasons. When you isolate the premises that you intend to use in support of a claim, your sense of what works is largely based on how you perceive the components to fit together in the argument. A complaint made against Mozart by another composer in the 1984 film, "Amadeus," is absurd because of its *uncommon* sense. A defect of Mozart's music, he said solemnly, was that it had "...too many notes." It is obviously a breach of common sense to judge music by counting the number of notes in a piece, but the comment was writer Peter Schaffer's astute way of showing how an insecure person might grasp for *any* reason, even a bad one. In Chapter 11, we will show how the search for good reasons can be put to work in the construction of persuasive speeches.

Fallacies: Traditional Indicators of Defective Reasoning

It is customary in almost every textbook that treats reasoning to provide readers with the logician's equivalent of the Rock of Gibralter: namely, some sturdy reference point that will simplify the problem of navigating between "good" and "bad" reasoning. The classification of logical fallacies has a long tradition of providing such guidance. If we know what "good" reasoning is, then it follows that there must be systematic methods to classify forms of "bad" reasoning. "A fallacy," notes philosopher Max Black, "is an argument which seems to be sound without being so...."[35] Black may be right when he concludes that "correct reasoning is as rare as perfect health."[36] Since reasoning in support of judgments depends on the validation of audiences, each defined by its unique set of values, any list of fallacies must be taken as advisory rather than absolute. Not only do audiences have different standards for assessing the appropriateness of arguments, but reasoning patterns useful in one context may be inappropriate in another. For example, one commonly cited fallacy is known as *ad hominem*, which means argument directed against a person rather than ideas. Imagine witnessing a debate between two people on whether religious organizations should continue to receive tax exemptions from a state. If the debater favoring continued exemptions attacked an opponent as "a known agnostic, a non-believer," you might justifiably feel that the personal religious beliefs of the advocates are not relevant to the issues in question. If this issue is going to be profitably discussed, the debate must focus on the principles involved (i.e., whether tax breaks for churches represent a violation of the long-standing tradition of separating church and state), rather than the personal affiliations of the advocates.

Consider a second case where two candidates for Congress are meeting in a debate. Since governmental officials are elected to make many decisions beyond those that can be presented in a campaign, you may feel that a candidate's character and personal affiliations should be relevant in determining a preference. It may indeed be useful to know that a candidate was once forced to declare personal bankruptcy, was kicked out of college for cheating on exams, changed his party affiliation, and so on. None of these traits would necessarily make the candidate unfit for public office. Our point is that fallacies like *ad hominem* are useful only when sufficient attention is given to the context in which a discussion takes place.

Here are four of the more common reasoning mistakes that occur in practical arguments.

False Cause

A persuader who has fallen victim to false cause assumes that because two superficially related events have occurred together, one has probably caused the other. Millions of readers believe that the paragon of perfect reasoning is Arthur Conan Doyle's famous detective, Sherlock Holmes. When the available evidence of a murder seems to indicate to readers that the butler did it, the more thoughtful Holmes invariably finds the true cause. Blows that could not have been made by a right-handed person, bodies that have been dead too long, and footprints left on a rug are only a few of the clues that have allowed Holmes to sort out real from false causes.

The child who notes that a rooster always crows before the morning sun might conclude that the sun responds to the rooster's call. He has made the same mistake as the angry constituent who complained that Congressional approval of Daylight Savings Time would result in "too much sun" for his garden. Each assumed that animals or legislators could cause the sun to violate the physical laws that govern the solar system. Similarly, most Americans identify the Great Depression with the famous stock market crash on October 24, 1929 "black Thursday." In reality, the crash was more a symptom of the weak 1929 economy than a cause of it. There were many causes of the depression including too much consumer debt, overproduction, and unstable foreign money systems; stock speculation was only the most visible sign of the economic house of cards that eventually collapsed as the 1920s ended.[37]

A final example of false cause comes from the social sciences. For many years it was an automatic reflex in educational circles to assume that television-viewing by young children *decreased* their interest in reading. In fact, some studies now suggest that television-viewing may encourage literacy in certain types of children, particularly slower learners.[38] There are few simple correlations that link television viewing to other kinds of behaviors; new evidence on how people use television may force us to re-think cherished but unjustified assertions.

Non Sequitur

A *non sequitur* is when a conclusion does not follow from the reasons that have been cited. Most *non sequiturs* have at least superficial connections that link claims to supporting "reasons," but under closer examination the connection is insufficient or inconsistent. Consider the wording of an advertisement for Alka-Seltzer Plus Cold Medicine, as reported by *Consumer Reports*.[39] In fine print, the ad notes that the "Product may cause drowsiness; use caution if operating heavy machinery or driving a vehicle." The same ad also contains testimony from Harold "Butch" Brooks, a truck driver who notes, "When I'm out on the road, bad weather, bad cold, my load's still gotta go, so I rely on Alka-Seltzer Plus." The ad is an example of a *non sequitur*; it contains conflicting and contradictory information. Its inconsistency is similar to the strange assertion on a package of D-Con mouse killer which proudly notes that the poison is made from a "scientifically balanced blend of natural ingredients."

Targeting advertisements to locate *non sequiturs* is the equivalent of shooting fish in a barrel. When we read beer ads that imply beer-drinking is the key to sociability or automobile ads that imply a new car will create respect and envy, we know that such product claims cannot stand up to logical scrutiny. The more dangerous *non sequiturs* are those that arise in debates on important social issues and in the rhetoric that is offered in defense of an official action. One of the most valuable services political reporters perform is to expose the sometimes confused reasoning of policy makers in government. The *New Republic's* Richard Strout, for example, always had a good ear for political statements that said less than they first seemed, as in the campaign speeches of Dwight Eisenhower:

> He has an effective little trick of non sequitur in which he begins, I do not think this," and after developing at length what he does not think, says suddenly and positively as though in a burst of confidence, "But I do think this," and comes out with the answer to quite a different question.[40]

Similarly, in their extensive reporting of the events at the 1968 Democratic Convention, Lewis Chester and his British colleagues recorded perhaps the most humorous accidental non sequitur made by any politician in that year. "Get the thing straight once and for all," began Chicago's Mayor Daley in answer to a question about whether his police had lost control. "The policeman isn't there to create disorder; the policeman is there to preserve disorder...."[41]

Circular Argument

Sometimes the reasons cited for a claim are little more than a re-wording of the claim. What are offered as supporting premises are really just re-statements which give the appearance of more support than actually exists. Ad slogans such as "When you're out of Schlitz, you're out of beer," and "When you say Budweiser, you've said it all"[42] have the structure of sentences that progress from one idea to another but actually start and end with the same idea. Parents regularly use this form of argument on their children in the familiar retort: "Do it because I said so." Obviously, what follows after "because" is essentially a duplicate of what preceded. Circular arguments can cut short public debate on pressing issues by narrowly focusing on only unchallengable claims. By August of 1968, for example, the United States had committed 541,000 troops to the Vietnam War. Many leaders in the Congress and the Johnson and Nixon Administrations argued that because we were so deeply committed to the defense of South Vietnam, we must remain to see the war through to a successful conclusion. Even those who regretted having become involved in an Asian land war felt that the enormous human and economic costs already expended prohibited a withdrawal of forces. A quagmire of circular reasoning developed because of the desire to give meaning to the enormous sacrifices which had already been made. The simple fact of being at war became its own justification for delaying our departure from Vietnam until the fall of South Vietnam in 1975. By that time, over 58,000 American lives had been lost.[43]

In the 1960's, confrontations between protesters and police forced many Americans to consider opposing points of view on the Vietnam War.

Wide World Photos, Inc.

Excessive Dependence on Authority

It is a legitimate pattern of reasoning to support a persuasive claim by citing the expertise of like-minded authorities. Excessive dependence on authority, however, is sometimes used to end discussion of an important issue prematurely. As Toulmin, Rieke, and Janik have noted, "appeals to authority become fallacious at the point where authority is taken as closing off discussion of the matter in question. No further evidence is considered; the authority's opinion has settled the matter once and for all."[44]

For the person on the receiving end, persuasion always implies the question, "Have I heard enough to change my mind?" The answer coming from an individual who has heard from only one source should probably be "not yet." Sometimes, however, a single source may have the power to change someone's mind or motivate them to act. There is no shortage of experts—real or self-styled—who are prepared to argue that they should have the last (and sometimes only) word. Some radio stations employ "psychics" who respond to phone requests for advice on personal, medical, and financial decisions. No information pertaining to the caller's personal circumstances is requested; special "powers" are used to "see" into a caller's future. An example: "My doctor says I need an operation to remove a cyst from my back. What should I do?" The advice: "If you get a second opinion, you will find you won't need the operation." It is troubling that people would ask a stranger for advice on decisions of great personal consequence.

Presidents, ministers, influential teachers, and therapists represent a few of the authorities who are sometimes consulted for conclusive documentation of a claim or a decision. Even good teachers can sometimes overstate the case for one kind—their kind—of perspective. Consider the implications behind the following sentence where the writers of a psychology text make psychology the sole source of wisdom about human behavior. "It is interesting to note that when ordinary people try to understand behavior, they are acting as naive psychologists."[45] The authors make the subtle assumption that "ordinary" people should not attempt to understand the diverse ways in which humans act. Only *real* authorities, academic psychologists, have the necessary qualifications. The sentence thoughtlessly excludes valuable insights about human behavior which playwrights, sociologists, journalists, political scientists, novelists, and scores of others have made. Phrases like "He said so, and that's enough for me," "The only person I trust said…," or "She has the advanced degree, so she must know what she is saying" are clues to attitudes that have been accepted on the slender thread of one person's advice. In Chapter 7, we will examine in more detail persuasion based on such appeals to authority.

Why Persuasion and Logical Argumentation
Are Not the Same

Thus far we have shown how a claim supported by reasonable premises can lead to persuasion. We labeled this single logical unit an "argument," and noted that Aristotle discovered forms of argumentation (enthymemes) that routinely appear in most forms of persuasion. Does it follow that we can use the words "persuasion" and "argumentation" interchangeably? Is persuasion always subject to the rules of practical reasoning? Philosophers and social scientists have debated these questions for years, but raising them is more than an empty academic exercise. *How* you answer them says a great deal about how you think you can influence others. Answering "yes" to both implies that persuasion should always involve the use of "good reasons." Answering "no" suggests that factors other than reasoning can and should influence what people believe. We close this chapter with an explanation of why we think persuasion is *more* than the construction of reasoned arguments, vital though they are. We start by noting a common misconception: that persuasion depends more on "emotional" than "rational" responses.

The Traditional Wisdom: Argumentation is Logical;
Persuasion Appeals to the "Emotions"

Ask the average person to analyze an advertising "pitch" or a pamphlet from a group seeking social change and the odds are good they will come up with some variation of a basic distinction that Aristotle made over 2000 years ago. They will identify some parts of the message as containing "logical" reasons and other parts containing "emotional" appeals.[46] No scheme for evaluating persuasion is more common than this frequently-made, but confusing, distinction. Among experts who study messages closely, the wording may be fancier, but the implication that logic and emotion are opposites is still present. A law school professor regrets that "emotion can activate any behavior which has not been inhibited by reason."[47] An expert on political communication similarly notes that the statements of most politicians are "nothing more than emotional appeals."[48] We think it is a mistake to assume that the presence of emotion indicates the absence of logic and that this represents a key difference between persuasion and argumentation. Argumentation is the art of finding reasoned support for claims. By comparison, we often assume that persuasion commonly uses appeals and rhetorical tricks which have little to do with reasoning.

The problem with this distinction is that reason and emotion are not opposites, but actually *complementary* processes. A sense of reasoned justification usually *increases* our emotional attachment to ideas. When we feel that we have a strong case for a point of view, our sense of urgency in communicating that commitment is stronger. Think about your experiences with the emotion of anger. Your anger probably develops in proportion to the "good reasons" you have for it. Reasoning motivates our emotions. We identify with film characters as diverse as "Clark Kent" (alias, Superman) and Clint Eastwood's "Dirty Harry" because we sympathize with their problems and share their feelings of anger. Even brutal "revenge" films like *Death Wish* are careful to make their villains so evil and cruel that their violent deaths at the hands of the enraged characters *seem* justified. There can be no doubt that anger is an emotion. Our point is that its presence may indicate an intensely felt chain of reasoning. The misplaced distinction between "reasoning" and "emotion" thus fails to provide a way to separate persuasion from argumentation, but does turn us in the right direction.

Persuasion's "Self Interest" and Argumentation's "Public Interest"

Persuasion and argumentation do not differ in the degree of reasoning that is present, but in the *kinds* of reasons that are offered in support of claims. All persuasion must provide a series of incentives or reasons for winning the approval of audiences, but not all legitimate persuasion involves "good reasons." As we have noted, the "good reasons" that occur in arguments are made with the hope that a wide diversity of people might also sense their reasonableness. By contrast, while persuaders frequently employ rational argumentation, they also rely on their abilities to use *appeals* to personal wants and needs.

The distinction between persuasive *appeals* and argumentative *good reasons* is revealing. As we will discuss more fully in the next chapter, all of us have legitimate personal needs for affection, for approval from others, for high self-esteem, and so on. We can be motivated by *appeals* that promise to satisfy those needs; however, when we present *arguments* for the approval of audiences, we know that our reasoning must move beyond individual needs and "make sense" to the public as a whole. For example, in a court of law, jurors are sometimes cautioned by a judge to ignore attempts at flattery directed to them by lawyers eager to win their cases. Appeals to a juror's personal vanity (i.e., to their occupations and religion) are as out of place in the courtroom as they are in argumentation's "court of reason" based on the accumulation of facts and evidence.[49] Persuasion frequently depends on just such flattery: efforts to recognize and appeal to personal needs and motivations. For instance, McDonald's previous advertising slogan, "You deserve a break today," was an undeniably persuasive appeal, but it was not an argument. The slogan struck a chord of self-interest by implying that a trip to McDonald's was a way to get out of the kitchen and at the same time give oneself a flattering reward. "I *do* deserve a break" was the anticipated response. A long-used slogan for FTD Florists offered the same kind of persuasive appeal. "When you care enough to send the very best" was effective because it made the purchase of flowers a certification of thoughtfulness. Both of these slogans successfully appealed to the need most of us have to raise our self-esteem, but neither slogan is meant to provide information about the merits of their products. Good reasons are explanations we would accept as relevant to others as well as ourselves. Appeals are statements that "work" because they favorably motivate us. One reason advertising works so effectively on television is that it reaches the viewer as a *private* rather than *public* person. We accept advertising appeals made to us in our homes that we might reject as a member of a "live" audience. It is revealing that an advertisement viewed passively at home is sometimes greeted by groans of disbelief when shown to a movie audience in a theater. Persuasion directed to us as persons with private needs may be inappropriate to public gatherings where there is an expectation that the persuader will seek consensus from everyone present. To put our point another way, while persuasion *can* employ reasoning from facts and general opinions, it also reaches individuals by appeals to subjective and personal needs.

This distinction between argumentation and persuasion is admittedly imprecise, but it is important. It explains why the understanding of persuasion is as much the study of individual psychology as the logic of argumentation. It also reminds us that persuasion is multi-dimensional. As recipients of messages, we are capable of assessing claims with the collective interests of others in mind, but we also consider ideas more personally. Wayne Booth, whose observations opened this chapter, reminds us that not all of our attitudes can be subject to rational argument:

> As a university professor I am committed to the supreme profes-
> sional standard of rationality: insofar as I am an honest professor,
> worthy of my own respect, I am sworn to change my mind if and
> when someone shows me that there are *good reasons* to change my
> mind. But both as a man who loves art and literature that I cannot
> fully explain, and as a human being who holds to many values the
> correctness of which I cannot easily prove with unanswerable
> rational arguments, I know how much of my life is not readily explic-
> able at the court of what is usually called reason.[50]

Our beliefs cannot always be measured by what we can support with good reasons, as a final example illustrates. A few years ago television was saturated with an advertisement for a cream that promised to remove "ugly age spots." The ad was a favorite subject for analysis in one of the authors' persuasion classes because its reasoning was obviously flimsy. Only recently has it become evident to the author that he mistakenly judged the commercial as an argument. The ad for Porcelana Cream opens with a picture of four middle-aged women playing a card game. One of the women is obviously ill at ease as she looks down at her hands holding the cards. She says to herself, "These ugly age spots; what's a woman to do!" Obviously, Porcelana Cream is the solution to her dilemma. From an argumentative point of view the commercial is hopelessly flawed. Would friendships be at stake merely because a person had a few spots on her hands? Of course not. But the woman's anxiety and embarrassment is dramatically plausible. Based on just a few seconds of the commercial, we can believe that there are people like us who are anxious to be accepted by their friends, and may believe (like or unlike us) that even minor blemishes put them at risk. The commercial appeals to the very private fear of rejection that most of us experience from time to time. To dismiss it as an "irrational" attempt at persuasion is to miss the point. The appeal to the fear of rejection is not intended to stand up under the close scrutiny that we give arguments containing good reasons. The appeal evokes subtle and fragile feelings that cannot be allayed by reference to what others think. You could easily argue that using the cream will not help maintain friendships, as its faulty logic seems to imply. That does not deny the strong possibility that users of the product may feel better in the knowledge that they have taken a step to improve their personal appearance. We have missed something important if we fail to recognize that a sense of personal well-being is an important outcome of persuasion. Argumentation is vital to our understanding of persuasion, but like any other single perspective, it is only a part.

Summary

In this chapter, we have looked at the role that reasoning plays in persuasion. Although philosophers have always viewed logical reasoning as a source of new knowledge, persuasive arguments usually attempt to defend existing attitudes. For our purposes we defined reasoning as the process of supporting controversial claims with premises that function as "good reasons." Reasons are "good" when we believe that they are as "sensible" for others as they are for ourselves. We noted that there is a great deal of misunderstanding about reasoning, and what it can and cannot do. For example, not all persuasion utilizes "good reasons" because sometimes the most direct route to attitude change is by appealing to private but powerful motivations, such as a person's need to feel wanted by others. These private appeals are not necessarily "irrational emotions" nor "unreasonable" grounds for forming attitudes, but neither are they the kinds of appeals that can stand up as reasons that would help shape a consensus of support in a public gathering. Advertising is full of such motivating appeals, often selling products as "rewards" that buyers bestow on themselves. Topics of greater consequence, such as efforts to reconstruct occurrences of violence in Chicago in 1968, demand more rigorous defenses.

Using the pioneering writings of Aristotle as a guide, we looked at practical arguments called "enthymemes." Enthymemes have two special features that distinguish them from the formal, "analytic" arguments used by scientists, mathematicians, and philosophers. First, usually one or more of their parts (claims or premises) are implied rather than stated; enthymemes typically "build from" what an audience already believes or accepts. Second, their claims are "probable" or "preferable" since they deal with practical subjects for which demonstrations of "eternal truths" are impossible. Like all forms of reasoning, enthymemes can have support which is misapplied. In fallacies like "false cause," "non sequitur," and "circular argument," premises may present the illusion of logical support for a claim.

Reasoning can create a sense of relentless power harnessed to convert listeners or readers to a predetermined conclusion. Your awareness of the basic problems and concepts associated with constructing arguments is the first crucial step in using or resisting this potent force.

Notes

[1] Wayne C. Booth, *Now Don't Try to Reason With Me* (Chicago: University of Chicago, 1970), 22.

[2] Dan Rather and Mickey Herskowitz, *The Camera Never Blinks: Adventures of a TV Journalist* (New York: Ballantine, 1978), 346.

[3] Norman Mailer, *Miami and the Siege of Chicago* (New York: World Publishing, 1968).

[4] Raymond Simon, "The Strategy of Confrontation," report prepared by the Corporation Council of the City of Chicago, 1968.

[5] Daniel Walker, *Rights in Conflict*, report submitted to the National Commission on the Causes and Prevention of Violence (New York: Signet, 1968).

[6] This comparison is based on an analysis of both reports' chronologies in Gary C. Woodward, "The Riots at the 1968 Democratic Convention: An Analysis

and Comparison of Documents of Public Inquiry," (Masters thesis, California State University-Sacramento, 1969), 80-89.

⁷Simon, 11.

⁸Walker, xx.

⁹Simon, 41.

¹⁰Walker, 319-320.

¹¹Stephen Toulmin, Richard Rieke, and Allan Janik, *An Introduction to Reasoning* (New York: Macmillan, 1979), 9.

¹²Aristotle, *The Rhetoric*, in *The Basic Works of Aristotle*, ed. Richard McKeon (New York: Random House, 1941), 1325.

¹³Walker, xxiii.

¹⁴Simon, 49.

¹⁵Simon, 19.

¹⁶Simon, 76.

¹⁷See Stephen Toulmin, *The Uses of Argument* (London: Cambridge University, 1964), 125-135.

¹⁸Chaim Perelman and L. Olbrechts-Tyteca, *The New Rhetoric: A Treatise on Argumentation*, trans. John Wilkinson and Purcell Weaver (Notre Dame, IN: University of Notre Dame Press, 1969), 2.

¹⁹For further discussion of this point, see Richard Weaver, *The Ethics of Rhetoric* (Chicago: Henry Regnery, 1953), 7-9.

²⁰Lloyd Bitzer, "Aristotle's Enthymeme Revisited," *Quarterly Journal of Speech* (December, 1959), 399-408.

²¹Aristotle, *Topics*, in McKeon, 188.

²²Aristotle, *The Rhetoric*, in McKeon, 1421.

²³Aristotle, *Topics*, in McKeon, 188.

²⁴Aristotle, *Topics*, in McKeon, 189. For further discussion of the differences between demonstrations and arguments, see also Perelman and L. Olbrechts-Tyteca, 13-14.

²⁵Toulmin, Rieke, and Janik, 9.

²⁶See Weaver, 11-12 and *Plato's Phaedrus*, trans. R. Hackforth (Indianapolis, IN: Bobbs Merrill, Library of the Liberal Arts, 1952), 119-122.

²⁷Lewis Chester, Godfrey Hodgson, and Bruce Page, *An American Melodrama: The Presidential Campaign of 1968* (New York: Viking, 1969), 594-595.

²⁸A paraphrase of Royko in Chester, Hodgson, and Page, 601.

²⁹A good case has been made by "Sociologists of Knowledge" and others that very little knowledge about human affairs is completely free of our own values. In a practical way, however, certain obvious facts are largely free of subjective interpretations. The reader interested in how social values can shape what we claim to "know" might start with Peter L. Berger's and Thomas Luckmann's *The Social Construction of Reality* (New York: Doubleday, 1967).

³⁰*Guinness 1984 Book of World Records* (New York: Sterling, 1984), 340.

³¹For a convincing case arguing Hauptmann's innocence, see Ludovic Kennedy, *The Airman and the Carpenter* (New York: Viking, 1985).

³²Ray Anderson and C. David Mortensen, "Logic and Marketplace Argumentation," *Quarterly Journal of Speech* (April, 1967), 150.

³³Kenneth Burke, *Permanence and Change* (Indianapolis, IN: Bobbs Merrill, Library of the Liberal Arts, 1965), 85.

[34]Karl R. Wallace, "The Substance of Rhetoric: Good Reasons," in *The Rhetoric of Our Times,* ed. J.J. Auer (New York: Appleton-Century-Crofts, 1969), 287.

[35]Max Black, "Fallacies," in *Readings in Argumentation,* ed. Jerry M. Anderson and Paul J. Dovre (Boston: Allyn and Bacon, 1968), 301.

[36]Black, 301.

[37]Geoffrey Perrett, *America in the Twenties: A History* (New York: Touchstone, 1982), 384-390.

[38]See, for example, Michael Morgan, "Television Viewing and Reading: Does More Equal Better?" *Journal of Communication* (Winter, 1980), 159-165.

[39]"Selling It," *Consumer Reports* (April, 1986), 279.

[40]Richard L. Strout, *TRB: Views and Perspectives on the Presidency* (New York: Macmillan, 1979), 109.

[41]Richard Daley, quoted in Chester, Hodgson, and Page, 595.

[42]Ivan L. Preston, *The Great American Blow-Up* (Madison, WI: University of Wisconsin Press, 1975), 18.

[43]This is admittedly a simplification of a very complex issue. There were obviously many reasons for the American commitment to support the South Vietnamese. One reporter who has written extensively on both the early and later phases of our involvement is David Halberstam, whose first book, *The Making of a Quagmire* (New York: Random House, 1965), points to the dilemmas brought on by heavy military involvement in a land war. His second book, *The Best and the Brightest* (New York: Random House, 1972), partially reconstructs the circular reasoning behind what became the United State's "no win" situation.

[44]Toulmin, Rieke, and Janik, 17.

[45]Philip G. Zimbardo, Ebbe B. Ebbesen, and Christina Maslach, *Influencing Attitudes and Changing Behavior,* Second Edition (Reading, MA: Addison-Wesley, 1977), 73.

[46]In *The Rhetoric,* Aristotle identified three forms of "proof" available to the persuader: logical, emotional, and who we are (our personal credentials). Although he did not specifically note that the presence of one meant the absence of another, popular usage of these categories has had that effect. An excellent review of this problem is Gary Lynn Chronkite's "Logic, Emotion, and the Paradigm of Persuasion," in the *Quarterly Journal of Speech* (February, 1964), 13-18.

[47]Gary L. Dorsey, "Symbols: Vehicles of Reason or of Emotion?" in *Symbols and Values: An Initial Study,* ed. Lyman Bryson, Louis Finkelstein, R.M. McIver, and Richard McKeon (New York: Cooper Square, 1964), 445.

[48]Murray Edelman, *The Symbolic Uses of Politics* (Chicago: University of Illinois Press, 1967), 137.

[49]A similar distinction is sometimes made between "persuasion" that moves us intellectually and "conviction" that moves us personally. See Perelman and Obrechts-Tyteca, 26-31.

[50]Booth, 20.

Questions and Projects for Further Study

1. Locate an argumentative essay written by a newspaper columnist. After studying the column, summarize the *claims* and *premises* the author has used. Be careful to look for *implied* as well as stated premises. Make a judgment about the quality and adequacy of the author's arguments.

2. Using examples from magazine advertisements, locate and explain messages that contain fallacies mentioned in this chapter: *ad hominem,* false cause, *non sequitur,* circular argument, and excessive dependence on authority.

3. This chapter describes "practical reasoning" by comparing several categories of opposites. Briefly explain the differences between each of the following contrasting terms, indicating which term identifies a characteristic of practical reasoning:
   "Demonstration" vs. "Argumentation"
   Reasoning to "Discover" vs. Reasoning to "Defend"
   "Analytic Arguments" vs. "Enthymemes"

Additional Reading

Anderson, Ray Lynn; and C. David Mortensen. "Logic and Marketplace Argumentation." *Quarterly Journal of Speech* (April, 1967): 143-151.

Booth, Wayne C. *Now Don't Try to Reason With Me.* Chicago: University of Chicago Press, 1970.

Perelman, Chaim; and L. Olbrechts-Tyteca. *The New Rhetoric: A Treatise in Argumentation.* Trans. John Wilkinson and Purcell Weaver. Notre Dame, IN: University of Notre Dame Press, 1969.

Toulmin, Stephen. *The Uses of Argument.* London: Cambridge University, 1964.

Toulmin, Stephen; Richard Rieke; and Allan Janik. *An Introduction to Reasoning.* New York: Macmillan, 1979.

Wallace, Karl R. "The Substance of Rhetoric: Good Reasons." In *The Rhetoric of Our Times.* Ed. J.J. Auer. New York: Appleton-Century-Crofts, 1969.

6

The Psychology of Persuasion

 OVERVIEW

The most serious offense many of the depth manipulators commit, it seems to me, is that they try to
invade the privacy of our minds. It is this right to
privacy in our minds — privacy to be either rational or irrational — that I believe we must strive to
protect.[1]

The history of human development is earmarked by a continual
struggle for control — control over people, places, or things. From birth
to death, we are influenced by others. Our attitudes, beliefs, values,
likes, and dislikes are all defined and influenced by others. At the heart
of social control is the control of individuals. In democratic nations,
individual control is expressed in laws that define the boundaries of
acceptable behavior.

The most extreme form of behavior control is coercion. In coercive
situations, there is no choice among behavior alternatives and usually
there is a threat of the use of force to insure compliance. Most of us,
however, believe that our beliefs, attitudes, and values are rather
stable. Few individuals are willing to admit to changing their minds
about various topics or issues. Yet, we know that attitudes and
behavior continually change. In this chapter we are going to
investigate various behavioral theories of persuasion. The persuader
who is thinking like a psychologist attempts to determine what happens
"inside" individuals when they are confronted with assertions urging
change. Specifically, we are going to consider models that attempt to
account for internal changes that occur when we feel compelled to
alter our beliefs, attitudes, and values. Also, we will discuss several
techniques most often used to enhance a persuasive effort.

Logic and Rationality

Why do people continue to smoke when the evidence clearly
indicates that smoking is a health risk? Why do people with children

keep loaded guns in their homes when evidence indicates that there is a great likelihood of a firearm accident? Why do people take drugs routinely when such usage is socially and personally harmful? Logic would dictate that we should avoid smoking, loaded firearms, and drugs. How can large numbers of people ignore the obvious?

Mr. Spock, on the television show *Star Trek*, was a totally logical person. He functioned as a computer, devoid of human emotion and motivation. In contrast, Dr. McCoy on the show was highly emotional, responding to situations based upon feelings and instinct. Captain Kirk, the hero of the show, was a combination of the two. When confronted with choices, he used both "logic" and instinct, reason and compassion.

As you recall from Chapter 5, human logic is a subjective notion comprised of more than mere "facts." How we interpret facts and assign meaning and significance to them will largely determine the structure of our logic. In short, logic is a product of the interaction between speaker and listener. A teenager, with a sense of immortality and subject to a great amount of peer pressure, can easily find enough evidence to suggest that cigarettes are emblems of adulthood. "Logical" alternatives are not obvious and thus must be discussed, argued, and debated.

Persuasion is more than an exercise in formal logic because humans are more than machines. There can never be absolutely predictable behavior as long as there are choice and human motives. There are too many situations, emotions, motives, and generic differences among people for there to be singular solutions or arguments.

Finally, there is often an easily recognizable difference between "social" logic and "private" logic. In terms of our society, it is "logical" for farmers to receive more money for their products, but as a consumer is it "logical" for me to pay more for food when there is such a large surplus of agricultural products? Whenever a politician advocates a policy for "the common good of the nation" you can be assured that the policy will cause individual hardships for some people. Some critics of the Reagan administration would argue that the price we paid to bring inflation under control in the mid-1980s was too costly in terms of unemployment and reduced governmental social services. The dichotomy between "social" and "private" logic also operates in the home. As family members we all must make certain sacrifices and tolerate specific inconveniences for the good of the whole. It takes a great deal of effort for us as individuals to view situations and events from the perspective of others. Such efforts will, however, make us better members of groups and society.

Attitudes, Beliefs, and Values

The clearest evidence of successful persuasion is some form of overt behavior in response to our suggestions. The goal of most persuasive endeavors is ultimately to get someone to do something. Accepting or maintaining an attitude is considered an "act." Traditional theory argues that behavior change or modification is predicated on attitude change. Consequently, attitude change is the core concept of nearly all theories of persuasion. According to Fishbein and Raven, there is an almost hierarchical relationship among the concepts of attitudes, beliefs, and values.[2] Therefore, before we can discuss behavioral theories of persuasion, we need to define the concepts of attitudes, beliefs, and values.

Attitudes are the "evaluative dimension of a concept."[3] They comprise our likes and dislikes of people, places, or things. As internal and private predispositions, attitudes influence our responses to stimuli and ultimately our behavior. Thus, when we evaluate some symbol in the world as favorable or unfavorable, we are forming an attitude. For example, when we say "abortion is bad" we are expressing an attitude.

Attitudes have three dimensions. The "affective" dimension focuses on the object of the attitude and how we feel about the object. The "cognitive" dimension of an attitude reveals what we know or believe about the object. And the "behavioral" dimension reveals the likelihood of acting as a result of the attitude. For example, as Figure 1 shows, supporters of more stringent gun laws have attempted to tap into strong feelings and memories by reference to rampant American handgun violence. Campaigns such as those waged by Handgun Control Inc. have associated the handgun with information about deaths that the widespread availability of guns promotes. Their ultimate goal, of course, is to combine negative feelings about guns with specific information that will encourage individuals to act on their attitudes. In this case, the behavioral outcome of the "right" attitudes is to give money to counteract the legislative clout of the powerful National Rifle Association. For their part, the NRA has used much the same attitude-behavior linkage. In The American Rifleman, editorials tap into existing attitudes that view gun control as a threat to basic freedoms. Members are encouraged to vote for political candidates who support the NRA. The motivating language is both graphic and masculine: "It means a total commitment to safeguarding your firearm freedoms on every front with a square jaw and an iron fist."

Attitudes serve four important functions.[4] Obviously, attitudes serve a utilitarian function by influencing our behavior. They help us maximize rewards or positive behavioral responses as well as help us to avoid negative or harmful responses. Attitudes also serve an ego-defense function by helping us know who we are and what we stand for, thus reducing internal, mental unrest. Third, there is a knowledge function of attitudes. They help give meaning to the world around us. Attitudes help us form the "do's" and the "don'ts" of our daily lives. Finally, attitudes perform a value-expressive function. They serve as the vehicle for expressing our core feelings, beliefs, and values.

Beliefs are the "probability dimension of a concept."[5] They are our estimates about the truth or falsity of a notion. A belief is what we personally "know" to be true, even if others disagree. For example, the belief in the uniqueness of life and that humans are special beings superior to common animals can contribute to the negative attitude toward abortion.

Values are defined as "an organized set of related attitudes."[6] They represent general assumptions (sometimes stated, but often implied) which serve as building blocks to support specific assertions of attitude. Thus, the negative attitude toward abortion can be one of several that contribute to the value of the sanctity of life which will, in turn, be applied to many contexts.

From this brief discussion, it is obvious that attitudes are perhaps easier to alter than beliefs or values. At least we can agree that beliefs and values are more complex and are developed over a longer period of time. We can also see from this discussion the interrelationship among the terms. Attitudes are revealed in our daily conversations, but values are more difficult to ascertain. We must often directly ask people to reveal their beliefs and values. We can assume that we generally have fewer core values than beliefs and fewer beliefs than attitudes. We now can address the broader question of how do attitudes become the objects of public debate and persuasion?

Public Issues

The process of policy formation in the United States consists of a continuous interplay between citizens and decision makers. Both groups concern themselves with the allocation of the nation's human and natural resources. There is an assumption that public opinion influences public policy. As we noted in Chapter 2, the transformation of public opinion to public policy is the result of public discussion, argument, and debate.

Opinions are the verbal expressions of attitudes. Public issues begin as "private opinions." Private opinions consist of verbal and nonverbal activities representing individual images and interpretations of specific objects in settings that people take into consideration.

Figure 6.1

—Mrs. James S. Brady—

"Help me fight the National Rifle Association."

"Five years ago, John Hinckley pulled a $29 revolver from his pocket and opened fire on a Washington street. He shot the President. He also shot my husband.

I'm not asking for your sympathy. I'm asking for your help.

I've learned from my own experience that, alone, there's only so much you can do to stop handgun violence. But that together, we can confront the mightiest gun lobby–the N.R.A.– and win.

I've only to look at my husband Jim to remember that awful day... the unending TV coverage of the handgun firing over and over... the nightmare panic and fear.

It's an absolute miracle nobody was killed. After all, twenty thousand Americans are killed by handguns every year. Thousands more–men, women, even children–are maimed for life.

Like me, I know you support *stronger* hand-gun control laws. So does the vast majority of Americans. But the National Rifle Association can spend so much in elections that Congress is afraid to pass an effective national handgun law.

It's time to change that. Before it's too late for another family like mine... a family like yours.

I joined Handgun Control, Inc. because they're willing to take on the N.R.A. Right now we're campaigning for a national waiting period and background check on handgun purchases.

If such simple, basic measures had been on the books five years ago, John Hinckley would never have walked out of that Texas pawnshop with the handgun which came within an inch of killing Ronald Reagan. He lied on his purchase application. Given time, the police could have caught the lie and put him in jail.

Of course, John Hinckley's not the only one. Police report that thousands of known criminals buy handguns right over the counter in this country. We have to stop them.

So, please, pick up a pen. Fill out the coupon. Add a check for as much as you can afford, and mail it to me today.

It's time we kept handguns out of the wrong hands. It's time to break the National Rifle Association's grip on Congress and start making our cities and neighborhoods safe again.

Thank you and God bless you."

"Together we can win."

Dear Sarah,

It's time to break the N.R.A.'s grip on Congress once and for all. Here's my contribution to Handgun Control, Inc., the million-strong nonprofit citizens' group you help direct:

☐ $15 ☐ $25 ☐ $35 ☐ $50 ☐ $100 or $_____.
☐ Tell me more about how I can help.

NAME

ADDRESS

CITY   STATE   ZIP

HANDGUN CONTROL

1400 K Street, N.W., Washington, D.C. 20005, (202) 898-0792

Used by Permission of Handgun Control, Inc.

A NOTE FROM THE PRESIDENT:
At the direction of the NRA Executive Committee, J. Warren Cassidy assumed the post of acting Executive Vice President in May of this year and was named Executive Vice President at the September meeting of the Board of Directors. Mr. Cassidy comes to the task with impressive credentials, both as a leader and as a manager. A benefactor member, Cassidy served on the NRA board, finance and legislative policy committees, before giving up his family business in 1982 to become Executive Director of the NRA Institute for Legislative Action. In that role he has achieved a 95 percent record of pro-NRA legislative victories. I ask you to join me in welcoming Mr. Cassidy with your full support.

—J. E. Reinke, President

There's uncompromising thunder in these three words:

HERE WE STAND

As an NRA member, I always turned first to this page in every issue to be informed and inspired by the powerful prose of Harlon Carter . . . to learn the latest of my Association in action . . . to be reassured of its dogged determination to defend my freedoms . . . to know where we stand.

Today I write these words as the new leader of the NRA and, with Harlon Carter's permission, under that same banner. My name and my face are not new to you, nor are my goals: to continue to help lead our beloved Association toward the next century with renewed dedication to individual freedoms.

And what does the next century hold for the NRA? Greatness.

But talk is talk and action is action. As the owner of a small business in New England, I learned the principles of taking action. To count every cost, to keep an open ear and open door, to work sleeves-up and hands-on with the brightest people I could find. All with one eye trained on a vision of excellence. You can expect no less of me now.

The NRA is stronger than ever in its 115-year history. But like a high-powered engine, fine-tuning can improve performance.

That means setting new standards of member service and responsive leadership. It means offering the finest firearms training courses anywhere to people everywhere. It means strengthening the thousands of NRA-sanctioned competitions held each year. It means total commitment to safeguarding your firearms

Here We Stand

J. Warren Cassidy
EXECUTIVE VICE PRESIDENT

freedoms on every front with a square jaw and iron fist. It means continually working to educate Americans about our philosophies, programs and goals. And it means giving you full access to all of those in whom you have entrusted the future of your Association.

This fine-tuning will come gradually. There will be no sudden turns or jolting stops. Instead we will take measured, deliberate steps, carefully calculated for permanent impact. And once a step is taken, there is no retreat.

Each step we take, however, relies upon the strength of our unity. It was our unity that defeated California's Proposition 15, and that enacted pre-emption laws in a score of states. And it was our unity that scored the NRA's most historic victory: passage of the Volkmer-McClure Firearm Owners Protection Act. It all worked because we worked together.

But make no mistake. These triumphs have further aroused our opponents. Their targets include the Firearm Owners Protection Act, handguns containing plastic parts, even semi-automatic firearms.

We shall face them together and we shall prevail. For we stand upon the undeniable direction of our forefathers to defend the right of all law-abiding citizens to keep and bear arms.

For victory we pay a price. The Firearm Owners Protection Act struggle left us battle-scarred. Wounded in that fight was our century-long relationship with the law enforcement officers of this country. Anti-gun propaganda convinced the media that America's police broke ties with the NRA over this issue, despite clear, evident support of thousands of rank-and-file peace officers. But the wound is real and must be healed. We will rededicate our commitment to this nation's police officers with action, not talk. We will continue to be leaders in police firearms training, pro-police legislation, and programs beneficial to their own communities.

I challenge you to demonstrate your commitment as well. Go to the polls in the primaries and November elections. Question your candidates about their constitutional convictions. Then apply the full force of your vote.

In return, my pledges to you are clear: to fight those who would usurp our freedoms; to keep open channels of communication; to be fiscally conservative and fully accountable; to restore our traditional ties with America's police; and to marshal the machinery of the NRA better to serve your needs.

And I call upon you, our three-million-strong membership, to stand shoulder to shoulder with one unified voice which thunders that unmistakable battle cry among friend and foe alike: *HERE WE STAND*

Used by permission of the National Rifle Association.

"Private opinions" become "public opinions" when they are widely shared through the collective activities of others. Thus, public opinions are a process involving personal, social, and political activities.

There are three steps in the development of a public issue:

1. There is an individual, private conflict over some behavior, attitude, belief, or value noted in society.
2. There is the emergence of leadership that articulates and publicizes the conflict.
3. There is the stimulation of public communication activities about the conflict through various communication channels.

Public issues have five characteristics:

1. They possess a content dimension (i.e., they are about "something").
2. They possess a direction of attitude either positive or negative, favorable or unfavorable.
3. There is an intensity of belief or attitude on the issue.
4. There is controversy, conflict, or division relevant to the issue.
5. The issue is persistent and continual with any "official" resolutions being only "temporary" in nature.

Thus, at the heart of social debate and public issues are the attitudes of individual citizens. To cause significant change in society or even to enact a specific piece of legislation involves the altering of public attitudes, beliefs, and values.

Behavioral Theories of Persuasion

The study of persuasion from a behavioral perspective began as early as World War I.[7] The focus of the research was on propaganda. Specifically, the research identified elements of the persuasive process. The researchers investigated predictable patterns of response predicated on various elements of information (and/or misinformation). This very early research laid the structural foundation for studies to follow. World War II once again stimulated research in the area. This time, however, the research was more exploratory and experimental rather than historical. The focus of the research included the concept of attitudes which was a new variable for study. The "Yale Studies" directed by Carl Hovland had a profound impact upon persuasion theory. Hovland and his colleagues perceived persuasion as "a process of teaching persuadees to learn new attitudes or modify old ones, in much the same way that animals in a learning laboratory are trained to traverse a maze or to modify past maze-crossing habits."[8] Thus, behavioral theories of persuasion are grounded in social psychology and are characterized by experimental, laboratory research. These theories focus on the impact beliefs, attitudes and values have on human behavior. There are four very basic and important behavioral theories that we wish to review.

Stimulus-Response Theory

The most basic and fundamental behavioral theory of persuasion is stimulus-response. The most famous example and perhaps the most extreme form of this theory is Pavlov's dog. With each feeding of the dog, a bell is rung. Soon, upon hearing the bell the animal begins to salivate. Throughout life we accept favorable rewards and avoid unfavorable ones. Positive rewards reinforce certain attitudes and behavior. If we are told enough that we are good, beautiful, or smart, we then begin to believe it and act accordingly. We tend to give more credence to attitudes and behaviors that occur in the presence of positive reinforcements. The stimulus of a teacher's praise for a student is obviously designed to reinforce the motivation of doing good work. To the extent this linkage works, a *conditioned response* is a predictable outcome. When there are concrete, positive reinforcements, we tend to give even more credence to the attitudes and behavior.

Advertising uses this concept daily. What do we think of when we think of Michelob—friends, good times,. women or men? Why? Advertisements continually give us messages that cause us to associate certain things with Michelob. Indeed, this is a form of stimulus-response. If you were to exchange an expensive wine and a cheap wine in the bottles, which do you think would win a taste contest among your friends? If you were to purchase two paintings from a local artist and sign one Smith and the other Picasso, which do you think would receive more money at an auction? The same process is used when advertisers use a famous spokesperson for ads. They hope we suspend judgment and rely upon the credibility of the person to alter our attitudes and enduce trial. We are conditioned to like someone (or their character) and carry those positive feelings to the product. As a result, we respond to the person and not the attributes of the product.

Although the structure of the stimulus-response model is rather simple, the variables of the model become complex. To focus on the nature of the stimulus considers factors of human motivation and conditioning. For example, what makes us recognize and value a Picasso painting more than one by Smith? To focus on the nature of response considers factors of choice and reasonableness. What rationale would we provide for a preference for the Picasso painting? And finally, to focus on the organism of response considers factors of background, beliefs, and values. Why does one have any interest in paintings, impressionism, etc.? In many ways, the stimulus-response model provides the basic premises for all the other behavioral theories of persuasion.

Attribution Theory

Attribution theory attempts to explain how people account for the actions of others. As humans, it is our nature to make sense of the world and the behavior of others. We receive messages, decode them, and interpret them. By interpreting messages, we make inferences about the motives of others. It is important to remember that an ever-present feature of all communication is the identification of a person's motives. For example, suppose you are a car salesperson and you begin a conversation with a potential customer by complimenting his or her clothing. How will the customer interpret the compliment? It could be read as a sincere gesture, as a ploy to gain rapport, or even as a sexual advance. The entire communication that follows is understood in terms of the customer's perception of the persuader's intent. Similarly, a fascinating feature of most films, plays, and novels is the way their authors leave cues about the intentions of particular characters. Part of the pleasure we derive from fiction is in learning whether we were right in judging that a character had evil or honorable intentions. Every James Bond story, for example, features at least one or two voluptuous women whose loyalty to Bond is in doubt. In Bond movies, love scenes can quickly turn into murder scenes, confirming our suspicions about the dishonorable motives of a gorgeous vamp.

The task for the persuader is to figure out how certain messages or behavior will be interpreted. What makes the process complex is that human perception plays a major role in interpreting the messages of others. Perception is comprised of a multitude of variables that function differently in separate individuals. Since no two people process information the same way, attributions of intent can vary within an audience exposed to the same persuasion. One person may praise a President for making a courageous defense of policy; another may condemn the same effort as a collection of cleverly worded half truths.

There are two kinds of attributions: situational and dispositional.[9] Situational identifies factors in the environment that are believed to cause people to act in certain ways. The classic example is attributing crime to environmental factors such as poverty, broken homes, etc. In Chapter 4, we noted that an important source of attitudes is the peer group and the varied audiences they represent. Dispositional attributions identify internal, personal factors that are believed to cause people to behave in certain ways. For example, elements of religion, philosophy, or attitude may influence behavior. In Chapter 7 we note that certain personality traits such as authoritarianism may correlate with predictable attitudes, such as excessive faith in the judgments of authority figures.

There are, however, problems with this approach. There is no certainty of interpretation of individual motives and such an approach encourages oversimplification of human behavior. Each day our actions are influenced by the roles we play. For the authors, we assume the roles of teacher, parent, husband, and citizen; all of which impact our behavior. We may show compassion as a parent and husband but show little sympathy for poor performance when functioning as teacher or citizen.

It is important to remember that although attribution theory appears to be less than precise, the fact is that we must account for the behaviors of others so that we can assess our own behavior.

Cognitive Dissonance Theory

One of the most important and powerful of all psychological theories is the concept of cognitive dissonance introduced by Leon Festinger in 1957.[10] The theory has been refined and modified by many since it was first proposed, but it is sufficient for our purposes to outline only its basic assertions. At the heart of the theory is the simple idea that we seek consistency between attitudes and other related attitudes or between attitudes and related behaviors. Persuasion occurs when it becomes apparent to a person that there is an inconsistency between two or more related attitudes or behaviors. The revealed inconsistency produces dissonance or mental stress. The removal of the stress may take the form of changing an attitude or behavior to reduce the inconsistency. Roger Brown has offered a concise summary of dissonance theory:

> A state of cognitive dissonance is said to be a state of psychological discomfort or tension which motivates efforts to achieve consonance. *Dissonance* is the name for a disequilibrium and consonance the name for an equilibrium. Two cognitive elements, A and B, are dissonant if one *implies* the negation of the other; i.e., if A implies not-B. Two cognitive elements are consonant when one implies not the negation of the other element but the other element itself; i.e., A implies B. Finally, two elements, A and B, are irrelevant when neither implies anything about the other. Dissonance is comparable to imbalance; consonance to balance....[11]

To imagine how dissonance produces change, consider that—for any attitude—there is at least one related attitude that should be consonant. If the related attitude is dissonant, pointing out that inconsistency may produce persuasive change. For example, a person with a high regard for the President may have a low regard for his decision to support a policy for which the person has a low opinion, such as reinstituting the military draft.

(President) **high** $\cdots\cdot+\cdots\cdots\cdots\cdots\cdots\cdots\cdots\cdots\cdots\cdots\cdots\cdots\cdots$ **low**

(draft) **high** $\cdots\cdots\cdots\cdots\cdots\cdots\cdots\cdots\cdots\cdots\cdots\cdots\cdots+\cdot\cdot\cdot$ **low**

How does a person resolve the discrepancy created when a respected person takes on a disliked idea? Dissonance theory predicts that the disparity is resolved by altering the two original attitudes. If respect for the president is roughly equal to dislike for the draft, we would expect a process of change that would bring the two elements in consonance. That is, the person's enthusiasm for the President

(President) **high** $\cdots\cdots\cdots\cdots\cdots\cdots\cdots+\cdots\cdots\cdots\cdots\cdots\cdots$ **low**

will *moderate* and his dislike of the draft will be *less* intense.

(draft) **high** $\cdots\cdots\cdots\cdots\cdots\cdots+\cdots\cdots\cdots\cdots\cdots$ **low**

In short, the dissonance is relieved by changing attitudes to create consistency. Comments such as, "I still think he's a pretty good president," or "I don't like the idea of the draft, but there may be times when it is necessary," reveal that there has been a change that reduces the inconsistency between the two elements.

Similarly, a person forced to do something against his will, such as saying some nice things about a disliked person, may in fact produce dissonance that leads to attitude change. Being forced to do something we don't want to do (in the military, in school, by parents, by employers, etc.) is sometimes called "enforced discrepant behavior" by psychologists. The dissonance that is created may set up a process of attitude change to lessen the discrepancy between the enforced behavior and the inconsistent attitude. The outcome may be that we may like a person more if we are forced to say nice things in public; or we may come to share the belief that military discipline is good training for later life. Such changes in attitude give meaning and consistency to behaviors that we have publicly undertaken.

Two important qualifications are important to remember when applying dissonance theory to the study of particular messages. First, there is no dissonance if two concepts are not related, or if a person's attitudes toward two concepts are similar. For example, if a President we did *not* like proposed a policy we feared, the model would read:

(President)   **high** · +· · ·   **low**

(draft)   **high** · +· · ·   **low**

As the model suggests, there is no need for a realignment of attitudes. Second, when confronted with an inconsistency, the mind provides many options: an individual may change an attitude, discount the source of the inconsistency, rationalize the behavior, or seek new supporting information to negate the inconsistency. What becomes critical are the various "cognitive elements" or bits of information that comprise the attitude. For example, the individual who smokes is confronted with the fact that smoking causes cancer.[12] But there can be other elements that mitigate the threat of cancer. If the individual smokes only low tar cigarettes, thinks smoking induces relaxation and helps control weight gain and believes the old adage that "you've got to die of something," then the single element of the relationship between smoking and cancer becomes less important.

Thus, there is no direct relationship between attitudes and behavior. Seldom is there one attitude that dictates behavior. There are many attitudes that influence us.

Social Learning Theory

Social learning theory is most closely related to attribution theory. At the heart of the theory is the simple notion that most of our overt behavior is learned from society. Through social interaction, we discover rather clear rules for acceptable behavior; other people provide models for how to behave. People learn behavior in several ways: direct experience, the observation of others, role-playing, reading and just listening to others. The rules we learn can change based upon age, situation, or reference group. Standards of behavior differ whether we are alone, with friends, or attending a formal affair. As a result, people must always use judgment and discriminate among various behavior options. As individuals, we quickly run through "if-then" scenarios; we recognize almost instantaneously the rewards or punishments associated with each alternative behavior. Etiquette books have always provided a ready source of examples about how we prejudge the consequences of our behavior. For example, "in meeting a friend whom you have not seen for some time, and of the state and history of whose family you have not recently or particularly been informed, you should avoid making allusions in respect to particular individuals of his family.... Some may be dead; others may have misbehaved, separated themselves, or fallen under some distressing calamity."[13]

Using one's fingers to eat chicken is acceptable up to a certain age and then only in the most informal situations. Does this rather minor "rule" really matter? Of course it does. If someone is attending a job interview luncheon, it is most likely that they want to be perceived as dignified, well mannered, and certainly not gross! The point is obvious—implicit rules of behavior govern our every action.

What Do We Know?

The four broad theoretical models discussed above have provided a general framework for testing persuasion effects. In the next chapter we examine some experimental studies focusing on audience perceptions of high and low credibility. In more capsule form, however, here are some key conclusions that experimental studies of persuasion have yielded in the last 50 years. It is useful to group these in terms of the persuader, audience, and message. Like all generalizations derived from specific studies, it is important to remember that these cause and effect assertions represent general tendencies rather than irrefutable "laws."

Persuader

1. A source of perceived high credibility will have greater success in altering attitudes than sources of low credibility.

2. A source that expresses similarities of views and background will have greater success in altering attitudes.

3. Hostility reduces openness to suggestion and thus should be avoided by a persuader.

4. Low or modest fear appeal is more effective in altering attitudes than direct threats to an audience. Extreme threats may have short term impact. In general, however, raising audience anxiety reduces the persuasiveness of a message.

5. It is more effective to link the advocated attitude or behavior to other more salient attitudes or behaviors. For example, linking the desired attitude or behavior to health, money, love, etc. will generally have a positive impact upon an audience.

6. Asking for an extreme opinion change will result in more actual opinion change than asking for a modest opinion change.

7. It is effective to demonstrate an inconsistency among the audience's beliefs, attitudes, values, and behavior.

Audience

1. Audiences seek messages of agreement rather than disagreement. Thus, audiences generally begin with a favorable predisposition toward the speaker's message.

2. Audience members with low self-esteem are easier to persuade than members with high self-esteem. A related issue is that framing the desired change in terms of raising self-esteem is an effective strategy.

3. Better educated and highly intelligent people are more difficult to persuade.

4. Generally, women have been found to be easier to persuade than men. This situation seems to be changing rapidly.

5. Increased age usually makes persuasion more difficult.

6. As an individual becomes more committed to a belief, attitude, or value, persuasion becomes more difficult. Likewise, the more extreme the position of an individual the less likelihood of a change.

7. Resistance to persuasion increases as belief or attitude patterns become more consistent.

Message Presentation

1. One-sided presentation is more effective when the audience is friendly, already accepts your position, or when you desire a quick, short-term change.

2. Two-sided presentation is more effective when the audience is hostile to your position or if the audience is likely to be presented with the opposing view.

3. Presenting counter-arguments to your own position is effective in disarming future persuasive attempts from the opposition.

4. Presenting weaknesses of the other side is more effective than just presenting counter-arguments.

5. Most studies argue that the views presented last will be the most effective and will probably be more readily remembered.

6. It is better to provide conclusions explicitly than to let the audience draw conclusions from the messages.

7. General cues that warn audiences of forthcoming manipulative attempts increase message resistance. The audience becomes suspect of the source's motives and will thus be more critical of message.

Summary

Social control is a fact of life. While we are all aware of overt attempts of control by force, we tend to ignore the equally powerful subtle attempts at human manipulation. We do not suggest that social cooperation is bad. We are more interested in understanding the process of human inducement—the role communication plays in inducing advocated human behavior.

Sociologists focus upon social structures. Behavior results from factors such as status, position, norms, values, and roles. Such factors are viewed as causing our behavior. Psychologists, on the other hand, focus on such factors as motives, attitudes, or hidden psychological processes. All these factors are important. We must also understand the influence of human interaction. To analyze human society, the starting point must be the analysis of humans interacting with each other. Individual behavior and self-control are the most basic elements of social control. The interrelationship between social control and self-control is the result of commitment to various groups which produce self-fulfillment, self-expression, and self-identity. Emotional commitments result from personal attachments among group members. Moral commitment results from identification of self to the values or principles of a specific group. Social control is not, therefore, just a matter of formal governmental agencies, laws, rules, and regulations. Rather, social control is a direct result of citizens identifying and internalizing the values of a group so that those values become essential to self-esteem. Thus, individuals will behave in a manner which supports the social order. Adherence to the rules of society becomes a fair price to pay for membership in the group. There is, however, a great deal of competition for various values and social commitments among groups. Thus, we are confronted daily with attempts to alter our beliefs, attitudes, and values. Direct coercion plays a very small role in altering our behavior.

In this chapter, we see how the concepts of attitudes, beliefs, and values provide the basis for our behavior. In addition, we recognize the importance of perception and social situations in influencing our daily behavior. Some attempts at influence are obvious and overt. Others are more subtle. Although we are humans and not mere machines, observation does provide patterns of behavior. These patterns also provide insight into techniques of changing people's attitudes and the resultant behavior. It is useful to see how these theories and techniques of persuasion are applied to everyday situations.

There is a very popular television advertisement that wants people to call a toll free number to subscribe to *Time* magazine. The ad begins with an attractive telephone operator who cues us that a special offer is coming. We are encouraged to pay attention to the forthcoming message. The promise of a reward or special offer plays upon our basic nature to seek reward and to avoid punishment (stimulus-response theory). The spokesperson assumes the role of an everyday person thereby creating a sense of commonality and identification with the audience. Although we know a sales message is coming, she is non-threatening and is offering us something "good" (attribution theory). The heart of the ad shows a series of people thoughtfully reading the magazine. Again, there is a representative group shown reading the magazine — men and women, young and old. The announcer reminds us of the responsibility of keeping informed about issues and the world situation (social learning theory). If we are not well informed and yet hope to make the world safe, then we need to subscribe to the magazine (cognitive dissonance theory). When the operator returns, she offers us a tangible reward or premium and discounted, low price to subscribe to the magazine. What appears to be a straightforward commercial utilizes many elements of psychology to induce purchase of the magazine.

Notes

[1]Vance Packard, *The Hidden Persuaders* (New York: Pocket Books, 1957), 229.

[2]Martin Fishbein and B. Raven, "The AB Scale: An Operational Definition of Belief and Attitude," *Human Relations,* 15 (February, 1962), 42.

[3]Fishbein and Raven, 42.

[4]Gerald Miller, Michael Burgoon and Judee Burgoon, "The Functions of Human Communication in Changing Attitudes and Gaining Compliance," in *Handbook of Rhetorical and Communication Theory,* eds. Carroll Arnold and John W. Bowers (Boston: Allyn and Bacon, Inc., 1984), 442-444.

[5]Fishbein and Raven, 42.

[6]Fishbein and Raven, 42.

[7]Miller et al., 404.

[8]Herbert W. Simons, *Persuasion: Understanding, Practice, and Analysis,* Second Edition (New York: Random House, 1986), 29.

[9]Philip Zimbardo, Ebbe Ebbesen, and Christina Maslach, *Influencing Attitudes and Changing Behavior* (Reading, MA: Addison-Wesley Publishing Co., 1977).

[10]L. Festinger, *A Theory of Cognitive Dissonance* (Evanston, IL: Row, Peterson, 1957).

[11]Roger Brown, *Social Psychology* (New York: Free Press, 1965), 584.

[12]Zimbardo et al., 66-67.

[13]Quoted in Erving Goffman, *The Presentation of Self in Everyday Life* (New York: Anchor Doubleday, 1959), 210.

Questions and Projects for Further Study

1. Select a television advertisement and see how many specific techniques and behavioral theories of persuasion you can find.

2. Select a magazine advertisement and see how many specific techniques and behavioral theories of persuasion you can find.

3. Select a contemporary, controversial political issue and identify the underlying attitudes, beliefs, and values on each side of the issue.

4. How would your persuasive strategies differ if you were to advocate mandatory military service speaking before audiences comprised of veterans, women, or college students?

Additional Reading

Festinger, Lee. *A Theory of Cognitive Dissonance.* Evanston, IL: Row, Peterson, 1957.

Fishbein, Martin; and Icek Ajzen. *Belief, Attitude, Intention, and Behavior.* Reading, MA: Addison-Wesley, 1975.

Lindzey, G.; and E. Aronson, eds. *The Handbook of Social Psychology.* Reading, MA: Addison-Wesley, 1968.

Miller, Gerald et al. "The Functions of Human Communication in Changing Attitudes and Gaining Compliance." In *Handbook of Rhetorical and Communication Theory.* Eds. Carroll Arnold and John W. Bowers. Boston: Allyn and Bacon, 1984.

Petty, Richard; and John Cacioppo. *Attitudes and Persuasion: Classic and Contemporary Approaches.* Dubuque, IA: William C. Brown, 1981.

Rokeach, Milton. *Beliefs, Attitudes, & Values.* San Francisco: Jossey-Bass, 1968.

Rokeach, Milton. *The Open and Closed Mind.* New York: Basic Books, 1960.

Smith, Mary John. *Persuasion and Human Action.* Belmont, CA: Wadsworth, 1982.

Zimbardo, Phillip et al. *Influencing Attitudes and Changing Behavior.* Reading, MA: Addison-Wesley, 1977.

Power, Credibility, and Authority

 OVERVIEW

There could be no mistaking he was a great
man—he looked like one, talked like one, was
treated like one and insisted that he was one.[1]

The Essential Role of Credibility: Two Cases

Prime time television has become a favorite place for celebrities to
play practical jokes on each other. In a recent episode, television's
well-known Dr. Joyce Brothers decided to trick her friend, Merv
Griffin. The pop psychologist asked him to come to a rehearsal studio to
observe a new "act" she and a group of professional dancers were
supposedly rehearsing. When Griffin appeared, Dr. Brothers
pretended to be busily involved in a run-through of her routine. She
asked Griffin to watch and to give her his honest opinion; a hidden
camera recorded his reactions. Instead of her usual conservative
clothes, Dr. Brothers wore a gown more appropriate for a Las Vegas
chorus girl than for a trusted professional psychologist. The alleged
"act" itself featured what only a generous person would recognize as
"dancing" and "singing." The dance steps made a stumble look
graceful, and Joyce's weak soprano voice warbled about the need to
face up to psychological problems. Dr. Brothers periodically
interrupted her "rehearsal" to explain that the act would extend her
"range" as a psychologist. Griffin was aghast at the thought of a friend
about to scuttle a well-developed image. Had the good doctor lost her
marbles? He searched for a way to let her down gently without hurting
her feelings, but he needed to communicate that the musical act would
endanger her livelihood. "Think about your credibility," he pleaded.
Dr. Brothers was a paragon of common sense for millions. How could
audiences take the advice of someone who had so little understanding
of her own limitations? This practical joke reminds us that often the
most valuable commodity we bring to social situations is our own
credibility.

Consider another case which generated debate within the music
world several years ago. In 1979, the much-anticipated "memoirs" of
the Soviet composer Dmitri Shostakovich were published in the United

148

States, but their appearance raised a storm of international controversy about their authenticity.[2] Shostakovich was a towering figure in modern Russian culture and remains one of the most frequently performed modern composers in Europe and the United States. Yet, *Testimony: The Memoirs of Dmitri Shostakovich* reveals a tormented man. He portrays himself as caught between the need to express his creativity and the need to write music that would placate the Soviet power structure. Until his death in 1975, he was alternately praised and vilified by the official press and the Communist Party. The frequently recorded Fifth Symphony was deemed appropriately "Soviet," but other works were severely criticized as "formalist," too personal, or despairing. Shostakovich had held important posts within the Party; yet his "memoirs" lashed back at his enemies within the official bureaucracy. He accused the power structure from Joseph Stalin onward of making life miserable for artists and musicians, and he expressed resentment at having to write what one critic called "propaganda poster music."[3]

Were these much-discussed indictments of the Soviet cultural world authentic? The memoirs appeared in print only after Shostakovich died at the age of 65, thus it was impossible to verify their accuracy. In addition, individual chapters were not written by the composer; they were dictated to the musicologist, Solomon Volkov. Shostakovich is said to have signed each of the drafts before they were smuggled out of the Soviet Union. Volkov later immigrated to the United States where he edited and annotated the memoirs. Some Soviet writers claim that *Testimony* is a forgery, and many Western observers have puzzled over the use of distinctly non-Soviet expressions in the text such as "con man" and "big shot." Today we are still uncertain that this book "sets the record straight" about one of the most important figures in twentieth-century music.

The Goals of this Chapter

As these dissimilar cases indicate, the power to persuade is almost always contingent on our assessment of the credibility or authority of a source. Even though we frequently pay lip service to "the integrity of ideas" or the "impartiality of facts," there is no doubt that the credibility of a communicator can be decisive in winning supporters. The first half of this chapter explores three very different perspectives that account for how authority is established and communicated to audiences. The first involves practical guidelines about "good character"; the second outlines common guidelines for assessing the reliability of sources in legal settings; the third is based on experimental research on the kinds of advocates audiences are likely to believe. The last half of the chapter concludes with an examination of four related strategies useful in understanding why certain advocates can dramatically affect audiences.

The Inexact Nature of Credibility

Because the subjects of credibility and authority are complex and inexact, it will become obvious that there is a gap between the questions that we raise and the relatively incomplete answers current research is able to provide. Power relationships between people are fascinating, but they are rarely reducible to simple formulas. Indeed, understanding the questions that arise in the course of explorations into authority may be more important than recalling the partial answers now available. The mysteries of human behavior cannot be revealed with the clarity that comes with discoveries in the physical world. The sciences yield concrete findings; studies of human action, in contrast, locate *patterns* which usually apply only to certain settings and to certain people. As with the subject of persuasion itself, *many* theories and partial explanations about authority are useful but not definitive. Also, it is important to remember that credibility applies to both individuals and groups. Sometimes it makes more sense to talk about the specific credibility of one individual, such as the President of the United States or a speaker in a persuasion course. At other times, it is more relevant to consider the credibility of a group or organization. Group credibility might be explored in polls such as a 1986 poll which asked a cross section of Americans if they thought "moral and ethical standards are higher in big corporations, or higher in the Federal Government?"[4]

The Three Meanings of "Credibility"

"Credibility" is a pivotal term in the study of persuasion, but those who use it frequently have different meanings in mind. Usually a term with inconsistent meanings is best discarded in favor of less confusing substitutes. In this case, however, the various ways credibility is used represent different but equally valid approaches for assessing how *who a persuader is* affects audience response. For some, credibility means *good character*. For others, it is a synonym for *truthfulness*. Social scientists apply a third meaning to the term: it is a trait identified with a source who is *believable* to others, even if "immoral" or "wrong." As we shall see, these three perspectives sometimes blend together. At other times, the diverse perspectives present an opportunity to explore the different ways in which sources use their power and authority.

Ethos **and the Idea of Good Character**

One of the oldest terms associated with the qualities of an advocate is the Greek word, *ethos*. For Aristotle, *ethos* was one of three major forms of influence. In *The Rhetoric* he wrote that the ideal persuader should put the audience in the right emotional frame of mind (*pathos*), state the best arguments (*logos*), and have the right kind of character or *ethos*. The persuader "must not only try to make the argument of his speech demonstrative and worthy of belief; he must also make his own character look right...."[5]

Aristotle labeled the components of good character as good sense, good moral character, and goodwill. "It follows," he noted, "that any one who is thought to have all three of these good qualities will inspire trust in his audience."[6] "Good sense" and "good moral character" center on audience perceptions that the judgments and values a persuader endorses are reasonable and justified. If the persuader seems to see the world in the same terms as the audience—a world in which "good" people are easily separated from less trustworthy people—the audience will be inclined to accept the speaker's evidence and conclusions. At a very practical level it is obvious that we are attracted to friends and even politicians on the basis of our perceptions of their similarity to ourselves. Add in the element of "goodwill"—the important idea that the persuader seems to have honorable intentions towards an audience—and we have a sense of which kind of advocates are likely to be successful.

Character Judgments in Everyday Life

We "read" every social setting for cues about the motives and competence of strangers as well as acquaintances. All interpersonal contact requires a degree of trust. Whenever someone encourages us to part with our money or to alter our attitudes, we want to be certain that our faith in them will not be abused.

In a book that describes both his cross-country motorcycle travels, as well as the journey into his troubled mind, Robert Pirsig provides examples of how we assess the abilities and sensibilities of people who present themselves as knowledgeable. At another level, Pirsig's *Zen and the Art of Motorcycle Maintenance* is also an eye-opening description of the confrontation between the Sophists and Plato discussed in Chapter 2. In the following excerpt, Pirsig describes the credibility-revealing behavior of two mechanics attempting to repair his motorcycle:

> The shop was a different scene from the ones I remembered. The mechanics, who had once all seemed like ancient veterans, now looked like children. A radio was going full blast and they were

> clowning around and talking and seemed not to notice me. When
> one of them finally came over he barely listened to the piston slap
> before saying, "Oh yeah. Tappets."[7]

The $140.00 repair bill that Pirsig paid failed to remedy the engine
problem. He later discovered that the noisy piston was caused by a
damaged twenty-five cent pin accidentally sheared off by another
careless mechanic. "Why," he asks, "did they butcher it so?" What
evidence did they provide that indicated they were less than fully
competent mechanics?

> The radio was the clue. You can't really think hard about what
> you're doing and listen to the radio at the same time. Maybe they
> didn't see their job as having anything to do with hard thought, just
> wrench twiddling. If you can twiddle wrenches while listening to the
> radio that's more enjoyable.
>
> Their speed was another clue. They were really slopping things
> around in a hurry and not looking where they slopped them. More
> money that way....
>
> But the biggest clue seemed to be their expressions. They were hard
> to explain. Good-natured, friendly, easygoing — and uninvolved.
> They were like spectators. You had the feeling they had just
> wandered in there themselves and somebody had handed them a
> wrench. There is no identification with the job. No saying, "I am a
> mechanic." At 5 p.m. or whenever their eight hours were in, you
> knew they would cut it off and not have another thought about their
> work. They were already trying not to have any thoughts about their
> work on the job.[8]

Pirsig argues that a good mechanic is a person who can match the
precise tolerances of machinery with a precise, analytic mind. The
ethos of an expert mechanic has little to do with "wrench twiddling,"
but a great deal to do with cultivating a gift for problem-solving.

Assessing the Character of Advocates

Ethos is the personal or professional reputation the persuader brings
to the persuasive setting or constructs in the process of
communicating. In more formal settings, it is customary to introduce a
speaker with a few flattering comments to intensify audience respect.
In other settings, the persuader must decide if something should be
said (usually in the early moments of a speech) to repair a negative
audience perception or to increase the likelihood of audience approval.
From the choice of a topic to the style of dress, speakers calculate the
elements of content and style that can be safely presented to an
audience as evidence of expertise and good character. Most of us have
little difficulty recognizing the general traits of credibility. We identify
high *ethos* sources as "fair," "trustworthy," "sincere," "reliable,"

and "honest." Their knowledge about a subject may be seen as "professional," "experienced," and "authoritative"; their manner of presentation may be perceived as "energetic," "active," "open-minded," "objective," "bold," or "decisive."[9]

No public figure from our recent past has shown more skill in using ethos-building devices than Ronald Reagan. He became a public figure nearly 50 years ago in the entertainment industry, first as a radio announcer, then as a Warner Brothers actor, and finally as President of Hollywood's powerful Screen Actors Guild. Later he served as a spokesperson for the corporate giant, General Electric, visiting hundreds of offices and factories and giving countless speeches in praise of G.E. and American free enterprise. It was from his G.E. forum that he successfully rose to the Governorship of California and later to the Presidency in 1980. Throughout this period, he was tireless in using the facts of his public biography as a basis for winning over suspicious audiences. His responses to attacks on his *ethos* as an *actor* were especially masterful. Throughout his long political career he was plagued by the question, "How can we take an actor seriously?" He made his background seem more appropriate and urgent to the world of politics than many would initially judge. Consider how he started an address to a California press club in 1961 before his move into electoral politics. At the time he was known only as a "nice guy" actor and former President of the actors union:

> It must seem presumptuous to some of you for a member of my pro-fession to stand here and attempt to talk on problems of the nation. We in Hollywood are not unaware of the concept many of our fellow citizens have of us and our industry. We realize that our merchan-dise is made up of tinsel, colored lights and a large measure of make-believe.[10]

By identifying and labeling the audience's likely assumptions about the mythical world of Hollywood, Reagan served notice that he was under no illusions about his occupation. His self-effacing description of his career was candid and fair-minded. He went on to add weight to his theme of "encroaching control" of government by pointing out that Hollywood itself was on the front line of a vital (and not so trivial) struggle. As he saw it, the key battleground was in Hollywood's important and powerful unions.

> However, a few years ago "a funny thing happened to us on the way to the theatre." Ugly reality came to our town on direct orders of the Kremlin. Hard core party organizers infiltrated our business. They created cells, organized Communist fronts, and for a time, deceived numbers of our people, who with the best intentions, joined these fronts while still ignorant of their true purpose. The aim was to gain

economic control of our industry.... The men in the Kremlin wanted
this propaganda medium for their own destructive purposes.[11]

In countless speeches like this one, Ronald Reagan presented himself
as more than an actor. His redefined *ethos* put him at the very
forefront of a battle with the Soviet Union for the hearts and minds of
the American public. Although there has been no substantial evidence
linking the Kremlin to attempts to take over the film industry's trade
unions,[12] Reagan made the seemingly enormous leap from Hollywood to
Washington precisely on his reputation as a fighter to prevent the
Soviets from using "our screens" for "the dissemination of Communist
propaganda."[13]

The Rational/Legal Ideal of Credibility

A second major way of estimating the quality of sources is through
the use of formal guidelines for judging expertise and reliability. In
the rational/legal view of credibility, statements or views deserve to be
believed if their sources meet certain general standards for accuracy
and objectivity. As described by Robert and Dale Newman, a source is
credible if it is "worthy of belief," hence probably telling the truth
"with no concern as to whether any specific audience or reader will in
fact believe it."[14]

The difference between a persuader's *ethos* and his rational
credibility rests on objective criteria that exist apart from the beliefs
of people in specific settings. Only an audience can determine if a
certain persuader has "good character," hence, high *ethos*. The legal
rules for judging sources are meant to apply to all audiences. Members
of a jury, for example, may have strong suspicions that a defendant of a
different race and social background is guilty of the charges brought
against him. Yet, under courtroom guidelines of credibility, they are
obliged to disregard their personal ethnic and racial preconceptions in
favor of the rules of evidence before them. The witness who is
outwardly most like them (in dress, race, and education-level, for
example) may only be capable of giving "hearsay" (overheard or
second-hand) evidence. Under the legal rules governing sources,
hearsay testimony will be discounted by a judge in favor of statements
from an eyewitness, even if the eyewitness' lifestyle is alien to most of
the members of the jury.

The challenge of rising above one's own prejudice to see the raw
truth is a dilemma posed in the classic American novel *To Kill a
Mockingbird*. In Harper Lee's story, an all-white jury in the 1930s is
asked to believe that a black man, Tom Robinson, is innocent in the
alleged rape of a white woman. As the novel unfolds, it becomes clear
that the charge is unfounded. Lee describes a young and disturbed

woman who coaxes Robinson into her house, kisses him, and then tries to erase her socially instilled guilt by claiming that she had been assaulted. The story pits the nation's most honored values of fair play and justice against the prejudices of our past. The sympathetic figure of defense attorney Atticus Finch (played in the film version by Gregory Peck) tries valiantly to point out that no objective review of the evidence can lead a thinking person to a verdict of guilty. In his stirring summation, he concludes, "I am confident that you gentlemen will review without passion the evidence you have heard, come to a decision, and restore this defendant to his family,"[15] The jury, however, accepts the dubious testimony of the white witnesses for the prosecution. The jurors' collective prejudices allow them to see only that a black man stepped out of his place in a rigid social hierarchy. From the moment Tom Robinson was charged, the narrator tells us, he was guilty "in the secret courts of men's hearts."[16]

What standards should have guided the jury? In the practice of law, guidelines for determining the quality of a source are relatively straightforward, although they are always harder to apply to specific cases than to summarize in the abstract. These guidelines raise two fundamental questions; one concerns the source's ability, and the other pertains to the source's objectivity.

Ability

How do we determine if someone has the ability to tell the truth or to make intelligent observations about a specific subject? The first crucial test spotlights the need to measure the extent to which an "authority" has been in a position to observe. In many walks of life, from legal proceedings to the reconstruction of historical events, we routinely estimate the credibility of claimants based on their expertise. Were they eyewitnesses to events or did they get information second-hand from another source? Do they have the training, experience, access to information, and knowledge to know what to look for? Can the testimony of one source be supported by others with knowledge in a similar area? We would expect, for example, that a persuader attempting to convince us that nuclear power plants emit "unsafe levels of airborn radiation" would base such claims on more than personal hunches. We would search for assurances that the advocate not only knows how such plants are designed and operate, but also understands the complex biological issues involved in assessing what constitutes "acceptable" levels of radiation exposure.

Expertise itself may not be enough. It is possible that a source may have the *ability* to make sound judgments but still not make them. An expert may have an overriding reason to ignore or to overlook what accumulated knowledge should indicate.

Objectivity

The second crucial factor in rational and legal discussions of credibility involves estimates of objectivity, the ability to understand an event without prejudging it according to prior standards or experiences. No one can be completely objective. In fact, it is testimony to our humanity that we are endowed with feelings and attitudes that make us more than simple recorders of events. Such interpretations of reality can sometimes intrude on what should be strictly accurate, objective judgments.

Consider, for example, the dilemma facing a well-paid and highly qualified research chemist employed by a major food processor. Suppose this expert in food chemistry stumbles onto evidence that moderate consumption of one of the company's most profitable products — a successful line of potato-based snack foods — creates an unusual chemical compound that slightly discolors tooth enamel. Our Ph.D. in chemistry is certainly expert enough to know how to design further studies to measure this effect accurately. However, she may be caught in a professional bind; she realizes that she has not been hired by the company to document all of the "marginal" side effects of processed foods. While manufacturers do not want to harm their customers, the limited effect of a slight dulling of tooth enamel color is problematic. The condition is certainly not life-threatening. It would take a company with a very broad view of its social responsibilities to support experiments that may confirm the presence of such low-grade, negative effects. Rather than thinking of her initial discovery as a matter of pure science, the chemist is likely to weigh her career investment before reporting her findings and doing more studies. She may conclude that research on this particular side effect is not worth the risk it poses to her position.

Thus, not only must we ask if a source has the ability to tell the truth and to make expert judgments, but also if the source is free from an overriding bias that could cancel out the advantages of expertise. Determining that a source is not objective is not simply a matter of labeling a person "deceptive" or "fraudulent." It is natural to see the world from a view of self interest. We expect certain investments to shape the comments and responses of groups and individuals. CBS does not routinely praise NBC's television programs. Political candidates usually see faults rather than strengths in the activities of their rivals.

We can judge a source's objectivity by determining if it is *willing* or *reluctant*. The Newmans write that the idea of reluctant testimony is based on a sturdy old principle: "It is assumed that sane individuals will not say things against their own interests unless such testimony is true beyond doubt." Sources are reluctant when they take positions that go *against* their own interests; hence, "The greater the damage of

Figure 7.1

ARE WE DOING SOMETHING WRONG?

It could only happen in an election year . . . Just when we thought we were doing everything right —

emphasizing the right issues — attacking the right people — exposing the right foul-ups and cover-ups . . . we get a compliment like this.

Sure, we have a lot of respect for Mr. Will and his journalistic ability. We've even published his thoughts on various issues. (We think it's fair to our readers to see both sides of the fence.)

But this is too much! What is he trying to do? Is he trying to ruin us with our faithful readers . . . or is this a sinister reverse psychology plot to undermine our own confidence?

The next thing you know, we'll be getting compliments from Jesse Helms, Ed Meese, and even the Great Communicator Himself.

We'd like your help in this matter. Please use the attached card (or the coupon on this page) to try us out. Then please let us know if we're losing our touch . . . or if The New Republic has finally gotten through to the other side.

❝ The New Republic is currently the nation's most interesting and important political journal. ❞

George Will, Syndicated columnist

THE NEW REPUBLIC 75A022
P.O. BOX 955
FARMINGDALE, N.Y. 11737-9855

☐ YES! Please enter my subscription for the term I've checked below. I save 60% off the $1.95 cover price with this special introductory offer.

  ☐ 32 issues only $24
  ☐ One full year (48 issues) only $36

Name _____

Address_____ Apt # _____

City _____ State_____ Zip_____

For new subscribers only. TNR'S basic subscription rate is $48 per year
OFFER SUBJECT TO CHANGE WITHOUT NOTICE.
Allow 3-5 weeks for delivery of first issue. All foreign orders must be prepaid.
Additional postage: add $22 per year to foreign orders and $10 to Canadian orders, payable in U.S. currency.

An advertisement based on the principle of reluctant testimony.

Used by permission of *The New Republic*.

his own testimony to a witness, the more credible it is."[17] When a political rival pays a compliment to an opponent, or agrees with the position the opponent has taken, it would appear that something other than self interest is at work. In Figure 7.1, for example, a liberal magazine uses the reluctant testimony of a conservative writer in an advertisement that promotes the quality of its articles. The ad encourages its readers to assume that the praise means more coming from a conservative rather than a liberal source. Testimony from a liberal would be willing because we would expect an author to praise a like-minded publication. Willing testimony always supports the testifier's *existing* attitudes and perceptions because, by definition, its utterance involves no risk to its author. Reluctant sources potentially have much more to lose, such as the Department of Defense "whistleblowers" who embarrassed their employers by exposing wasteful spending practices. (See Figure 7.2.)[18]

In reality, the gap between the willing and the reluctant source is an unbroken continuum that is heavily weighted at the willing end of the scale. Reluctant testimony is understandably rare. The task left to audiences searching for advocates worthy of belief is to find high-ability sources who, though perhaps not completely reluctant, are at least not so deeply tied to one fixed point of view that they are incapable of seeing merit and truth in positions opposed to their own.

Source Credibility and Believability

A third perspective on credibility comes from comparatively recent experimental studies on the formation of attitudes. The redefinition of credibility as believability received support in the important work of psychologist Carl Hovland in the early 1950s and spawned hundreds of studies examining the range of source-related traits that can affect audience acceptance of a message.[19]

Source Credibility as Audience Acceptance

In some ways, scientific interest in the personality traits of advocates was an updating of Aristotle's interest in the attributes of the persuasive speaker. As we have seen, the idea of *ethos* implies an idealized view of the advocate as someone with "good character" and strong virtue. In contrast, social psychologists—struck by the dramatic effectiveness of Hitler and many other demogogues within the first half of the twentieth century—separated the analysis of an advocate's effectiveness from his or her ethical obligations. They noted that a persuader might be believed by a particular audience, but still be unworthy of belief by more traditional standards. In the words of one set of researchers, "Credibility and like terms do not represent

Figure 7.2

"Oh-oh — another whistleblower who called attention to excessive costs" — from *Herblock Through the Looking Glass* (W.W. Norton, 1984).

attributes of communicators; they represent judgments by the listeners."[20] We think both views are valuable. The newer tradition of focusing on what audiences think and what they will accept is important. For example, there is no other way to account for Adolph Hitler's successes than to consider his credibility in a *descriptive* sense. Belief in Hitler was grossly misplaced, thus the older *prescriptive* standards outlined by Aristotle and carried on by the rationalistic tradition remind us that some sources are untrustworthy.

Measuring Source Credibility: Problems and Selected Research

A 1951 study of audience responses to high and low credibility sources by Hovland and Weiss is considered a classic.[21] The researchers asked students at Yale to complete opinion questionnaires that measured the students' attitudes on four different topics. Afterwards subjects were given pamphlets to read arguing pro and con positions on the four areas where their attitudes had been determined. The students were then randomly subdivided so that different groups could be exposed to the views of ostensibly different advocates. Hovland and Weiss deliberately picked some sources with obvious high or low credibility and then told the students that a particular source was the author of a certain point of view. Although the opinions were attributed to different sources, all of the students actually read the same opinions on issues. For example, on the subject "Can a practicable atomic-powered submarine be built at the present time?" (in 1950), an identically worded opinion was attributed to different sources for several sets of students. One group was told that the opinion they were reading was from the Russian daily, *Pravda*. Another group was told that the source was the widely respected physicist, J. Robert Oppenheimer. An additional topic was on whether the popularity of television would decrease the number of movie theaters in operation. Again, the *same* view was attributed to a high credibility source for some readers (*Fortune Magazine*) and a low credibility source for others (a movie gossip columnist). The study was designed to hold every variable constant except for the attributed sources who had allegedly made the comments.

Would the attributions make a difference? Would there be greater attitude change from the groups who believed in the integrity of their sources? Not surprisingly, many of the experimental subjects agreed with opinions when they were attributed to high credibility sources. Oppenheimer and *Fortune*, for example, were ranked as more believable than *Pravda* and the columnist. Did high credibility translate into greater agreement with the source? The answer was a qualified yes. The experimenters measured shifts in attitudes by comparing the results of the initial questionnaires with the results of attitude surveys given after the attributions of the opinions were made known. The net change in attitudes was not enormous, but always greater for readers of "trustworthy" sources.[22] Even so, other analysts who have studied and replicated this research have since noted that

> in order to demonstrate a measurable effect upon attitudes, the researchers had to create extreme differences in communicator credibility that, nevertheless, gave only a slight edge to the credible source in producing attitude change. In real-life situations, where the naturally existing differences between communicators would be much less extreme, would there still be the same enhancement of the communication by virtue of its attribution to a slightly more credible source? Some of the data suggest there would not.[23]

The problems involved in designing precise experimental studies are far more complex than can be outlined here.[24] It is important to realize that source credibility has many relevant dimensions. As is the case with this study, it is difficult to reduce a many-sided concept to just one measurable dimension (i.e., a single source assigned to one topic). "One persistent theoretical problem," notes Arthur Cohen, "is that of disentangling the main components of credibility. Is it expertness or trustworthiness, perception of fairness or bias, disinterest or propagandistic intent, or any combination of factors which is responsible for the effects of credibility on attitude change?"[25] Among other things, sources can be studied by focusing on one special dimension (dress, sex, age, perceived intelligence, the decision to include both sides of an argument), or on a broader identity (a writer for The New York Times, a representative of the United States government, a member of the Chamber of Congress, or a felon). We may link communicator traits to the content of a message, as has been done in studies of how the race of a speaker affects attitudes on the subject of racism.[26] Other traits may be topic-neutral, as when listeners are asked to classify sources as "honest," "aggressive," "crude," "sincere" or "boring."[27] Even the simplest communication setting contains a multitude of variables and varieties of people with different expectations and experiences reacting to a message in diverse ways. It is hardly surprising that efforts to "control" for all of these factors have tended to raise more questions than answers.

In spite of these limitations, some useful observations have come from research into the believability of sources. The following summary represents several well-documented conclusions about how sources are judged by audiences:

1. *For many people, high credibility means trustworthiness.*
   Receivers are more willing to accept ideas from a persuader whose intentions are honorable. Credibility, notes George Gordon,

"depends upon the implications of intention."[28] Trustworthy sources are seen as people who will not abuse their access to audiences. Audiences who believe that they are being "used," "deceived," or carelessly misled will pay little attention to an advocate's opinions.

2. *Similarities between communicators and audiences do not necessarily pave the way for influence.*
   Researchers have sometimes found that listeners judge similar sources "as more attractive than dissimilar sources."[29] Most of us would expect as much. However, recent research has cast some doubt on the view that "attitude similarity" translates into positive attraction toward a persuader.[30] The fact that there is prior agreement between people on a range of topics does not guarantee that they will more easily influence each other.

3. *Physical attractiveness increases a persuader's chances with audiences of the same and opposite sexes.*
   While there is obviously no universal standard for attractiveness, a number of researchers who have studied audience reactions to persuaders have concluded that attractive, well dressed, and well-groomed advocates are likely to be more successful than "unattractive persuaders."[31]

4. *Most surveys of audience attitudes indicate that the high prescriptive standards for judging sources (as noted in our previous discussion of "rational" standards) are not routinely applied.*
   Many audiences can be induced to believe sources with questionable credibility. Persuaders, for example, who state where their information was obtained generally do not fair any better than less candid advocates.[32] Experimenters on credibility have discovered that audiences seem to learn information regardless of a source's reliability.[33] Thus, a political campaign commercial on television may teach the viewer more about the political views of a candidate than an objective news report with ostensibly higher credibility.[34] We absorb views regardless of our assessments of the quality of the teacher.

5. *Audiences tend to have a shorter memory for the qualities associated with a source than for the ideas expressed.*
   Demonstrating what is known as the "sleeper effect," some studies have shown that people tend to forget their initial impressions of an advocate while retaining at least a general sense of the point of view expressed. The work of Carl Hovland and others has pointed out that "the increased persuasion produced by a high credibility source disappears. Similarly, the decreased persuasion produced by a low credibility source vanishes."[35]

6. *When compared with radio, newspapers, and magazines, television retains the greater believability, especially as a news source.*[36]
   Although studies looking at the mass media in the aggregate provide only general impressions, television consistently ranks high as a "believable" medium. (See the Roper Poll data in Figure 7.3). The preference of Americans for television as a source of news is a constant reminder of the medium's power. The results are also further evidence that what experts consider to be "ideal" mass media sources are not necessarily what general audiences will accept. Even though television is consistently ranked as the most believable by audiences, most professional journalists — including many working in television — give the print media higher marks in their abilities to explain accurately complex issues and events.[37]

Figure 7.3

"If you got conflicting or different reports of the same news story from radio, television, the magazines and the newspapers, which of the four versions would you be most inclined to believe — the one on radio or television or magazines or newspapers?"

Most believable	1959 %	61 %	63 %	64 %	67 %	68 %	71 %	72 %	74 %	76 %	78 %	80 %	82 %	84 %
Television	29	39	36	41	41	44	49	48	51	51	47	51	53	53
Newspapers	32	24	24	23	24	21	20	21	20	22	23	22	22	24
Radio	12	12	12	8	7	8	10	8	8	7	9	8	6	8
Magazines	10	10	10	10	8	11	9	10	8	9	9	9	8	7
Don't Know/ No Answer	17	17	18	18	20	16	12	13	13	11	12	10	11	9

Source: Television Information Office.

Roper poll results on the credibility of the mass media: 1959-1884.

7. *The needs of receivers often override extensive consideration of a persuader's credibility.*
   The acceptability of a source is sometimes based on factors far removed from "rational" source credibility criteria. "Do listeners always attend to public and television speakers because they con-

sider the sources to be believable?," Gary Cronkhite and Jo Liska ask. "Sometimes that is the reason, of course, but persuasion in such formats also proceeds as a matter of mutual need satisfaction." At times, "likability, novelty, and entertainment are valued more highly" than traditional standards of competence and trustworthiness.[38]

Credibility Reconsidered

As we have seen, the qualities which make a given source attractive to a particular audience have been the subject of much speculation. For the early Greeks who first sytematically thought about the role of the advocate in persuasion, credibility was inherent in the quality of a person's character. A good persuader had to be a good and virtuous person. For logicians and historians, credibility resides in sources who have high expertise and reasonable objectivity. To social scientists who are concerned with how attitudes are formed, source credibility means believability, and it is determined by the standards of an audience rather than the logician or expert. Figure 7.4 presents a brief summary of these perspectives.

Not surprisingly, our discussion points as much to the failure of individuals to consider sources carefully as to "universal" standards

Figure 7.4

Three Perspectives on Credibility

Prescriptive		Descriptive
1. *Ethos* as "good character"	**2.** *Legal* Standards for Judging Sources	**3.** *Behavioral* Studies of Believability
Good sources have...	Good sources have...	Traits of "acceptable" sources vary, but sometimes include...
Good sense Good moral character Goodwill, etc.	Ability to make accurate observations Objectivity (or are more "reluctant" than "willing")	Trustworthiness Honesty Expertise Similarity to receivers, etc.

applied consistently. The widespread lack of care in considering the credibility of persuaders has many social and financial costs. Harper Lee's novel is a reminder that lives may literally hang in the balance when sources are not judged for their fairness and objectivity. A similar disregard for the signs of integrity and honesty is probably one reason why Americans lost over $500 million dollars in 1984 in mail order frauds perpetrated by low-credibility businesses.[39]

Four Source-Related Persuasion Strategies

Often a message can stand more or less on its own, on the inherent weight of its ideas and arguments. This is not the case with the four strategies we turn to now. Each represents a dimension of persuasion that depends upon an advocate's attributes as much as the ideas presented. These include the use of a source's prestige to make ideas acceptable, the use of "mystifying" language to protect a source's power, the exploitation of charisma as a basis for leadership, and the sometimes dangerous substitution of appeals to authority in place of more open, idea-centered persuasion.

Prestige and Legitimation

Within every level and sub-group of society, there are a few leaders who have the power to give an aura of legitimacy to almost any idea or cause they endorse. Their presence may add a sense of success or importance to a gathering, such as when a President chooses a local forum for an appearance. These high *ethos* figures may be politicians, business leaders, entertainers, artists, clergy, or local civic leaders. Their names may be as recent and familiar as Chrysler's Lee Iacocca, CBS's Dan Rather and NBC's Bill Cosby, or more distant as the folk heroes Charles Lindburgh and Edward R. Morrow. What all of these figures have exhibited is the power to gain acceptance for a point of view *because of who they are.*

Few audiences are immune to the renowned person's prestige. During his first term as President, for example, Ronald Reagan frequently spoke before groups of fundamentalist religious leaders and broadcasters. His presence gave them new hope that the weight of his popularity would help gain acceptance for their goals of public school prayers, private school tuition tax credits, and an end to legal abortions. No group attempting to influence American public opinion overlooks the beneficial effects of such endorsements. While the advocate gets a forum from which to express his or her opinions, the immediate audience receives an endorsement of its objectives from a prestigious source. Jim Jones used this strategy. Even as he moved the People's Temple toward the fringes of society, he continued to participate in meetings and conferences featuring major local and national figures in politics, such as former First Lady Rosalyn Carter.[40] The legitimacy such contacts gave the People's Temple was important to the insecure Jones.[41]

In advertising, the counterpart of political legitimation is the product endorsement — as in Figure 7.5 — in which an attractive figure appears as a contented user of a product. As early as the 1880's, tobacco companies sought to identify their products with athletes and actors.[42] Endorsements by celebrities reached their peak on network television in the late 1950s when many stars, program hosts (including Ronald Reagan), and even some news reporters were expected to sell their sponsors' products. Today endorsements remain a standard advertising strategy, but in recent years a wide variety of attractive "high achievers" have been used as frequently as film and television stars to promote products.

Authority and Mystification

In the strategy of legitimation, a high-ethos figure is used to endorse a point of view. Imagine reversing this pattern. What happens when persuasive language is used to protect the influence of a persuader? There are times when an impressive display of language itself can become a way to persuade, or to ward off challenges from opponents. Such "mystification" is a common, fascinating, and at times troubling form of influence.

Two Forms of Mystification

In its broadest form, mystification involves the use of ideas to legitimize class distinctions, for example: defending slavery or oppression by calling it "God's will." Some of Karl Marx's most perceptive ideas deal with this use (and misuse) of "ideologies" to justify the domination of one class of people by a higher "ruling class."[43] We use mystification here, however, in a narrower sense. In its simplest form, it is the use of jargon to imply that the persuader has special authority and expertise to which others should defer. Mystification is a way of "pulling rank" because its use decreases the likelihood that an advocate's authority will be challenged. Anything but obedience seems wrong or risky.[44]

When a persuader acquires formal or legal authority, he usually inherits verbal and symbolic references that serve as emblems of his prestige. A special status usually comes with its own set of ideas and terms. As Hugh Duncan explains:

> Fathers teach us that if we disobey them the family will suffer, not
> simply that father will be "unhappy." School principles convince us

Figure 7.5

Legitimation and prestige in a product endorsement.

Used with permission of Schenley Industries, Inc. Copyright © 1984.

(more or less) that our disobedience hinders group activities and that we spoil the fun of being together. Christian priests teach that a sin against the church is a sin against God, and since God upholds order (in nature as well as society), sin threatens the very foundation of the world.[45]

Typically, challenges to individuals are treated (and re-named) as challenges to authorities or institutions. A persuader may not employ mystifications in a calculated attempt to suppress opposition, but the result may be the same. Our contacts with others are normally within a framework of hierarchies which either suggest expertise and authority or indicate the lack of it.

The Potent Effects of Technical Symbols

One fascinating feature of ancient and modern medicine is the "placebo effect." A placebo is presented to a patient as "treatment" for an illness, but it actually has no physical or chemical powers. The most common form of a placebo is a sugar pill. When administered by medical authorities, placebos can have powerful therapeutic benefits. Patients who believe they are receiving "help" for a medical problem — even when taking only placebos — often report improvements. Why? The power of suggestion based on both expectations and faith in authority produces its own physical and mental changes. "Physicians have always known that their ability to inspire expectant trust in a patient partly determines the success of treatment," notes Jerome Frank.[46] The patient's *inability* to understand the medical terminology, complicated apparatus, medicines, and equipment may actually *enhance* the possibilities for cure. There is irony in the fact that a more thorough understanding of the limitations of treatments might only serve to take away the mystery that is the basis of a "cure." As Frank notes, "a patient's expectations have been shown to affect his physiological responses so powerfully that they can reverse the pharmacological action of a drug."[47]

Other forms of authority share the mystifications of medicine. Consider Thurman Arnold's analysis of the confusing mysteries of "jurisprudence," the impressive term for the study of legal philosophy. "Here is a subject," he notes, "which not even lawyers read. Its content is vague; its literature abstruse and difficult. Nevertheless there is a general feeling that under this title are hidden the most sacred mysteries of the law."[48] He notes that the confusing and jargon-laden language of the law "performs its social task most effectively for those who encourage it, praise it, but do not read it."[49] For most of us legal jargon remains a mysterious but impressive set of codes which provide the basis for faith in the legal system. Persons practicing a craft filled with impressive Latin terms give us reason to put our trust in their expertise. Advertisers seek those same advantages for products such as cars and electronic equipment. The ads emphasize a bewildering array of specifications which evoke the imagery of high technology through the use of statistics, charts, graphs, and impressive technical words.

Assuming that the easiest persuasion involves the course of least resistance, nearly every advocate will occasionally look for ways to use symbols of authority to lessen audience resistance. Mystifications, then, are appeals to the legitimacy of authority based on symbols which indicate expertise. An advocate is unlikely to impress us by simply stating:

> "Too many cooks spoil the broth."

But even this cliche can be easily whipped into a tall verbal concoction that overflows with the imagery of expertise:

> Undue multiplicity of personnel assigned either concurrently or consecutively to a single function involves deterioration of quality in the resultant product as compared with the product of the labor of an exact sufficiency of personnel.[50]

The Charismatic Persuader

Although charisma is frequently misused, it remains a unique form of persuader authority. Its essence is best illustrated through an extended example.

Kennedy in Berlin

President John Kennedy gave a short speech in West Berlin in June of 1963 which dramatized the power of his charisma. As part of a European trip, Kennedy told his West German hosts that he would like to see the famous wall which divides the former capitol into East and West Berlin. The popular President planned to make a few brief remarks at the nearby Rudolf Wilde Platz after his visit to the concrete and barbed-wire wall. Historian Arthur Schlesinger, Jr. recalls that no one anticipated the passionate speech Kennedy delivered nor the reaction from the audience. Over half of the city's population filled the streets "clapping, waving, crying, cheering, as if it were the second coming."[51] People had packed themselves into the plaza, "compressed into a single excited, impassioned mass." Kennedy, routinely dubbed "the leader of the free world" by journalists, came to pay homage to the Berlin wall, but the audience had come to pay homage to him.

The speech itself was a taunt at Soviet power and noticeably lacked the tone of conciliation that surfaced in subsequent speeches. Visibly moved by the sight of a city and its people, Kennedy put aside most of

President John F. Kennedy at Rudolf Wilde Platz, Berlin.

Wide World Photos, Inc.

his planned text to direct a dramatic challenge to the secrecy and suspicion of the Kremlin:

> There are some who say that communism is the wave of the future.
> Let them come to Berlin!
> And there are some who say in Europe and elsewhere we can work with the communists.
> Let them come to Berlin!
> And there are even a few who say that it is true that communism is an evil system, but it permits us to make economic progress.
> Lass sie nach Berlin Kommen! Let them come to Berlin![52]

Schlesinger's description of the event is a classic account of the effects charismatic leaders often leave with listeners:

> The crowd shook itself and rose and roared like an animal. Absorbed in his short remarks, Kennedy hurried on. In a moment he concluded: "All free men, wherever they may live, are citizens of Berlin, and therefore, as a free man, I take pride in the words 'Ich bein ein Berliner.' [I am a Berliner.] The hysteria spread almost visibly through the square. Kennedy was first exhilarated and then disturbed; he felt, as he remarked on his return, that if he had said, "March to the wall—tear it down," his listeners would have marched.[53]

A sample of Kennedy's handwritten notes for this speech is reproduced in Figure 7.6.

Charisma as Extraordinary Power

In its modern usage, the term charisma comes from the turn-of-the-century work of sociologist Max Weber. Weber was fascinated by the fact that some public figures gain respect and power from their followers that dramatically exceeds whatever legal authority they may have. He knew that social movements and persuasive campaigns frequently have been headed by individuals with limited formal power but enormous personal support. In more recent years, Mahatma Gandhi in India and Martin Luther King in the United States, for example, were at least as powerful as the legal "legitimate" authorities they confronted in their separate quests for independence and improved civil rights. As Edward Sills has noted,

> According to Weber's usage, charismatic quality may be attributed to religious prophets and reformers, to dominating political leaders, to daring military heroes, and to sages who by example and command indicate a way of life to their disciples.... Charismatic quality is attributed to expansive personalities who establish ascendancy over human beings by their commanding forcefulness or by an exemplary inner state which is expressed in a being of serenity.[54]

Figure 7.6

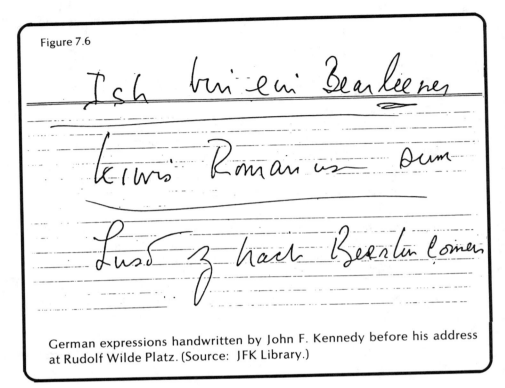

German expressions handwritten by John F. Kennedy before his address at Rudolf Wilde Platz. (Source: JFK Library.)

John Kennedy garnered an enormous following even on foreign soil. He followed a number of leaders who owed part of their effectiveness to the force of their public images and personalities: Adolph Hitler, Franklin D. Roosevelt, Louisiana's Huey Long, France's Charles de Gaulle, Cuba's Fidel Castro, and Dwight Eisenhower, to name a few. Their modern counterparts are now largely in the entertainment industry where a number of film and music celebrities create intense excitement, even when their performances are mediocre. Charisma has come to be synonymous with the "electrifying personality."[55]

Charisma remains an idea that is better illustrated than analyzed because it is so multi-dimensional. One important dimension seems to be deep emotional identification with a leader's victories, defeats, and enemies. Charismatic figures are able to mobilize resentments, anxieties and fears to the extent that personal attacks on them are taken as attacks on their followers as well. "I do not know how to describe the emotions that swept over me as I heard this man," recalls one of Hitler's followers. "His words were like a scourge. When he spoke of the disgrace of Germany, I felt ready to spring on any enemy."[56] The use of vividly portrayed and sharply defined enemies as a basis of support is common. Strongly felt emotions may start within one region or a particular social class, but before long a charismatic leader is able to mobilize the feelings of a larger constituency.

The popular leader often becomes the symbol of a moral cause. Almost every aspect of his or her life comes to be interpreted as illustrating a vital moral issue. It was not surprising, for example, that a young and photogenic Kennedy came off so well as an anti-communist cold warrior. He gave American foreign policy against Soviet interests a crusading quality that it did not have under less attractive leaders. He was a naval hero, so there was credibility to his dangerous showdown with Soviet ships carrying missiles to Cuba. He talked like a man who was prepared to back up his words with actions when faced with Soviet threats to "free" West Berlin from the control of France, Britain, and the United States. Kennedy is still remembered for how he "stood up to the Russians." In contrast to the older and overweight Soviet leader, Nikita Khrushchev, he personified a nation that was certain about its place and aggressive in its desire to control the growth of Soviet power.

Therein lies a dilemma for the typical persuader who faces opponents lead by a charismatic leader. Charisma can divert attention from a detailed analysis of ideas to a simplified portrayal of threats and reassurances. Modern life is saturated with public discussion dominated by people who have greater claims to celebrity than expertise. The popularity of celebrity journalism (i.e., *People Magazine* or its television counterparts) reminds us that having something to say may be secondary to simply being charismatic. Fascination with personalities over ideas is fraught with danger. In politics, for example, Richard Sennett reminds us that we have a tendency to trivialize issues in favor of attention to superficial personalities and gossip. For too many of us

> the reality of politics is boring — committees, hassles with bureaucrats, and the like. To understand these hassles would make active interpretative demands on the audience. This real life you tune out; you want to know "what kind of person" makes things happen. That picture TV can give you while making no demands on your own responsive powers....[57]

In a television commercial, the ties between fame and persuasion may be dubious, but they are mostly harmless (as when a baseball player gives a testimonial for a local bank). The stakes are obviously larger if charismatic leadership replaces public debate on important issues with public admiration for heroes.

Authoritarianism and Acquiescence

History is filled with examples of strong leaders who have been able to re-shape the attitudes and actions of compliant people. During World War II Hitler, Mussolini, and Japan's Tojo were widely portrayed in the United States as having hypnotic control over their followers. Many thought that they could persuade their supporters to do almost anything. Like the Reverend Jim Jones, their powers seemed strong enough to promote mass suicide. The popular press often portrays such persuasion in overly simple but familiar terms. A group of "gullible" people are taken in by a "cult" and "brainwashed" by a clever and demonic figure. These terms are reassuring, even if mass movements are rarely successful because of just one strong leader. Yet the problem of excessive deference to authority remains. In describing the "true believer," for example, Eric Hoffer summarizes what seems an immutable feature of ordinary life. For millions of people who see themselves as society's victims rather than beneficiaries, social causes espoused by strong leaders are especially seductive. In Hoffer's words,

> People whose lives are barren and insecure seem to show a greater willingness to obey than people who are self-sufficient and self confident. To the frustrated, freedom from responsibility is more attractive than freedom from restraint.... They willingly abdicate the directing of their lives to those who want to plan, command and shoulder all responsibility.[58]

The Concept of the Authoritarian Personality

People who are excessively respectful of authority and strong leadership have been called "authoritarian personalities." Since the 1950s, an enormous amount of research in the social sciences has focused on obedience to authority. In the 1930s, Sigmund Freud wrote about the manipulation and "re-infantilization of the masses" in pre-war Europe.[59] The first major English language analysis of enslavement to mass movements was The Authoritarian Personality by T.W. Adorno, Else Frankel-Brunswik, and their associates.[60] The 1950 study is considered a classic, although serious questions have been raised about its complex attitude-research methodology.[61] The authors (some of whom had been displaced from Austria by Nazi advances) sought to trace the origins of a multitude of personality traits, including anti-semitism, "susceptibility to anti-democratic propaganda," ethnocentrism (judging others only from one's own cultural values), and predispositions toward fascism. All of these "pathologies" appear in movements such as Nazism where there is a central charismatic figure and an inviolate set of core beliefs. The authors' efforts to determine how patterns of upbringing instilled such traits is less important here than the fundamental issues their study brought into focus. Are certain kinds of listeners overly susceptible to appeals based on authority, especially "official" sources? Are some types of audiences too willing to look past the natural ambiguities of everyday life for the rigid ideological certainties of a demogogue (i.e., Hitler's stereotypes of Jewish "failings")? What psychological needs are met by giving total allegiance to a leader?

The F (Anti-Democratic) Scale questionnaire which Adorno, Frankel-Brunswik and their associates used to locate the "authoritarian type" consisted of several agree-disagree claims. They sought to discover the signs of "authoritarian submission" and evidence of an "uncritical attitude toward idealized moral authorities." Among some of the typical statements in the questionnaire used to measure authoritarianism were the following:

- Obedience and respect for authority are the most important virtues children should learn.
- Every person should have complete faith in some super-natural power whose decisions are obeyed without question.
- What this country needs most, more than laws and political programs, are a few courageous, tireless, devoted leaders in whom the people can put their faith.[62]

The authors of *The Authoritarian Personality* verified their expectations that anti-semitism, rigidity, ethnocentrism, undue respect for power, and other personality traits tend to cluster and are probably tied tc certain styles of family life. They learned that authoritarianism can be identified and recognized in segments of any population. What remains unanswered, however, is whether such people represent a unique persuadable type.

The Dilemma of Obedience to Authority

The idea of obedience to authority raises a significant social dilemma that pits a society's stake in the "rule of law" against the corruptions that come with formal or official powers. On one hand, we regard the "loss of respect for authority" as a problem when people ignore laws or established social customs. We equally regret the failure of ordinary people to challenge the seductive appeals of demogogic leaders and the unjust laws enforced by governments. There are times (in colonial America, for example, or in the Civil Rights marches and sit-ins of the 1960s) when disorder arguably brings about a *better* order, and when an illegal act can be justified as obedience to a *higher* moral code. From the perspective of the present, order and obedience almost always seem preferable to their opposites. The advantage of hindsight, however, helps gauge when the price of obedience has been too costly. For instance, it is now easy to criticize the average German soldier's obedience to Hitler and his lieutenants during World War II. Nearly every discussion of the Second World War includes the question, how could so many decent people accept the vile racism implicit in the Third Reich? Yet many ordinary Americans were acquiescent to official decisions during the war to incarcerate thousands of Japanese-Americans. Why did decent Americans allow 117,000 *American* citizens of Japanese ancestry to be imprisoned in camps on the West coast?[63] What made the official propaganda line that a San Francisco "Jap" could be as dangerous as a Tokyo "Jap" acceptable? The rhetoric of our leaders and slick Hollywood war films played their parts.[64] A more complete answer must include the fact that governments, businesses, and institutions have enormous interests in respect for authority and order. Of course, a stable society needs clearly defined codes of conduct and leaders who are respected by their followers. Unfortunately, there are no guarantees that "legal," "expert," or "official" authorities will use their persuasive powers wisely.

Evidence of how "decent" people can be made to obey oppressive authority has been strikingly illustrated in the research of psychologist Stanley Milgram. His well known and controversial work in the 1960s measured the degree to which ordinary people would follow problematic orders from a responsible official. The design of his study was quite simple. Milgram advertised for volunteers to help conduct a "learning experiment." The volunteers were asked to assist him in the teaching of a "learner" (in reality, a Milgram confederate). Every time the learner incorrectly answered a question, the white-coated researcher explained, an electrical shock would be administered by the volunteer "teacher." In fact, no shock would be given. The real purpose of the study was to chart the extent to which the volunteer would follow an authority figure's orders to inflict pain on the learner. In *Obedience to Authority*, Milgram explained how the teachers were introduced to the setting:

> After watching the learner being strapped into place, he is taken into the main experimental room and seated before an impressive shock generator. Its main feature is a horizontal line of thirty switches, ranging from 15 volts to 450 volts, in 15 volt increments. There are also verbal designations which range from *slight shock* to *danger — severe shock*. The teacher is told that he is to administer the learning test to the man in the other room.
>
> . . . .
>
> The learner, or victim, is an actor who actually receives no shock at all. The point of the experiment is to see how far a person will proceed in a concrete and measurable situation in which he is ordered to inflict increasing pain on a protesting victim.[65]

The dilemma the "teacher" faced was one of traumatic obedience. At what point should he reject the commands of the experimenter to "keep going."

> For the subject, the situation is not a game; conflict is intense and obvious. On one hand, the manifest suffering of the learner presses him to quit. On the other hand, the experimenter, a legitimate authority to whom the subject feels some commitment, enjoins him to continue.[66]

Many did continue, even when the "learner" cried out in agonizing pain. Had the learners actually been wired to the shock box as the volunteers were lead to believe, many would have died a slow and painful death.

To the casual observer, volunteers who continued to obey Milgram would appear to be incredibly sadistic. Milgram, however, concludes otherwise, citing the very human tendency to shift responsibility to a higher and seemingly legitimate authority. He notes that "relatively few people have the resources needed to resist authority. A variety of inhibitions against disobeying authority come into play and successfully keep the person in his place."[67]

Admittedly, there are differences between a setting in which a volunteer agrees to carry out the orders of a researcher, and a persuasive situation in which a popular advocate elicits support from a more autonomous collection of individuals. The volunteer's desire to be helpful is probably greater than the average listener's motivations to accept the views of the mass persuader. We doubt that most people in open societies are the "servile flock...incapable of ever doing without a master" that Gustave Le Bon described in his famous study of social movements.[68] Even so, demonstrations of authority represent a major class of legitimizing appeals: appeals which are potent tools of persuasion.

Summary

In human communication, the content of a message must always be understood in terms of the quality and acceptability of a source. As we noted at the beginning of this chapter, there are many questions about the nature of authority that still need answers, and there are many ways to describe how credibility enables persuaders to succeed. Three forms of credibility were outlined. Audiences expect that those seeking their support will demonstrate traits of character, common sense, and goodwill—beginning with Aristotle, students of persuasion have attributed such traits to worthy advocates. In settings where audiences are prepared to weigh evidence to determine truth—such as in the courtroom or the laboratory—sources are best measured by their abilities to observe events accurately and objectively. We called this second form the "rational-legal" model of credibility. A third type involves the idea that specific personal attributes of persuaders are likely to be attractive or unattractive to particular types of people. This "believability" standard has less to do with the search for Truth or "good character" than with the recognition of audience attitudes as they *are* rather than as they *should be*.

However inconclusive our present understanding of credibility is, it remains central to the study of persuasion. An audience's awareness of the personal biography of an advocate is often the first important moment in the communication process. In addition, for public figures and persuaders reaching large audiences, the presence of charisma or mystifying expertise may double or redouble the impact of a message. The sheer force of a dominating public character can generate an intensely loyal following. Sometimes the audience responds to the extraordinary nature of an advocate's leadership; other times, the audience reflects the inclination of many people in every society to take comfort in obedience to simple ideas and dominating leaders.

Notes

[1]Daniel Webster, described by John Kennedy in *Profiles in Courage*, Memorial Edition (New York: Harper and Row, 1964), 56.

[2]Dmitri Shostakovich, *Testimony: The Memoirs of Dmitri Shostakovich,* ed. Solomon Volkov, trans. Antonia W. Bouis (New York: Harper and Row, 1979).

[3]Harold C. Schonberg, "Words and Music Under Stalin," *New York Times Book Review* (21 October 1979), 1, 46-47.

[4]Adam Clymer, "How Americans Rate Big Business," *The New York Times Magazine*, Part II (8 June 1986), 69.

[5]Aristotle, *The Rhetoric,* in *The Basic Works of Aristotle,* ed. Richard McKeon (New York: Random House, 1941), 1379.

[6]Aristotle, in McKeon, 1380.

[7]Robert M. Pirsig, *Zen and the Art of Motorcycle Maintenance: An Inquiry Into Values* (New York: William Morrow, 1974), 32.

[8]Pirsig, 33-34.

[9]These are high credibility indicators cited by Jack L. Whitehead, Jr. in "Factors of Source Credibility," *Quarterly Journal of Speech* (February, 1968), 61.

[10]Ronald Reagan, "Encroaching Control," *Vital Speeches* (1 September 1961), 677.

[11]Reagan, "Encroaching Control," 677.

[12]Robert Sklar, *Movie Made America* (New York: Vintage, 1975), 256-268.

[13]Reagan, "Encroaching Control," 677.

[14]Robert P. Newman and Dale R. Newman, *Evidence* (Boston: Houghton Mifflin, 1969), viii. We are indebted to the authors of this book for the general scheme developed in this section.

[15]Harper Lee, *To Kill A Mockingbird* (New York: Popular Library, 1962), 208.

[16]Lee, 244.

[17]Newman and Newman, 79.

[18]Another interesting and widely reported case involving potentially reluctant testimony grew out of the widely publicized death of Karen Silkwood. An employee of a chemical company involved in the manufacture of nuclear fuel, Silkwood became concerned about health and safety procedures at her Oklahoma plant. She died in a suspicious automobile accident, minutes before she had planned to turn over allegedly damaging documents to a *New York Times* reporter and a union official. See Richard Rashke, *The Killing of Karen Silkwood* (Boston: Houghton Mifflin, 1981).

[19]See Carl Hovland, Irving L. Janis, and Harold Kelley, *Communication and Persuasion* (New Haven, CT: Yale University Press, 1953).

[20]Carolyn W. Sherif, Muzafer Sherif, and Roger E. Nebergall, *Attitude and Attitude Change* (Philadelphia, W.B. Saunders, 1965), 201.

[21]See Carl Hovland and Walter Weiss, "The Influence of Source Credibility on Communication Effectiveness," *Public Opinion Quarterly* 15 (1951), 535-650.

[22]For a critique and review of this study, see Philip G. Zimbardo, Ebbe B. Ebbesen and Christina Maslach, *Influencing Attitudes and Changing Behavior*, Second Edition (Reading, MA: Addison-Wesley, 1977), 94-98, 125-127.

[23]Zimbardo, Ebbesen, and Maslach, 126.

[24]For more detailed analyses of experimental research on source credibility, see Kenneth Andersen and Theodore Clevenger, Jr., "A Summary of Experimental Research in Ethos," in *The Rhetoric of Our Times*, ed. J. Jeffrey Auer (New York: Appleton-Century-Crofts, 1969), 127-151; Jesse G. Delia, "A Constructivist Analysis of the Concept of Credibility," *The Quarterly Journal of Speech* (December, 1976), 361-375; Icek Ajzen and Martin Fishbein, *Understanding Attitudes and Predicting Social Behavior* (Englewood Cliffs, NJ: Prentice-Hall, 1980), 13-27, 218-228; and Dominic A. Infante et al., "A Comparison of Factor and Functional Approaches to Source Credibility," *Communication Quarterly* (Winter, 1983), 43-48.

[25]Arthur R. Cohen, *Attitude Change and Social Influence* (New York: Basic Books, 1964), 26.

[26]Andersen and Clevenger, 132.

[27]Don A. Schweitzer, "The Effect of Presentation on Source Evaluation," *The Quarterly Journal of Speech* (February, 1970), 33-39.

[28]George Gordon, *Persuasion: The Theory and Practice of Manipulative Communication* (New York: Hastings House, 1971), 46.

[29]Herbert W. Simons, Nancy N. Berkowitz, and John Moyer, "Similarity, Credibility, and Attitude Change: A Review and Theory," *Psychological Bulletin* (January, 1970), 3-4.

[30]Michael Sunnafrank, "Attitude Similarity and Interpersonal Attraction in Communication Processes: In Pursuit of an Ephemeral Influence," *Communication Monographs* (December, 1983), 273-284.

[31]For general discussions of these findings, see Mark L. Knapp, *Nonverbal Communication and Human Behavior* (New York: Holt, Rinehart, and Winston, 1972), 63-90; and Raymond S. Ross, *Understanding Persuasion: Foundations and Practice*, Second Edition (Englewood Cliffs, NJ: Prentice-Hall, 1985), 61-62.

[32]Wayne N. Thompson, *Quantitative Research in Public Address and Communication* (New York: Random House, 1967), 54-55.

[33]Thompson, 59.

[34]Thomas E. Patterson and Robert D. McClure, *The Unseeing Eye: The Myth of Television Power in Politics* (New York: G.P. Putnam, 1976), 22-23.

[35]Charles A. Kiesler, Barry E. Collins, and Norman Miller, *Attitude Change: A Critical Analysis of Theoretical Approaches* (New York: John Wiley and Sons, 1969), 108.

[36]Burns W. Roper, *Public Attitudes Toward Television and Other Media in a Time of Change* (New York: Television Information Office, 1985), 5.

[37]See, for example, Robert MacNeil, *The Right Place at the Right Time* (Boston: Little Brown, 1982), 300-311; and Walter Cronkite's remarks in Marvin Barrett, *Rich News, Poor News* (New York: Thomas Y. Crowell, 1978), 24-26.

[38]See Gary Cronkhite and Jo Liska, "The Judgment of Communicant Acceptability," in *Persuasion: New Directions in Theory and Research*, ed. Michael Roloff and Gerald Miller (Beverly Hills, Sage Publications, 1980), 104.

[39]"Shearing the Suckers," *Consumer Reports* (February, 1986), 87.

[40]Jean Mills, *Six Years With God* (New York: A and W Publishers, 1979), 197-201.

[41]For another discussion of groups seeking legitimacy, see John Waite Bowers and Donovan J. Ochs, *The Rhetoric of Agitation and Control* (Reading, MA: Addison-Wesley, 1971), 19-20.

[42]Daniel Pope, *The Making of Modern Advertising* (New York: Basic Books, 1983), 228.

[43]For wide-ranging discussions of mystifications, see Kenneth Burke, *A Rhetoric of Motives* (Berkeley, CA: University of California, 1969), 101-110; and Hugh Dalziel Duncan, *Communication and Social Order* (New York: Oxford, 1962), 190-237.

[44]More contemporary examples are noted in Robert E. Denton and Gary C. Woodward, *Political Communication in America* (New York: Preager, 1985), 347-352.

[45]Duncan, 285-286.

[46]Jerome D. Frank, *Persuasion and Healing* (New York: Schocken, 1974), 137.

[47]Frank, 139.

[48]Thurman Arnold, *The Symbols of Government* (New York: Harcourt, Brace and World, 1962), 46.

[49]Arnold, 70.

[50]Quoted in Richard Weaver, *The Ethics of Rhetoric* (Chicago: Henry Regnery, 1953), 200.

[51]Arthur M. Schlesinger, Jr., *A Thousand Days: John F. Kennedy in the White House* (Boston: Houghton Mifflin, 1965), 884.

[52]Schlesinger, Jr., 884-885.

[53]Schlesinger, Jr., 885.

[54]Edward Shils, "Charisma," in *The Encyclopedia of the Social Sciences*, Vol. 2, ed. David Sills (New York: Macmillan, 1968), 387.

[55]Richard Sennett, *The Fall of Public Man* (New York: Vintage, 1978), 271-272.

[56]Quoted in Doris A. Graber, *Verbal Behavior and Politics* (Urbana, IL: University of Illinois Press, 1976), 182.

[57]Sennett, *Fall of Public Man*, 285.

[58]Eric Hoffer, *The True Believer: Thoughts on the Nature of Mass Movements* (New York: Harper and Row, 1966), 109.

[59]Richard Sennett, *Authority* (New York: Alfred A. Knopf, 1980), 24.

[60]T.W. Adorno et al., *The Authoritarian Personality* (New York: Harper and Brothers, 1950).

[61]See, for example, Roger Brown, *Social Psychology* (New York: Free Press, 1965), 509-526.

[62]Adorno et al., 248.

[63]Charles Goodell, *Political Prisoners in America* (New York: Random House, 1973), 87.

[64]David Hwang, "Are Movies Ready for Real Orientals?" *The New York Times* (11 August 1985), Sec. 2, 1, 21.

[65]Stanley Milgram, *Obedience to Authority: An Experimental View* (New York: Harper and Row, 1974), 3-4.

[66]Milgram, 4.

[67]Milgram, 6.

[68]Gustave Le Bon, *The Crowd* (New York: Viking, 1960), 118.

Questions and Projects for Further Study

1. Working with a partner, list some specific items of background information you would want to know about a speaker addressing a campus forum arguing that "all 18 year olds in the U.S. should spend one year in national military service."

2. Observe some of the experts or spokespersons who appear in a network news program (i.e., The McNeil-Lehrer News Hour, ABC's "Nightline," etc.) They may be seen making observations about the day's events from their vantage points in government, business, the arts, and so on. Using the rational/legal model as well as their own explanations, assess the credibility of one or two experts.

3. Locate several magazine ads which use prestige and legitimation as a persuasive strategy. Describe the verbal and visual symbols that help sell the product.

4. Attend a portion of a criminal trial in your area. Study the way the prosecution and defense attorneys attempt to establish or discredit the credibility of specific witnesses.

5. Recall films or television programs you have seen recently. From among your examples, locate a character that seems to exhibit some of the characteristics of the authoritarian personality.

6. Using textbooks, self-help manuals, news or magazine articles, locate some examples of persuasion by mystification. Explain the elements in your samples that qualify them as good instances.

7. You may have noticed that this chapter poses a dilemma. Persuasion requires deference to many types of experts and authorities. However, we concluded with a caution about the dangers of persuasion which exploits the symbols of expertise and authority (as illustrated by Milgram). Attempt to explain the differences between persuasion based on genuine credibility and persuasion that abuses an audience's faith in authority. Cite a real or hypothetical example.

8. In "Factors of Source Credibility" by Jack Whitehead [*Quarterly Journal of Speech* (February, 1968), 59-63] a number of traits identified with high credibility sources are listed. Choosing from his list below, identify and defend 8 credibility traits that would most help (1) a male member of a persuasion course advocating a compulsory year of government service for all American 18 year olds, or (2) a Senator from your state urging a cross section of citizens to support a 15% pay increase for all members of Congress. The traits include the following:

fair	good speaker	respectful
good	right	honest
trustworthy	loyal to listeners	admirable
just	patient	correct
sincere	straightforward	reliable
valuable	unselfish	nice
virtuous	has good will	calm
moral	frank	friendly
professional	experienced	has professional manner
authoritative	has foresight	energetic
aggressive	active	bold
decisive	proud	open-minded
objective	impartial	

Additional Reading

Ajzen, Icek; and Martin Fishbein. *Understanding Attitudes and Predicting Social Behavior.* Englewood Cliffs, NJ: Prentice-Hall, 1980.

Adorno, T.W. et al. *The Authoritarian Personality.* New York: Harper and Brothers, 1950.

Cronkhite, Gary; and Jo R. Liska. "The Judgment of Communicant Acceptability." In *Persuasion: New Directions in Theory and Research.* Ed. Michael Roloff and Gerald Miller. Beverly Hills: Sage Publications, 1980, 101-139.

Delia, Jesse G. "A Constructivist Analysis of the Concept of Credibility." *Quarterly Journal of Speech* (December, 1976): 361-375.

Hovland, Carl; Irving L. Janis; and Harold Kelley. *Communication and Persuasion.* New Haven, CT: Yale University Press, 1953.

Kiesler, Charles A.; Barry E. Collins; and Norman Miller. *Attitude Change: A Critical Analysis of Theoretical Approaches.* New York: John Wiley and Sons, 1969.

Knapp, Mark L. *Nonverbal Communication in Human Interaction.* New York: Holt, Rinehart and Winston, 1972.

Milgram, Stanley. *Obedience to Authority: An Experimental View.* New York: Harper and Row, 1974.

Newman, Robert P.; and Dale R. Newman. *Evidence.* Boston: Houghton Mifflin, 1969.

Ross, Raymond S. *Understanding Persuasion: Foundations and Practice,* Second Edition. Englewood Cliffs, NJ: Prentice-Hall, 1985.

Sherif, Carolyn W.; Muzafer Sherif; and Roger E. Nebergall. *Attitudes and Attitude Change.* Philadelphia: W.B. Saunders, 1965.

Shils, Edward. "Charisma." In *The Encyclopedia of the Social Sciences.* Vol. 2. Ed. David Sills. New York: Macmillan, 1968, 386-390.

Whitehead, Jack L. "Factors in Source Credibility." *Quarterly Journal of Speech* (February, 1968), 59-63.

PART 3

PERSUASION INDUSTRIES

It takes little effort to realize that there are scores of occupational categories which are — broadly speaking — primarily about persuasion. Preaching, teaching, sales, public relations, fund raising and marketing are only the most obvious cases. In this section we focus on two basic and pervasive institutions which are organized around the constant imperative to alter behaviors or change public opinion. In Chapter 8 we look at persuasion organized to encourage the use of products or services. In Chapter 9 we explore the efforts of political leaders to shape our attitudes toward themselves during election campaigns, and to encourage our acceptance of laws and policies. The primary goal of advertisers is to create favorable attitudes towards products and the companies that provide them. In politics the process of consensus-building is a never-ending feature of both electoral and legislative cycles. Our look at these two key industries provides useful information that can be applied to virtually every type of persuasion in every kind of setting.

8

Advertising as Persuasion

 OVERVIEW

Advertising depends upon the simple precepts of human persuasion. And these have to do, for the most part, with treating the other party as a unique, important individual, letting him recognize your distinct positive identity and starting off by getting him nodding in agreement.[1]

There is a tendency with most books dealing with persuasion to focus primarily on political issues and topics of concern. Yet, advertising is the most pervasive form of persuasion in our society. According to John O'Toole, we are exposed to 1,600 advertising messages a day![2] Often more time and talent are spent in making television commercials than on network programs.[3] Indeed, consumers pay dearly for those programs and commercials. According to Donna Cross, 20% to 40% of a product's price represents the production costs of commercials.[4] In her opinion, this amounts to "double shafting." Manufacturers convince us to purchase their products and then charge us for their advertising efforts.

Commercials are not only a fact of daily life, but many Americans seemingly enjoy commercials. We can easily identify our favorite commercial characters, slogans, and songs. Thus, in some way, we are all experts on advertising. We know what we like, what is in good taste, what is clearly right or wrong. Ironically, according to Stewart Alter, we don't believe advertising influences our buying decisions.[5] In a telephone survey, only 14% of the respondents said they were influenced by advertising. Interestingly, however, respondents believed that women, young people, and people in low income groups are more affected by advertising than other groups. Individuals of those groups disagreed. As a society we endure, remember, and enjoy advertising messages, but we are quick to dismiss their value or impact.

In this chapter, we investigate the persuasive dimensions of advertising. By identifying the tactics and techniques of persuasion, we can become better critics of advertising and more knowledgeable consumers.

What is Advertising?

There are several ways to discuss the essential nature and characteristics of advertising. In the traditional sense, advertising is a function or tool of marketing. Most definitions from this perspective emphasize four major characteristics:

1. Advertising is a *paid* form of communication. The message is shared resulting from financial payment for each iteration.
2. Advertising is a *nonpersonal presentational* form of communication. Advertising is distinct from face to face sales presentations.
3. Advertising messages are concerned with the presentation of *ideas, products, and services.* All too often we only associate advertising with products, but increasingly advertising addresses political, social, and philosophical ideas. Due to the drastic increase in service occupations and employment, much advertising espouses the virtues of the various service industries.
4. Sponsors of advertising messages are *identified.* Sponsorship identification contributes to message accountability and financial responsibility.

Another perspective is to define advertising in informational and persuasive dimensions. This perspective tells what advertising *does* rather than what advertising *is.* Most commercial messages contain a great deal of information about product purpose, usage, price, or availability. Although messages do inform, they are also tightly controlled. Great care is given to message content, direction, and time. In the early 1900's, N.W. Ayer, who later founded the first advertising agency in America, defined advertising as "keeping your name before the public."[6] Later, the sales function was combined with information and awareness; persuasion became an essential element of advertising. Advertising does not pretend to present both sides of a purchasing decision, nor is it required to do so. By design, advertising is perhaps the strongest form of advocacy. Finally, a communication definition of advertising recognizes the importance of the mass media in carrying the messages. The various media impact the style, content, and presentation of any message.

Still another way to gain insight into the nature of advertising is to review methods of classifying advertising. One classification scheme is by audience. Some ads are aimed at large, general audiences while others are aimed at small, perhaps regional audiences. Some are designed for audiences with specific demographic characteristics such as age, sex, income, or occupational status while other ads appeal to specific lifestyles or psychographic variables based on audience beliefs, attitudes, or values. Advertising is also classified according to the types of advertisers: national (general) or local (retail); business (industrial, trade, professional) or noncommercial (government, civic groups, religious groups); product (service, goods) or corporate (image, ideas); primary (create a demand for generic product for entire industry) or selective (create demand for a specific brand of product).

To define advertising is not a simple task. It is a vital force in our economy as well as a powerful means of communication. It influences who we are, how we live, and how we judge others. For our purposes, advertising is defined as *"one to one communication by a specific group or industry utilizing mass media for purposes of selling a product, service or idea."* This definition has several advantages. First, it recognizes that the most effective form of persuasion is that which is created with a *specific audience* in mind. An effective commercial is one that speaks to me—my wants, desires, problems. It is one that gains attention, addresses needs, and solves problems. And the definition also recognizes the importance of media adaptation. Today's technology is more than just a conduit for the transmission of symbols. Its role is as important to the reception and understanding of the message as is the package in enticing us to select a product. Finally, advertising, as with most persuasion, is both an art and a science. As a science, advertising must observe, measure, and analyze individuals, groups and institutional behavior. It must seek to establish cause and effect relationships and provide rationale and evidence for conclusions reached. It is also art, for advertising embraces intuitive judgment, encourages creative application of symbols (both verbal and nonverbal), and harnesses subjectivity when confronted by experience and hard data.

Functions of Advertising

From the various definitions, we can identify five basic functions of advertising. There is, of course, a marketing function of advertising. Ads must ultimately increase the sales of products to make money. Advertising is the link between markets and products. Especially in our society, advertising provides an important, efficient, large-scale, economic function by encouraging consumption and, hence, production. Advertising also has a basic social function. As we will discuss later, advertising not only informs us about products but indirectly informs us about ourselves, society, social values and behavior. We learn from the roles and models presented in ads.

The functions of advertising, then, certainly go beyond increasing sales and corporate profits. We must not only be aware of the world presented but also of the tactics and techniques of presentation. As Vance Packard warned in 1958, "the result is that many of us are being influenced and manipulated far more than we realize, in the patterns of our everyday lives."[7]

The Evolution of Advertising
From a Communication Perspective

The focus of advertising has changed since 1900.[8] Early advertising focused on product benefits and attributes. Ads stressed the unique qualities of the product, price, and provided general product information. By 1930, advertising messages moved away from describing the product to focusing on the user of the product. Attributes of the product were associated with the user. Testimonials became the primary structure of most ads. Durable goods, food and

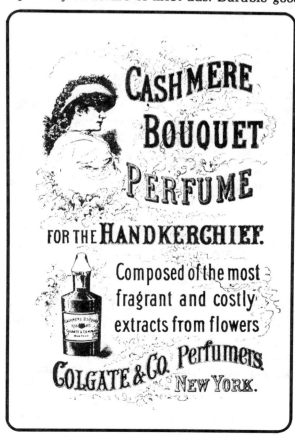

tobacco were advertised heavily and the advertising played upon themes of family, status, health, and social authority.

By the mid-1950's, advertising moved away from the user of the product toward a defined image associated with the product. Instead of certain people using certain products, the products promised a transformation of the user. Although subtle, this is an important shift of emphasis. Such an approach to advertising encourages an internalization of product values. Personal gratification and narcissism become goals of product usage. Happiness, romance, glamor are all ours if we only use the prescribed product. This "image era" of advertising is attributed to David Ogilvy whose primary concerns were product image, long term brand identification and loyalty.

Finally, by the early 1970s there had been another major shift of emphasis in American advertising. Products became emblems for group identification. From an advertiser's perspective, the strategy was to utilize behavioral and social science research techniques. According to William Myers, "advertisers found that the only way to create successful advertising was to address consumers' psychological needs and help solve their personal problems."[9] Thus, designer jeans become status symbols and special brands of cologne guarantee romance and sexiness. To be "in," "rich," "enlightened" demands the use of certain products.

Advertising messages, then, have evolved from what a product *"does"* to what a product *"says."* Clothes are worn for fashion rather than for warmth, social status rather than durability, personal style rather than utility. Even the appeal of toilet paper is not based upon its function but rather on its range of colors, designs, or softness. Does brown toilet paper really work better than white? The absurdity of the question demonstrates the potential problems with today's focus of advertising messages. Products have unique personalities, emotions, and significance beyond the chemical and physical characteristics of the item. Recall the American public's outcry over Coca-Cola changing the flavor of its product in 1985. The emotional attachment to the product went beyond mere taste preference. Since 1886, we were told that "things go better with Coke," "it's the real thing," "have a Coke and a smile," "Coke adds life," and "Coke is it." The product represents a significant element of American life. It would have, perhaps, been easier to change the Washington Monument.

The structure and nature of advertising is directly related to the political and social structure of society. In countries where tradition and the status quo are valued and there is little technological innovation, advertising is not needed and thus has little social impact. In authoritarian countries, advertising is tightly controlled and is used to promote national goals and specific consumption patterns. In America, which values the ideas of self-interest, individualism, rationality, competition and the freedom of choice, advertising is less restrictive. Capitalistic society encourages consumerism. For many immigrants, America was presented as a land "of milk and honey" where they might find an abundance of goods. Thus the wage system of labor encouraged consumption. Advertising is vital to advanced capitalistic societies where it is necessary to motivate people to work hard so they can accumulate money which can then be used to buy products.[10]

From this brief overview of the evolution of advertising, we can make several assumptions about its practice in America. Advertising must be considered within the cultural context of a nation. Advertising messages are extremely complex, utilizing rational, emotional, and social elements. Thus, the messages are open to various interpretations and actual effects are not clearly known. But what does the practice of advertising today say about human nature? According to Vance Packard, humans are "simply reactors to stimulus from the environment" and are "creatures of almost limitless plasticity."[11] This skepticism stems from the heavy reliance on modern techniques and theories of psychology in advertising.

The Role of Psychology in Advertising

As early as 1954, several professional publications began devoting more and more attention to what they called "motivation research."[12] Advertisers began looking for those "extra-psychological values" to give products a more potent appeal. The concern is not with specific psychological strategies or tactics but with a general orientation to product definition that plays upon individual strengths, weaknesses, hopes, and fears. In the "industry," such an orientation is known as product positioning.[13] From this perspective, the advertiser does not begin with the product but with the *mind of the consumer*. That is, advertising does not try to change minds but links product attributes to the existing beliefs, ideas, goals, and desires of the consumer. Our minds accept attitudes or behaviors which match prior knowledge and experience. To say that a cookie tastes "homemade," or "like mother used to make" does not tell whether the cookie is good or bad, hard or soft, sweet or bland. Rather, the statement elicits the aroma of fresh-baked cookies and fond memories of mother's baking. The point is rather obvious. Advertisers are more successful if they "position" a product to capitalize on established beliefs or expectations of the consumer.

A "positioning" approach to advertising is a response to an "overcommunicated" society. Today, communication itself is a problem. Over 35,000 new books are introduced in America each year. It would take 17 years of reading 24 hours a day to finish that many books. Even an 8-ounce box of TOTAL cereal has over 1,268 words of copy. Each year over 5,000 new products are introduced to the American public.[14] There is a great deal of competition for our attention. Product positioning provides a way to cut through the clutter and to take a shortcut to the brain. Simplified messages based upon consumer experience and knowledge do not require logic, debate, or lengthy explanations.

There is another important reason why psychology invaded the advertising community. By the early 1970s, the age of affluence was over for most Americans. The purchasing power of the dollar decreased by 60% and many households required two paychecks to survive.[15] As inflation grew, the "Woodstock Generation" became cynical. Bigger was not better. Change for the sake of "progress" was suspect. The advertising industry needed to stimulate the public to buy. The solution to the problem was image transformation. Advertisers sought to increase the perceived value and worth of mass products. The primary strategy was to offer an *emotional* reward for using a product. In short, brand "personality" became more important than brand "performance." Sexy jeans have a stronger appeal than long lasting jeans. A stylish designer watch is favored over an accurate one.

How Advertising Works

There are four basic models of buyer behavior.[16] Psychological models are based on the notions of stimulus—response. Humans respond to external stimuli in the environment. Such models become predictive and focus on the various forms of stimuli that can be created to ensure mass response. Economic models assume that people are rational and make "reasoned" purchasing decisions based on such reasons as price, quality, pleasure, or esteem. The difference between the two models lies in their assumption concerning human behavior. The psychological model views humans as robots; buying decisions are automatic as long as the right "stimulus" is used. In contrast, the economic model assumes that people at least process available information and have reasons for decisions. The model does not judge the quality of the reasons—only that we can identify and/or justify reasons for decisions.

Sociological models of buying behavior argue that specific social groups directly influence consumer desires, preferences, and purchases. Thus, such variables as status, lifestyle, and reference groups dictate buying habits. Finally, statistical models of buying behavior focus on the purchasing patterns of groups or types of consumer. For example, a certain "type" of individual buys items from direct mail or catalogs (i.e., upper income, post-high school graduate professionals). In addition, if individuals buy from one catalog, they will buy from any catalog. Frequency of catalog purchase is directly related to recency of purchase. The more recent the last purchase from a catalog, the greater the likelihood of another purchase from a catalog when given the opportunity.[17] For a retailer, this means that a family purchasing from catalogs can receive several a month and not decrease the likelihood of purchase.

Each of these models provides insight into why people buy when they do. Basically, all advertising attempts to move a consumer along a continuum from awareness to knowledge, to "liking," to preference, to conviction, and finally to purchase.

At each stage of the continuum ads attack different behavioral dimensions and use different types of appeals and techniques. Awareness to knowledge ads attempt to provide the consumer with product information and facts. Creatively, the ads use descriptive copy and slogans or jingles to capture attention. To move the consumer from the stages of liking to product preference, the ads play upon emotions and feelings. The ads use image, status, and glamour appeals. To reinforce conviction and repeat purchases, ads attempt to stimulate and direct consumer desires. Price appeals and testimonials are useful techniques at these stages of consumer reactions.

From this rather simple continuum of consumer reaction, we can see four distinct levels of persuasion.[18] The most simple and basic level is what Kim Rotzoll and her colleagues call "precipitation." Here, the persuasive goals are brand awareness and knowledge. The advertising messages must fight clutter and penetrate the mind of the consumer. The second level they simply call "persuasion." At this level, the messages appeal to human feelings and emotions and attempt to induce purchase. This level is the most powerful and perhaps the most subtle. The third level of persuasion is "reinforcement." Here the goal is to legitimize existing purchases and to validate previous purchasing decisions. "Reminder" is the final level of persuasion identified in advertising. The nature of persuasive efforts at this level is to reinforce brand loyalty. Many ads are designed to counter the competition in order to insulate the consumer. Most of the McDonald's ads are simply to keep "top-of-mind" awareness rather than describe product attributes.

According to William Leiss, Stephen Kline, and Sut Jhally, advertising creates demand in three ways.[19] First, through

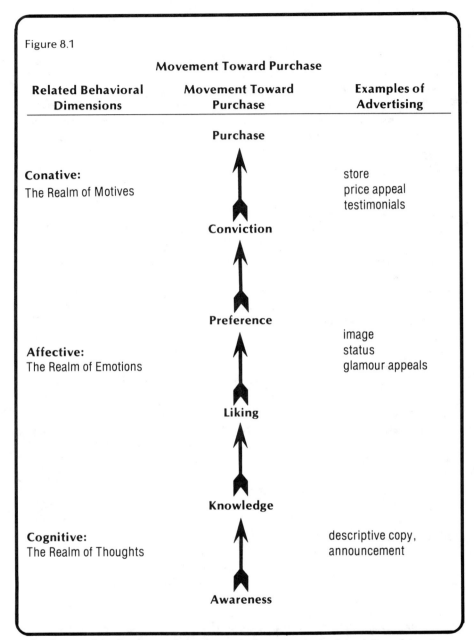

Figure 8.1

Movement Toward Purchase

Related Behavioral Dimensions	**Movement Toward Purchase**	**Examples of Advertising**
	Purchase	
Conative: The Realm of Motives	↑ Conviction	store price appeal testimonials
Affective: The Realm of Emotions	↑ Preference ↑ Liking	image status glamour appeals
Cognitive: The Realm of Thoughts	↑ Knowledge ↑ Awareness	descriptive copy, announcement

This hierarchical scheme for setting and measuring advertising objectives was developed by Robert Lavidge and Gary Steiner and has become the standard model for both scholars and the advertising industry. Robert Lavidge and Gary Steiner, "A Model for Predictive Measurements of Advertising Effectiveness," *Journal of Marketing*, 24 (October 1961), 59-62.

"technological manipulation" advertising utilizes the latest in psychographic (consumer beliefs, attitudes, and values) and demographic (consumer characteristics such as age, sex, income, etc.) research to identify tactics and techniques of mass appeal. The production techniques and drama of the various media heighten the impact of and response to creative advertising messages. The second method of advertising creates demand through "false symbolism." The concern here is how products become symbols for desired attributes. Why do specific articles of clothing represent status or group identification or why do certain perfumes promise sex? The third way advertising creates demand is through "false claims." Leiss and his colleagues argue many ads simply promise more than they can deliver and are deceptive in nature.

Another interesting explanation of how advertising works is provided in a model developed by the advertising agency of Foote, Cone and Belding (FCB model).[20] Their model suggests that purchasing decisions are based upon the degree of "involvement" in the decision and the degree to which "thinking" or "feeling" provides the basis for making a decision. If we think of these elements as crossing continuums forming a matrix we have as one set of end points high and low involvement. The other set of end points is thinking and feeling. (See Figure 8.2.)

Each quadrant of the matrix suggests a different "learn-do-feel" orientation in making a purchasing decision. In other words, we buy something ("do") based upon product information provided ("learn") or based upon some feeling or emotion about use of the product ("feel"). In order to illustrate these orientations, let's consider each quadrant separately.

High Involvement — Thinking

According to the model, purchasing major expensive items such as houses, cars, or major furnishings requires high consumer involvement and careful thinking. Consumers seek product information to insure product value and quality. The consumer is reflective, seeking the best deal, and will base the decision on product information and demonstration. From this perspective, consumers follow the "learn-feel-do" sequence in making a purchasing decision. Note too that this sequence provides insight into how to create the advertising. Advertising for products in this category would require much information, long copy, comparative product analyses, and visual demonstration.

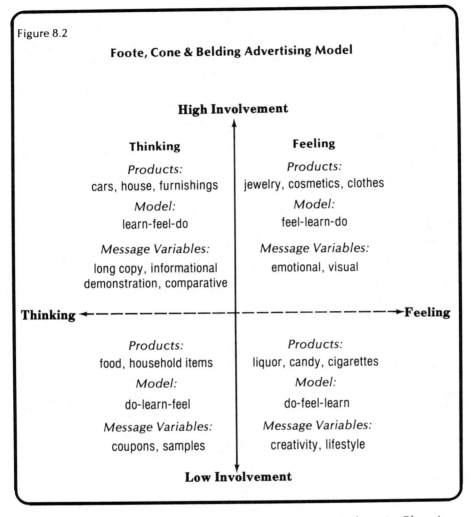

Figure 8.2

Foote, Cone & Belding Advertising Model

High Involvement

Thinking	Feeling
Products:	*Products:*
cars, house, furnishings	jewelry, cosmetics, clothes
Model:	*Model:*
learn-feel-do	feel-learn-do
Message Variables:	*Message Variables:*
long copy, informational demonstration, comparative	emotional, visual

Thinking ← — — — — — — — — — — | — — — — — — — — — — → Feeling

Products:	*Products:*
food, household items	liquor, candy, cigarettes
Model:	*Model:*
do-learn-feel	do-feel-learn
Message Variables:	*Message Variables:*
coupons, samples	creativity, lifestyle

Low Involvement

Source: Richard Vaughn, "How Advertising Works: A Planning Model,"*Journal of Advertising Research* (October 1980), pp. 27-33.

High Involvement — Feeling

Some products are based primarily on subjective, emotional reactions, but demand a great deal of consumer time and involvement such as jewelry, cosmetics, clothing, or other fashion products. The products often have more expressive, symbolic meaning than functional usage and thus purchase decisions are rather personal.

Because product information is less important than consumer attitudes, the purchasing sequence is "feel-learn-do." Advertising for products in this category must rely upon emotional and visual elements as well as the psychological needs of the consumer. The products are selected to tell others how we want to be perceived and understood.

Low Involvement — Thinking

Food and household items comprise the low-involvement — thinking category of products. Just how excited can we get over toothpaste or washing detergent? For most consumers, brand loyalty is strong for these products and purchasing is based upon habit rather than major product differentiation. Developing brand loyalty does involve some rational thinking. We ultimately decide to use a product because it is cheaper, better, etc. The buying sequence here is "do-learn-feel." Most of the advertising for this category is to provide "top-of-mind" awareness and to counter the "invasion" of other product ads. You also find a great number of free sample offers, coupons, and quantity pricing for such products to encourage loyalty and to provide a "real" reason for purchase.

Low Involvement — Feeling

In many way, the low involvement — feeling category is a "catch-all" for a variety of products ranging from candy, cigarettes, and liquor, to movies. The key is that these products are highly subjective and depend upon personal taste. They are low involvement primarily because they are inexpensive and consumed quickly. They involve feelings because preferences are personal and many of the items are promoted using imagery. The sequence for this category is "do-feel-learn." Quick self-satisfaction and gratification is the primary goal of much of the advertising. The messages stress creativity and self-indulgence. Some products in this category, such as certain liquors and drinks, also stress lifestyles.

Although the model is rather challenging, it is useful in many ways. It recognizes that there are many reasons and variables in making a decision to purchase an item. The model also attempts to link products to the process of consumer decision making. The model suggests appropriate approaches to create effective advertising messages based upon the sequence of buying decisions. Perhaps most importantly, the model demonstrates the complexity of consumer buying decisions ranging from what type of gum to buy to what type of house to purchase. This is also part of the reason why advertising is so persuasive.

It is important to recognize that advertising, in many ways, counters traditional ideas about how we learn and how we acquire attitudes. Many scholars argue that the learning process is linear and consistent. Information is transmitted; once the information is understood, attitudes may change or some reorganization of belief structure will occur. Once an attitude alters, then a corresponding behavior follows. The FCB model counters this notion. We purchase some products simply because we recall the ads from television and just want to try them. We may then like the product and will form a favorable attitude. In other cases, the advertising causes an attitude to form without ever experiencing the product, as in the belief that Mercedes are superior automobiles. We attach emotional significance to the products such as status or prestige before any purchase takes place. Thus, with this example, we start with an attitude change, develop emotional ties, and then, if circumstances allow, purchase the car.

Perhaps the most questionable practice in the advertising industry is the use of subliminal messages. Such messages are aimed to reach the consumer below the threshold of consciousness. Wilson Bryan Keys, in his books entitled *Subliminal Seduction* and *Media Sexploitation*, provides numerous examples of sexual symbols, words, and pornographic pictures embedded in ads.[21] According to Keys, such messages succeed on two levels: people remember the ads and the targeted behavior is stimulated. The notion of subliminal advertising originated in the famous study which projected messages of "eat popcorn" and "drink Coca-Cola" on movie screens for 1/3,000 of a second.[22] The messages increased sales of popcorn by 57% and of Coke by 18%.

There are several problems with the notion of subliminal advertising. First, the original study was conducted during the movie *Picnic* that contained several scenes of people eating and drinking during hot summer weather. In addition, the study has never been replicated with the same dramatic results. Also, industry professionals continue to deny widespread use of the techniques because they simply do not work. John O'Toole, former chairman of the advertising agency of Foote, Cone, & Belding emphatically states "I don't like to destroy cherished illusions, but I must state unequivocally that there is no such thing as subliminal advertising. I have never seen an example of it, nor have I ever heard it seriously discussed as a technique by advertising people."[23] Of course, as we have already argued, the appeals are subtle indeed. Subliminal advertising may be in the eyes of the beholder because many of the appeals are a matter of perception. For example, a product that uses a movie star as a spokesperson uses the same principle of gaining attention as showing an attractive couple in bed. One appeal is the person, the other sex. One approach is direct, the other is more subtle and plays upon our human interest in sex. Such uses, we believe, are not subliminal but subtle. They utilize deeply ingrained desires and motives of human nature.

The advertising industry relies upon the subtle and the obvious, the rational and the absurd, the everyday and the novel in order to lead us from awareness to ultimate purchase. Keeping that in mind, let's now consider some of the more common tactics and approaches to persuasion in American advertising.

Common Advertising Appeals

There are countless ways advertising attempts to motivate consumers to purchase products. As we have already mentioned, the process is complex. Some ads hope to accomplish more than motivating the public to purchase a product. It is beyond the scope of this chapter to identify all the various techniques advertisers use. However, there are several basic appeals that are common to most advertising messages.

Power

There are several kinds of power: economic, physical, political and social, to name only a few. Many advertising messages offer the products as a means of obtaining power. The consumer is placed in a power-seeking position. Advertisements present vignettes, images, icons, or emblems of power which can be had for a price. For example, the classic Marlboro cigarette ads offer more than image association. Few of us really want to be cowboys. We can, however, aspire to be strong and independent like him if we adopt his emblem of manhood and power — the cigarette. The appeal to physical power goes beyond ads for muscle building and weight machines. Many truck and car ads emphasize the power of the automobile. Cologne ads for both men and women promise sexual strength and power. Some ads offer economic power with such headlines as *"You can lease a BMW for only $200 per month"* or *"You now qualify for an additional $2,000 line of credit on your Visa or Mastercard."* Of course, many political ads offer us power as members of certain groups whose views and needs will be heard in Washington if we elect the right person. Sometimes the product itself is used to epitomize power. For example we know that Dodge trucks are "Ram Tough," that Sears Die-Hard batteries are "heavy duty," and that Glad's Alligator garbage bags are "puncture proof." Most products, we are told, give us some kind of additional power or strength.

Meaning

We live in a complex world and advertising offers products that will provide individual effectiveness or will help give meaning to our complex environment. We can combat hunger by giving $10 per month to sponsor a child in a foreign country. We are assured: "Weekends are made for Michelob," "GE adds life," "Coke is it," "Allstate is the good hands people," "Pierre Cardin provides the look that's right," and American Express is "a part of a lot of interesting lives." Ads tell us what is the "best," the "ultimate," the "chic," and so on.

Norms

Advertising not only purports to provide meaning for our lives, but it also tells us what is good or bad, in or out, right or wrong. Ads reveal how we should look, dress, and eat. Product usage defines us socially and can even disclose what we believe. Fashion advertising, in particular, establishes specific norms for behavior. What are the characteristics of style? Where did you get such criteria? It is most likely that you received them from advertising. It is interesting to note the transformation of blue jeans from pants indicating a lower working class to a status symbol of high fashion. During the Civil Rights movement and anti-Vietnam years, jeans symbolized resentment, protest, and denial of high fashion. Jeans were the uniform of the counterculture. Then in 1977, Jordache used television commercials to advertise tight jeans using sexy models. They became emblems of sexiness rather than rebellion. Soon many designer jeans competed for the newly created market. Some products, rather than establish norms, attempt to show they meet expected norms. "Miller, made the American way" and "At Ford, quality is Job 1" are examples of companies portraying themselves as meeting consumer expectations.

Isolation

Many ads play upon the fear of individual isolation and loneliness. Product appeals provide a means of identifying with a particular crowd or protecting against an imagined faux pas. Examples include "The Pepsi generation" or Coke's "Catch the wave." Many liquor ads depict a man or woman in a party setting with friends. A well-known vodka ad proclaims "Friends are worth Smirnoff." The message not only establishes a norm, but the visual implies popularity by using or associating with those who use the product. To be liked and accepted as a part of a group is a powerful appeal.

Self-esteem

A growing number of ads play upon our fear of low self-esteem. Products promise to deliver better looks or health; they promise to make us better as friends or lovers. Most people want to look their best. The message of a Diet Center ad reads, "First I changed my body, then I changed my mind... I'm more confident, more in control." The headline in an ad for women proclaimed, "I just hated being flat-chested." The product, of course, offers a solution that would increase self-esteem. Ford Motor Company has an employee stating in an ad that "It's a good feeling to know you're helping build the highest quality American cars and trucks."

Guilt

Perhaps the most prominent appeal used in advertising is guilt. Parents must buy products to ensure the safety, health, intelligence, and social well being of children, and they are told they must buy certain brands or spend a certain amount of money in order to show their love for spouses, friends, or parents. Thus, by playing upon our guilt, norms of buying behavior are established.

Fear

There are many types of fears: physical, social, psychological. Products will either prevent disaster, solve our problems, or at least reduce risk of embarrassment. Again, this appeal is so basic that it is difficult to find an ad that does not play upon it in some fashion.

How to Critique Ads

A primary goal of this book is not just to explain persuasion as practiced in contemporary American life, but to provide tools of analysis for various contexts. Because of the extensive daily exposure to advertising, it is useful to discuss two general approaches to analyzing advertising.[24]

Judith Williamson claims advertisements are one of the most important cultural factors molding and reflecting our life today.[25] Every ad creates structures of meaning. Their function is to transform statements about things into statements of significance to people. For example, if a characteristic of a car is high gas mileage, then this characteristic is translated to notions of economy and rationality. The key is in transforming a language of objects to a language of people. Thus, as a critic, one should look at the textual relationships between the parts of the message and the meaning created. Through ads, diamonds come to mean love—a transformation beyond mineral and rock to a purely human sign. In some ads, the objects communicate the human message such as "... say it with flowers" or "... gold says I love you." In other ads, people are identified with the objects that project significance such as "I'm a Pepper" or "become part of the Pepsi generation." The visual image created plays a very important part of the meaning created. In fact, the more prominent the visual in an ad the more ambiguity that is created. Today, the visual implies the meaning. In a now famous television ad for Apple Computers, reminiscent of George Orwell's 1984, a striking woman hurls a sledgehammer through the video screen that hundreds have been watching in a trance. Words cannot, of course, adequately describe the visual power of the commercial. The meaning was totally implied. The new Apple MacIntosh Computer would allow individual creativity and freedom, releasing us from the world of domination and "big brother" control. Thus, from a textual approach, we look for meanings within the ad. What are the appeals? What does the product promise in human terms? The product may promise smooth skin but imply younger looks. The product may promise a close shave but imply greater female approval. Such analysis of advertising forces us to become more critical of the claims made.

A second approach to analyzing advertising is to focus on surface meanings to detect patterns of similarities and differences. For example, how are women portrayed in print ads—as housewives or executives, smart or dumb, fat or thin? How frequent are certain roles portrayed? Surface meanings often include sex roles and modes of expected behavior. This systematic approach to viewing ads reveals cultural roles and stereotypes. Thus, by analyzing surface and implied meanings of advertising messages we can better recognize the persuasive appeals used and assess their validity.

Criticisms and Social Effects of Advertising

Although we accept advertising as a daily practice, there has always been some criticism of the industry. We seem to have a "love—hate" relationship with advertising. For most businesses, advertising is a "necessary evil." For consumers, the commercial interruptions are sometimes pleasant, sometimes informative, but always intrusive. There are several issues of advertising that deserve our special attention.

Deception

Most of us would agree that advertising is a business based on deception and half-truths. In reality, however, most of the factual messages presented in ads are true and the factual statements can be

verified. The problem is that there are few factual statements in most advertising messages. Consumers do not make distinctions between factual statements and value judgments. As noted in Chapter 5, statements of fact are verifiable whereas statements of value express opinions that are, to say the least, very subjective and judgmental. What does it mean when an ad claims that a restaurant has the "best" hamburgers? Does it mean they have the best hamburgers in terms of taste, size, toppings, or price? Certainly, several restaurant chains can claim to have the "best" hamburgers but can they all claim to have the "biggest?" Perhaps they can because some restaurants may have the biggest based upon weight before cooking or after cooking, or based upon size by using very large buns or by using thin but large in circumference hamburgers. There is a difference, therefore, between "false advertising" and "misleading advertising." The latter is most problematic and cause for our concern.

Some ads are misleading because of the nature of the comparisons made in their presentations. Bayer Aspirin claims that "All aspirin is not alike. In tests for quality, Bayer proved superior." The implication is that Bayer is better in relieving pain than other aspirins. The tests referred to in the ad were tests for quality conducted by Bayer and showed that Bayer's tablets were "superior" because they were whiter and less breakable than other brands tested.[26] We must be careful in accepting the claims made in comparative advertising.

Other ads are misleading when they imply false promises. We must always challenge the rationality of claims made in ads. Can the product really make us more beautiful, rich, young, successful, or sexy? Is there a logical relationship between the problem presented and the solution offered? For example, consider the Coast Soap commercials. If you feel sleepy and sluggish in the morning, all you have to do is use Coast Soap and magically you feel alert, happy, and energetic!

Advertising is misleading when it provides incomplete or exaggerated descriptions of products or services. An ad may state that a desk is made of "all wood" but will omit that the wood is actually "compressed wood parts." The more ludicrous ads will often contain small print qualifications with caveats concerning claims made. Ads touting high yield investments will tell you in small print that they require a large amount of money for participation; free checking requires a large minimum monthly balance; a new car for $100 a month requires a large down payment; the examples are limitless.

Most advertising also focuses on the trivial aspects of products elevating the insignificant to significant status. Minor qualities are exaggerated. In fact, differences among most brands or product categories are slight. Much of the distortion in advertising is accomplished in the visual accompanying the message. Frequently food looks better, clothes fit better, and gadgets are handier in commercials and pictures than after a purchase has been made.

In addition to exaggerating product differences, much of the competition is rather phony.[27] For example, White Cloud and Charmin toilet papers are both owned by Proctor & Gamble; Miracle and Parkay margarines are Kraftco brands as are Sealtest, Breyers, and Checkerboard ice creams; Maxwell House, Maxim, Sanka, and Yuban coffees are all produced by General Foods; Biz, Bold, Cheer, Duz, and Ivory belong to the Procter & Gamble stable of detergents. Such abundance of products gives us the illusion of choice and each tells us they are superior to their "sisters."

Perhaps the most difficult question involving deception concerns the motives of the advertiser. Many local retailers advertise a sale on low-end merchandise hoping to sell more expensive models once the consumer gets in the store. Thus while the ads are not deceptive, their purpose is not to offer the consumer a good value or necessarily a good product; the primary purpose is "bait-and-switch."

Language

Advertising has a tremendous impact upon us and many educators are concerned that advertising debases our language. The violation of rules of grammar and punctuation is commonplace. For years there was a running debate about the grammar used in the phrase, "Winston tastes good like a cigarette should." Advertising copy contains a multitude of dashes, hyphens, and sentence fragments. The United States Army receives hundreds of letters each year from teachers and students questioning the punctuation in the slogan, "Army. Be All You Can Be." The most frequent complaint is that there cannot be one word sentences.

Consumerism

The word "consumer" did not always have positive connotations. In its original French usage, consumption was viewed as an act of pillage, destruction and waste. With industrialization, the idea of using things up became associated with prosperity, and today the word consumer is a positive description. The focus in the 1960s was on conserving and preserving natural resources. Since the sole purpose of advertising is to induce the purchase of products, critics argue that it makes people too materialistic. Our happiness and success are frequently measured by the things we possess. The race to "keep up with the Joneses" is a never ending cycle. Advertising perpetuates the cycle by supplying images which may cause us to be unhappy with ourselves and our possessions.

Advertising can play upon our fears about situations as diverse as fire in a home to smelling bad at a party. In fact, some critics have suggested that American Express commercials have heightened fears about foreign travel almost as surely as fears about terrorists. Before products can solve problems, they must first convince us that we have a problem. When advertising raises our expectations it also intensifies our disappointments and fears of failure.

Advertising can sell us things we don't really need or want. Did "pet rocks" really make us happier and healthier human beings? Admittedly, an impulse item does not really cost much and is probably harmless. The item, while cute, is not an essential part of daily life. "Cabbage Patch" dolls were an incredibly successful example of such items. However, advertisers not only encourage us to buy what we don't need, but they go to great lengths to make what we have obsolete so we have no choice but to update equipment, cars or appliances. The Huffy Corporation came out with a new 12-speed bike despite the fact that market research revealed that most people did not even use ten speeds when riding. Why? According to President Harry Shaw, "People don't really need the two extra speeds... The bike may not do so much for you but it should help to obsolete the 10-speeder."[28] John O'Toole, former chairman of Foote, Cone, & Belding acknowledges that advertising sells things people don't need. He claims that people only need air, food, and water. For him, the distinction is that advertising can't sell things people *don't want*.[29]

Social Effects

There is growing concern about the effects of advertising on children. They will be future consumers, and they have learned the "rituals of purchase" at a tender age. Children, just as adults, learn what they need and want. Some children may actually suffer lower self-esteem if they do not own a popular toy such as the Cabbage Patch Doll of 1985. Advertisers long ago learned that children greatly influence adult food purchasing decisions and behavior. The concept behind using Ronald McDonald is to entice young children to ask parents to take them to McDonald's. Perhaps more alarming is how products are presented to children. Commercials take advantage of children's rational capability by distorting product attributes. Toys seem larger, more exciting, and easier to operate than is actually the case. Television studio sets for G.I. Joe and He-Man commercials are as elaborate as movie sets. Finally, many commercials encourage poor eating and health habits. Candy today is presented as "nutritional snacks."

As already mentioned, commercials tend to stereotype people. Women; old people, and minorities in particular are frequently stereotyped in terms of looks, occupations, roles, and behavior by the advertising industry.

There is also concern about the impact of advertising upon the cultural climate of our nation. Some ads are in poor taste, yet find public approval. Fashion designer Perry Ellis deliberately employed a four-letter word considered among the most offensive terms of American obscenity[30] in some of his advertisements. Twenty years ago

"And we thought some product commercials were offensive" — from *Herblock Through the Looking Glass* (W.W. Norton, 1984).

advertisements for hemorrhoid treatments, contraceptives, and douche products would have shocked the audience. Advertisements have become increasingly suggestive and now frequently challenge traditional values.

Freedom of Speech

There is also growing concern on the impact of advertising upon freedom of speech in America. In terms of special issues or political advertising, only those with money can have access to the media. Some critics suggest that influential sponsors of programs direct the content of newscasts by threatening withdrawal of advertising support. Perhaps more damaging is the impact upon how we address each other about the social issues confronting us. Politicians compete for exposure and must speak in "sound bites" so that they fit in a one minute news story. It is common to hear on the radio that "the news is brought to you by...." Yet, shouldn't we have access to news regardless of whether or not someone will pay for it?

Private versus Public Interests

John Kenneth Galbraith argues that ads largely serve private rather than public interests. "Advertising operates exclusively, and emulation mainly, on behalf of privately produced goods and services.... Every corner of the public psyche is canvassed by some of the nation's most talented citizens to see if the desire for some merchantable product can be cultivated. No similar process operates on behalf of the nonmerchantable services of the state."[31]

Summary

Advertising is the most pervasive form of persuasion in American life. Our society is characterized by possessions which often carry symbolic significance for the owner. The health of our society depends upon the consumer. We are commodities to be bought and sold based upon demographic characteristics such as age, sex, income, or lifestyle. We are slaves to the marketplace rather than in the marketplace. Varda Leymore, author of The Hidden Myth, argues that consumption is a kind of primitive religion. Leymore concludes that advertising plays the same role today in society as myth did in primitive societies.[32] Corporations, by seducing us with commodities, condition us to believe that there are no greater sources of reward. In the process, the large corporations become identified with what they produce and tend to take on all the psychic authority once associated with God, family, or nature.[33] Advertising is unarguably an important ingredient of modern culture.

Our purpose in this chapter was to identify the functions, techniques, tactics, and appeals of contemporary advertising. Advertising is as powerful, subtle and intensive as any face-to-face encounter. It is both a creative and scientific process. Advertising messages are inherently persuasive; they seek to convert the individual by playing upon human emotion, hopes, and fears.

Although critics suggest that advertising should be monitored and perhaps regulated, legal avenues or governmental regulation are possible only in cases of obvious deception and fraud. As consumers we must become informed about products and serve as our own critics of ads. John O'Toole argues that there is an implicit contract between advertisers and consumers and that the conditions of the contract are clearly understood by both parties.[34] Terms of the contract include acknowledgement that advertising performs a sales function, will not address other product attributes, won't lie, won't bore you, and in return will support the media, give you choice and information. A contract implies that both parties willingly enter an agreement and understand the terms. In light of the information presented in this chapter, you should decide if that is the case between the advertising industry and the American public.

Notes

[1]John O'Toole, *The Trouble with Advertising* (New York: Chelsea House, 1981), 113.

[2]O'Toole, 5.

[3]Donna Cross, *Media-Speak* (New York: Mentor Book, 1983), 14.

[4]Cross, 15.

[5]Stewart Alter, "Influenced by Ads? Not Me, Most Say," *Advertising Age* (10 June 1985), 15.

[6]O'Toole, 15.

[7]Vance Packard, *Hidden Persuaders* (New York: Pocket Books, 1957), 1.

[8]William Leiss, Stephen Kline, and Sut Jhally, *Social Communication in Advertising* (New York: Methuen, 1986), 229.

[9]William Meyers, *The Image-Makers* (New York: Times Books, 1984), 43.

[10]Arthur Gerger, *Media Analysis Techniques* (Beverly Hills, CA: Sage Publications, 1982), 57.

[11]Vance Packard, *The People Shapers* (Boston: Little, Brown, and Co., 1977), 11.

[12]Packard, *Hidden Persuaders*, 21.

[13]See Al Ries and Jack Trout, *Positioning: The Battle for Your Mind* (New York: McGraw-Hill, 1981).

[14]Ries and Trout, 11-14.

[15]See Meyers, *The Image-Makers.*

[16]Don E. Schultz, *Essentials of Advertising Strategy* (Chicago: Crain Books, 1981), 16-17.

[17]See William Cohen, *Direct Response Marketing* (New York: John Wiley & Sons, 1984), 267.

[18]Kim Rotzoll and James Haefner, *Advertising in Contemporary Society* (Cincinnati, OH: South-Western, 1986), 87.

[19]Leiss et al., 19-23.

[20]R. Vaughn, "How Advertising Works: A Planning Model," *Journal of Advertising Research* 20 (1980), 27.

[21]See Wilson Bryan Key, *Subliminal Seduction* (New York: Signet Books, 1973) and *Media Sexploitation* (New York: Signet Books, 1976).

[22]Courtland Bovee and William Arens, *Contemporary Advertising* (Homewood, IL: Irwin, 1986), 152.

[23]O'Toole, 21.

[24]See Leiss et al., 150-156.

[25]Judith Williamson, *Decoding Advertisements* (New York: Marion Boyars, 1983), 11.

[26]Cross, 16.

[27]Cross, 28-29.

[28]Cross, 21.

[29]O'Toole, 53.

[30]The line of controversy included: "Then I smiled my best f— you smile and walked out." See *Advertising Age* (12 May 1986), 3.

[31]John Kenneth Galbraith, *The Affluent Society,* Third Edition (Boston: Houghton Mifflin, 1976), 198.

[32]Arthur Berman, *Advertising and Social Change* (Beverly Hills, CA: Sage Publications, 1981), 47.

[33]Berman, 31.

[34]O'Toole, 29.

Questions and Projects for Further Study

1. By thumbing through a monthly or weekly magazine, find examples of ads that create appeals to an individual sense of:
   a. power
   b. meaning
   c. norms
   d. isolation
   e. self-esteem
   f. guilt
   g. fear

2. Select a magazine ad and perform a detailed content analysis of both the explicit and implicit meanings and promises contained in the ad.

3. Select an issue of *Gentlemen's Quarterly* and *Vogue*. How are men and women portrayed in each magazine? Do the portrayals differ? If so, how? What type of relationships, roles, and social status are the models portraying?

4. Record each ad you see in one day from all sources: television, radio, newspapers, magazines, billboards, and "point of sale" displays in stores. How does your number of ads seen compare with others?

5. Think about the items you have purchased in the last two weeks. How did you learn about them? Why did you select the brand you did rather than some other?

Additional Reading

Berman, Ronald. *Advertising and Social Change*. Beverly Hills, CA: Sage Publications, 1981.

Cross, Donna. *Media-Speak*. New York: Mentor Book, 1983.

Fox, Stephen. *The Mirror Makers*. New York, NY: Morrow, 1984.

Key, Wilson. *Media Sexploitation*. New York, NY: Signet Books, 1976.

Key, Wilson. *Subliminal Seduction*. New York, NY: Signet Books, 1973.

Leiss, William; Stephen Kline; and Sut Jhally. *Social Communication in Advertising*. New York, NY: Methuen, 1986.

Meyers, William. *The Image-Makers*. New York, NY: Times Books, 1984.

Ogilvy, David. *Ogilvy on Advertising*. New York, NY: Crown, 1983.

O'Toole, John. *The Trouble with Advertising*. New York, NY: Chelsea House, 1981.

Packard, Vance. *Hidden Persuaders*. New York, NY: Pocket Books, 1957.

Packard, Vance. *The People Shapers*. Boston, MA: Little, Brown, and Co., 1977.

Ries, Al; and Jack Trout. *Positioning: The Battle for Your Mind*. New York, NY: McGraw-Hill, 1981.

Rothschild, Michael. *Advertising*. Lexington, MA: D.C. Heath, 1987.

Williamson, Judith. *Decoding Advertisements*. New York, NY: Marion Boyars, 1983.

9

Political Persuasion

 OVERVIEW

News Story: *National Public Radio, March 28, 1979, narrated by reporter*
Steve Curwood:

Man: I saw a plume of steam rise several hundred feet in the air. You could see it — white steam — from the lights around the plant. And it roared. It woke me up. I looked out the window and I saw this huge column going up in the air and roaring.

Curwood: The worst commercial nuclear-power accident in history has begun.

Official: Everything is under control. There is no danger to public health and safety.

Pennsylvania Lt. Gov.: There was a small release of radiation to the environment. Metropolitan Edison has been monitoring the air in the vicinity of the plant constantly since the incident. No increase in normal radiation levels has been detected.

Curwood: But when a Nuclear Regulatory Commission team reaches the scene, they report to their superiors that things inside the reactor are anything but normal.

Men's voices on phone: (garbled)

Sam?

Yeah.

Couple of radiation levels

Okay.

200 R per hour...

Yeah...

... inside containment building

Holy Jesus!

That all the numbers you got?

Yeah. Those are the only numbers.

Okay. Keep us posted. That's a serious, serious damn event.[1]

Aristotle said "Man is by nature a political animal." Although we suspect many Americans would cringe at that thought, he was probably right. The National Public Radio report of disaster at a nuclear power plant is an excellent example of how the public is subject to the decisions made by political leaders. Governors, presidents, and legislators frequently shape our lives. We give them the power to make decisions on our behalf. Some regulations may barely affect us; others may determine whether we live or die. From the organizations we voluntarily join to the municipal, state, and federal regulations that govern us, we are restricted by rules that others impose.

Politics is the process of "negotiating" decisions that bind individuals, organizations, and societies together. In open societies, political activity involves the use of legal and persuasive powers to gain favorable decisions. We could rightfully talk about the "politics" of the National Collegiate Athletic Association or a corporate main office just as easily as we could describe the politics of tax reform in the U.S. Congress. At various times we use our own political skills to shape the opinions of others and, hence, to shape policies and guidelines. There is probably no single set of traits that makes political communication completely unique, but we can identify features that are inevitably a part of political appeals. This chapter explores some of those features as they pertain to governmental and electoral politics.

The Forms of Political Persuasion: Three Cases

Political persuasion is usually concerned with three broad kinds of goals: the explanation of administrative decisions made by leaders, the election of individuals to public office, and the adoption of legislation. The first half of this chapter considers three representative cases of these forms.

Lyndon Johnson and "The Treatment"

It is a common mistake to assume that presidents and other powerful elected officials have enormous powers to order actions to be taken. In fact, even presidents soon realize that their powers are frequently limited to what they can persuade others inside and outside of government to do.[2] Few were more successful in motivating colleges and reporters than Lyndon Johnson, especially in the Senate and in his first three years in the White House.

Johnson's presidency began unexpectedly in 1963 when a bullet ended the life of John Kennedy. Five years later Johnson surprised the nation by announcing on television that he would not seek re-election. The turbulence from 1963 to 1968 took its toll on the nation's patience. Political assassinations, urban riots and the increasingly controversial Vietnam war had shaken American confidence. The subject of Lyndon Johnson himself was equally controversial. The legend of the man and his Texas-sized appetites began in 1952 when he was elected to

Congress. He had tremendous compassion for the poor, enormous expectations about the range of legislation he could move through the Senate, an over-sized ego, and a reputation for persuasion that grew even larger as he assumed the Presidency. Ironically, Johnson's power usually faltered when he gave a public speech. He loved crowds, but he found it difficult to motivate *large* groups of listeners to share his goals and dreams. His political effectiveness was based on what came to be called "the treatment." If someone controlled what Lyndon Johnson needed—for example, a vote on a piece of legislation or a favorable comment in a newspaper article—that person became the target of a direct personal campaign. Even the most hardened of Johnson's critics found it difficult to withstand his one-on-one persuasive assaults. Legislators and reporters swapped stories about the Texan's efforts to further his objectives through intense personal persuasion. "The treatment" encompassed old-fashioned armtwisting, shameless flattery, and severe scolding. The objective was always the same: to win the victim's support for a decision the President had already made.

Dan Rather vividly remembers when, as an unknown Houston radio reporter, he made the mistake of assuming he could deal with Johnson on equal terms. At the time, Johnson was the Majority Leader in the Senate. He had called a press conference at his Pedernales River Valley home prior to returning to Washington after an illness. The young Rather decided to tag along, although his reputation at that time was insignificant compared to the renowned print and television journalists who had been summoned. The eager cub reporter soon confronted the Johnson presence. As Rather recalls it, he had made the innocent mistake of assuming he could use a phone in the Johnson home to call his station.

> I was sitting on a daybed. At that point the phone was yanked from my hand and this towering figure loomed up behind me and roared into the mouthpiece, "This is Lyndon Johnson. I don't know who the hell you are, and I don't know who this rude pissant is. But I can tell you this: He doesn't belong here, I'm throwing his ass out, what he told you is bullshit and if you use it, I'll sue you.
>
> By the time he banged down the receiver I was already fleeing out the door, my tape recorder flapping against my back, mike and cord dragging behind me. I hurried across the driveway... I tried to use the old Boy Scout pace: you know, trot fifty, walk fifty, across the river bridge and into the trees and onto the blacktop beyond, heading in the direction of Stonewall, Texas.[3]

It was Johnson's wife who finally drove her car along the dusty road to track down the reporter, still in shock from his encounter with the legendary politician.

Figure 9.1

Lyndon Johnson talking to Caribbean leaders at the White House in 1965.

From *The Vantage Point: Perspectives of the Presidency 1963-1969* by Lyndon Baines Johnson. Copyright © 1971 by HEC Public Affairs Foundation. Reprinted by permission of Henry Holt and Company.

Veteran UPI reporter Helen Thomas remembers when one of her colleagues faced the same combination of intimidation and persuasive power after Johnson had assumed the Presidency:

> Once when Charles Mohr of *The New York Times* was trying to find out the salaries of the White House top echelon, a focal point of abrasion, Johnson decided to give him the "treatment." [An aide]...

summoned Mohr one day to go walking with Johnson, and in their
chat Mohr told LBJ of his problems in getting queries answered.
"You didn't call me," said LBJ. "Ask me anything." Mohr put the
same question to him, inquiring about staff salaries. Johnson stalled,
saying: "Here you are the reporter for *The New York Times* walking
with the leader of the Western world and all you can think of is that
chickenshit question. Here you have the most powerful man and he
says he'll tell you anything...." Johnson, of course, never answered
the question.[4]

For television journalist Robert MacNeil "the treatment" involved
more flattery than intimidation. During the Vietnam war, Johnson
desperately wanted the three major television networks and the wire
services to share his own domestic political agenda. The President
rightly feared that his Vietnam policy was destroying his chance to
build a "Great Society" which would end poverty and racism. Three
television sets were installed in the oval office so that all of the network
evening newscasts could be viewed simultaneously. Visitors recall
hearing the constant clatter of the wireservice teletype machines just
outside the door. The President wanted to reach the American public
by persuading the press to report the official Johnson interpretation on
the controversies confronting the nation in the mid 1960s. Then a
correspondent for NBC, MacNeil remembers the remarks made to
him and to Frank Cormier of the Associated Press. Never one to be
subtle, Johnson's approach was to offer exclusive information to the
reporters that could help their careers:

> Now what impresses your bosses up there in the Associated Press
> and NBC? Is it you guys reporting what everyone else reports?
> President Johnson did this? What really makes them pay attention
> is when you have something the other reporters don't have. When
> you have inside information.... Now you fellas are good reporters
> and you're smart. You play it straight with me and I'll see that both
> of you get lots of little bits of information, special information.[5]

Comments like these make it painfully evident that Lyndon Johnson
operated under the mistaken assumption that everyone could be won
over by promises of power and prestige. Even so, it would be simplistic
to dismiss his attempts at persuasion as just the coercion of a crude
politician. When they were directed at others within the Washington
establishment they often produced solid administrative victories and
progressive legislation.

Bill McKay and the Politics of Glitz

For millions of Americans the political images that are most deeply
etched into memory are those that are formed during political
campaigns. Elections are always news; the activities of the 500,000

campaigns that occur every four years in the United States represent an almost unbroken spectacle of debates, campaign rallies, and political commercials. For most of us, the political campaign is a bewildering mixture of patriotic ritual, popular theater, and superficiality.[6] We know campaigns are necessary in an open society, but we are uneasy about whether they really provide opportunities for judging the abilities of would-be legislators and administrators.[7]

Perhaps the most authentic treatment of a political campaign ever attempted by Hollywood was the 1972 film, *The Candidate*, starring Robert Redford. The Academy Award winning film was written by Jeremy Larner, a speechwriter for Senator Eugene McCarthy. The movie reflects American ambivalence towards political campaigns; it is a cautionary tale about the increasing use of product marketing techniques in the "packaging" of candidates and ideas. It accurately reflects the fact that television exposure and audience research have partially replaced political parties in determining who will run for important elective offices.

Redford plays the idealistic Bill McKay, a California legal aid lawyer who represents the poor from the *barrios* and slums of Los Angeles. McKay's life is changed forever when a college friend, Marvin Lukas, pays him a visit. Lukas is a shrewd political consultant who has made a career of supporting his expensive lifestyle by organizing and running political campaigns. Played by character actor Peter Boyle, the balding and bearded consultant is a sharp contrast to the photogenic McKay. Oblivious to the ethics of politics, Lukas picks his candidates because of their potential to generate excitement and plenty of campaign cash. His proposition to McKay is simple: he wants the handsome liberal to run against the current Senator from California, a well-financed incumbent named Crocker Jarmon. McKay initially rejects the offer. He fears that becoming a candidate for a major party will require him to sell out his principles, but he is finally attracted by the prospect of reaching thousands of voters with hard-hitting criticisms of the complacent Jarmon.

McKay reluctantly enters the campaign and is increasingly absorbed by the necessity of attracting voters—a process that slowly puts the squeeze on his "new" ideas and fresh approach to politics. The film shows his transformation from an idealist to a figure who is increasingly molded and shaped to fit the needs of a winning campaign. Every time he is convinced by his staff to "soften" his statements on abortion, school busing, and industrial pollution, his ratings in statewide polls go up. At his first press conference, for example, he is asked how he feels about whether public school children should be bused to achieve racial balance in schools. "I'm for it," he says, jarring the sleepy members of the press to attention by this unexpected candor. He is equally straightforward about his position favoring liberal guidelines for abortion. It is only later, after the crowds get bigger and his chances for victory increase, that we see different responses to the same issues. McKay continually "refines" his answers to attract more votes. By the time he is well into his campaign, McKay has discovered that abortion and busing are issues "that need further study."

Lukas hires a "media consultant" to prepare the television commercials which will be the public's only real contact with the candidate. The consultant uses the tired formulas of image politics; advertisements create a manufactured candidate with all the sharp edges neatly smoothed over. "We'll give the people 30 seconds of McKay the statesman" is his offhand response to complaints that not enough time is being devoted to issues. We also see members of the press who generally confine their coverage, in the manner of television, to 20 second "sound bites" that will fit the available news slots in local television newscasts. Television reporters following the candidate typically leave after filming the opening minute of a speech. As Larner's screenplay describes it, McKay's campaign slogan "There must be a better way" is more than just a routine political catch phrase, it is also a symbol of the superficial nature of modern political campaigns. We leave the film believing there must be a better way to elect our leaders.[8]

Art rarely imitates life exactly. Candidates, for example, are usually not recruited by their campaign managers. Our suspicions about the intentions and motives of politicians are never far below the surface. The Candidate reflects those fears, and at the same time points out that American politics is not solely the manipulation of voters by cynical politicians. The film also shows apathetic voters, superficial reporters, and scheduling demands that would leave an Olympic athlete weak from exhaustion. In the end, it suggests a campaign process that has become burdened by the demands of public relations. It is a system that no one would abolish; after all, elections are the heart of democracies. The process, however, regularly points out the large gap that exists between the ideal of democracy and the realities of political life.

Winning the Vote in 1920

Politics has always inspired intense distrust within Americans, although the rules which govern our daily conduct are made through political action.[9] We cannot escape the grip of political decisions. How fast we can legally drive, how much tuition we pay, when we are declared legally dead, when we may marry or divorce, even how many hours we work in a day are a few examples of the local and national codes that affect our lives. Basic privileges we now take for granted such as the right to vote were won through diligent political action.

Women in the United States won the vote only in 1920 when Tennessee became the 36th state to ratify the Constitutional Amendment. Congress had passed the legislation three years earlier proclaiming that "The right of citizens of the United States to vote shall not be denied or abridged... on account of sex..." The first meeting to campaign for the "social, civil, and religious rights of women" had been organized by Elizabeth Cady Stanton, Lucretia Mott, and others 72 years earlier.[10]

Like most other causes, the women's suffrage movement depended on mastery of the art of political persuasion. Virtually every technique and strategy used in the years prior to ratification are still used today. The most dramatic persuasive tactics involved pickets in front of the White House ("Mr. President, How Long Must Women Wait for Liberty?") mass parades, and rallies. Arrests of women in virtually every major city of the United States made daily headlines. Some of those given jail sentences went on hunger strikes, undergoing agonizing pain when jailers resorted to the use of stomach feeding tubes.[1]

The most effective forms of persuasion undertaken by supporters of women's suffrage were less dramatic but no less important. The key activity involved lengthy and sustained efforts at lobbying individual legislators and members of congress. The well organized National American Woman's Suffrage Association was especially effective at securing the agreement of individual members of Congress and the state legislatures. One of the lobbyists, Maud Wood Park,

> was concerned with finding just the right woman to make a favorable impression on the member being interviewed. She always sent a woman from a man's own region if possible, recognizing the difficulty a New England woman might have, for example, with a congressman from Georgia. She thought on balance her most successful lobbyists were women from the Middle-West, middle-aged, and "rather too dressy," but "possessed of much common sense and understanding of politics in general, as well as of the men from their districts."[12]

Like most movements, the campaign for women's rights faced internal disputes about the kinds of tactics that were appropriate to produce change. Park and others in N.A.W.S.A. favored quieter persuasion and less open conflict than the more confrontational Congressional Union.

Lobbying is the process of supplying facts and arguments to legislators, usually prior to a key legislative vote. The term itself comes from the fact that before legislators had private offices they used to meet individuals seeking to influence legislation in the foyer immediately outside a legislative chamber. The noun has become a verb; to "lobby" is to attempt to influence a legislative or administrative decision in government.[13] For many Americans, lobbying carries sinister connotations of overpowering persuasion, for example, using money, food, sex, or whatever represents a legislator's weakness in order to win special favors. To be sure, lobbyists have power, but their persuasion tactics are far less exotic. The most common lobbying strategies include telling the legislator what constituents back home think, making suggestions for how he or she can defend a vote, and supplying arguments about the positive or negative consequences of a certain legislative decision. Most lobbying is low-key and directed to sympathetic or undecided lawmakers.[14] Virtually every major business, interest group and union lobbies legislators. General Electric, state student organizations, the Catholic church, the National Aeronautics and Space Administration, the National Rifle Association and the National Education Association are all lobbyists. This kind of persuasion is sometimes called "wholesale" politics because it is not directed to the general public; it focuses on lawmakers and opinion leaders. "Retail" political persuasion involves activities intended for general public consumption such as speeches, press conferences, television or direct-mail advertisements.

Major Features of Political Persuasion

The Substance of Politics: Character, Concerns, and Policies

When we think about persuasion, we most commonly associate it with selling *things*. The material benefits of most products are of less lasting consequence than the people and ideas which represent the prime subjects of political persuasion.

Character

"Character," in journalist Charles Peter's words, "is the ability to rise above all the forces that keep us from thinking clearly—not only about what will work, but about what is right."[15] We expect that election campaigns will provide evidence of the fitness of a candidate's character. It is by no means an easy job to judge the ability of an aspiring president, governor, mayor, or legislator, but we know that we must try. As important as specific issues are, we realize that they will change over time while the fundamental capacities and good sense of a leader will remain essentially unchanged. How will a president handle the stress of high office? When will a leader resort to the Marines or

Air Force to resolve a conflict that has not yielded to diplomacy? How will a governor deal with charges of rampant corruption, poverty, or industrial decline? And how will a legislator respond to yet unknown contingencies and emergencies? If our abilities to detect decency, good sense, fairness, and honesty are far less precise than our ability to analyze a simpler product like soap, it is only because the elements of responsible character involve many dimensions of personality that are difficult to identify.

When we talk about particular politicians it is usually not in terms of their ideas, but rather what kind of person we think they are. We see them as generous, ambitious, serious, calculating, friendly, obsessed, self-serving, or hundreds of other traits. Political commercials in election campaigns generally feature candidates in the same way that dramatists might introduce a character as a film or play unfolds. We see them making statements and taking positions, but many of the statements are secondary to the image or *public persona* that is projected. In 1976, for example, political commercials for presidential candidate Jimmy Carter often featured the former rancher and governor at his home, clad in jeans and a western shirt. While Carter made suitably presidential comments about the state of the nation and the economy, the deepest impression the commercials left was of a competent "grass roots" leader far removed from official Washington. Carter's effective campaign slogans emphasized the need to build a "government as good as its people," and fostered the image of a leader who was still close to his Georgia roots.

Even though 30 second political commercials are by definition superficial, character remains an important aspect of political dialogue. The most important "issue" in any campaign may be the candidate's fitness to make decisions on contingencies yet unknown. As presidential scholar James David Barber has noted, "The issues will change, the character of the President will last."[16]

Concerns

"Concerns" are expressions of awareness on general priorities or values. Statements of concern are often used to symbolize a person's awareness of a problem, frequently in place of more specific plans or policies. They are intended to show solidarity with a segment of the population that needs reassurance that a threat to the welfare or safety of some group has not been forgotten. A president, for example, may use many different public occasions to demonstrate his compassion and sensitivity. Concerns about the breakdown of order in the Middle East, or the decline of an industry such as textiles, or the fate of farm families who can no longer manage their debts might all be expressed. In many ways, these kinds of statements are the bread and butter of politics. General expressions of interest on certain issues are important to audiences who want evidence that their priorities are shared by their leaders. A question and answer session meeting between President Ronald Reagan and a group of farmers worried about Japanese restrictions on imports presents a typical case:

> Question: Mr. President, I'm in the cattle business. I'd like to know what is being done to help cut down the barriers for foreign trade, especially in Japan. Now, they've sent all their products over in the area, and we do not put any restrictions on their products, and yet they put the restrictions on our products. ...I feel that your admini-stration...is doing a lot, but I feel that there should be a lot more done.

The farmer's comment is an invitation for the President to declare a firm policy of reciprocal restrictions on Japanese goods. Because he had gone on record in opposition to a formal policy of tariffs on foreign goods, Reagan answered with an empathetic restatement of the problem and an expression favoring "quiet diplomacy" rather than "protectionist" legislation. His measured response focused on responding to the *concerns* of his listeners but not on the *policy* solutions sought by his audience.

> The President: This gentlemen is talking about cattle farming and the restrictions that are put on our exported cattle, for example, to Japan, and yet the unlimited way in which they can come in here. He says he knows we're doing something but [he is] not sure it is enough. Well, maybe one of the reasons is because we believe in quiet diplomacy. Instead of putting some fellow on the other side on the spot, and holding him up to public view, we have been working very hard... to change some of these and to tell them that the only alternative is start to go down the road to protectionism, which we don't want to do.[17]

As President Kennedy once noted, "every Presidential speech cannot reveal a major decision."[18] There are clearly many times when a political message is more a ritual of reassurance than a call for action.

Policy

The most important political messages address policy proposals. A policy is a specific plan of action or a set of guidelines which is intended to alleviate a problem. Before an election, only a small number of proposed policies will gain public attention. Debates on the merits of particular policies form the prime "issues" of a campaign. The complete agenda of issues that emerges is determined in part by the candidates and partly by the mass media. How does a candidate feel about the death penalty? Does he or she support increases in

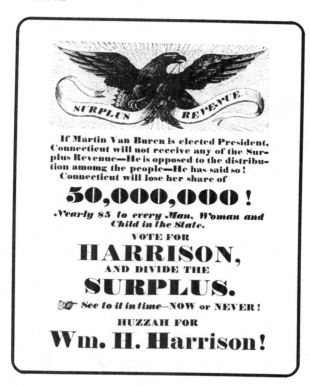

If Martin Van Buren is elected President, Connecticut will not receive any of the Surplus Revenue—He is opposed to the distribution among the people—He has said so! Connecticut will lose her share of

50,000,000 !

Nearly $5 to every Man, Woman and Child in the State.

VOTE FOR

HARRISON,

AND DIVIDE THE

SURPLUS.

☞ See to it in time—NOW or NEVER !

HUZZAH FOR

Wm. H. Harrison!

defense spending? Is the candidate willing to raise taxes in order to pay for government services? Voter studies generally conclude that the average American may have only a vague sense of where candidates stand on a variety of issues.[19] Most voters seem to have more precise feelings about the candidate's general qualifications.

Policy discussion is usually more detailed and prolonged after the campaign when proposals are introduced and debated in the nation's legislative assemblies. In the endless cycle of democratic politics new initiatives are proposed; the problems they are intended to remedy are discussed, and decisions are made which eventually result in the enactment or defeat of legislation. The single most important function of any kind of legislative body—from local town councils to the United States Congress—is the consideration of laws. The policy under discussion may be as narrow as a town council's ruling on whether satellite dish antennas can be placed in front yards or as complex as a constitutional amendment prohibiting abortions. Persuasion representing one side of the latter issue is presented in Figure 2. In addition to legislative bodies, it is obvious that powerful executives such as governors or the President has the power to set their own guidelines on spending, law enforcement, and executive organization. Chief executives are more than policy enforcers; they are *de facto* policy makers as well.

The careful reader will recognize policy discussion as one of the forms of persuasion to which the authors have returned again and again. As we noted in Chapter 2, democracy serves no higher function than to provide an orderly way for the public discussion of rules that will govern the population. In Chapter 3 we noted that political persuasion offers an ideal way to study how language works to create powerful symbols and to shape attitudes. In every chapter there are countless examples of persuasion intended to alter either the rules by which society lives or, on a smaller scale, the rules which govern a specific organization or group.

Since policies are specific actions taken to remedy social or economic problems, their explanation and defense usually hinges on a problem-solution sequence. Successful policy defenses are based on convincing persuadees that (1) a problem is severe and real, and (2) that a proposed course of action will alleviate either the causes of the problem, or at least its worst symptoms.

The Presidency of Lyndon Johnson again serves as an excellent example. Between 1963 and 1965, Johnson introduced a number of major proposals to deal with racial discrimination, hunger, and poverty. The ambitious and widely publicized persuasive campaigns had no shortage of critics (Ronald Reagan, for instance, long maintained that the policies of the "Great Society" treated symptoms rather than basic causes). However, Johnson was dramatically successful in following up statements of concern with specific policy proposals intended to provide concrete action. He persuaded members of Congress to pass the landmark Civil Rights and Voting Rights Acts of 1964 and 1965 which guaranteed the right to vote, to work, and to use public facilities. Johnson's speeches on the effects of racial segretation and the need for legislative remedies were uncharacteristicly eloquent and effective. On the subject of voting rights, he cited basic American values as good reasons to sweep away decades of inaction. He did more than pay lip service to the Constitutional promise of equality; his legislation provided stiff penalties for states which continued to use dubious devices such as poll taxes and literacy tests to restrict the rights of black citizens to vote. "We cannot, we must not, refuse to protect the right of every American to vote in every election that he may desire to participate in," he told the Congress.

> "So I ask you to join me in working long hours—nights and weekends, if necessary—to pass this [Voter Rights] Bill. For from the window where I sit with the problems of our country I recognize that outside this chamber is the outraged conscience of a nation... and the harsh judgment of history on our acts."[20]

Figure 9.2

"Do I look like a mother to you?"

She does if you look at the statistics.

The United States is the only industrialized nation where the teenage pregnancy rate is going up. Forty percent of all girls who are now fourteen will get pregnant before they're twenty. One million each year.

The social consequences are enormous. Because most teenage mothers are single mothers, trapped in a cycle of poverty that costs billions extra each year. In malnutrition. Disease. Unemployment. Child abuse.

But the tragic effects of motherhood on each individual teenager can't be measured in dollars and cents. And it isn't reflected in the statistics. She's robbed of her childhood and her hope.

While we must do everything we can to help *prevent* unwanted pregnancy, we must also preserve the option of safe, legal abortion.

A teenage girl shouldn't be forced to become a mother if she's not ready.

But there's an increasingly vocal and violent minority that disagrees. They want to outlaw abortions for all women, regardless of circumstances. Even if her life or health is endangered by a pregnancy. Even if she is a victim of rape or incest. And even if she is too young to be a mother.

They're pressuring lawmakers to make abortions illegal. And that's not all. They also oppose birth control and sex education—ways of *preventing* abortion. They've already tried to slash federal funding for these and other family planning programs. And to get their way, they've resorted to threats, physical intimidation and violence.

Speak out now. Or they just might succeed. Use the coupon.

The decision is yours.

☐ I've written my representatives in Congress to tell them I support: government programs that reduce the need for abortion by preventing unwanted pregnancy; and keeping safe and legal abortion a choice for all women.

☐ Here's my tax-deductible contribution in support of all Planned Parenthood activities and programs: ☐ $25 ☐ $35 ☐ $50 ☐ $75 ☐ $150 ☐ $500 ☐ or: $_____

NAME _____ AT 1-1

STREET/CITY/ZIP _____

P Planned Parenthood®
Federation of America, Inc.

810 Seventh Avenue
New York, New York 10019

This ad was paid for with private contributions. © Copyright 1985

A Planned Parenthood advertisement on birth control and abortion.

Used by permission of Planned Parenthood Federation of America, Inc.

Johnson was "political" in the full sense of the word. He could seem petty and arrogant, but he was sometimes able to use his considerable persuasive talent to achieve the ultimate goals of American politics: the use of law and policy to assure the freedom, safety and welfare of millions.

Short-Term Orientation

One of the clearest features of political persuasion is that it is usually governed by a limited time frame. Products have a far longer "shelf life" than issues. In the computer industry, large firms like IBM and Apple may do battle everyday for what they perceive as their rightful share of the world's market. Political candidates and legislators follow opportunities which are far more episodic. Political persuaders must work to have public attitudes "peak" at just the right moment, for example, when a bill comes up for consideration or when election day approaches (see Figure 3). The idea of the "campaign" itself owes its "do or die" imagery to the battlefield. "Strategies" and "tactics" are defined, and the "troops" are "mobilized" on voting day to produce a final victory. In war as in politics, battles may not always be decisive, but on any given day there is inevitably a "winner." Laws are passed or they are not; people are elected or they are not; political persuasion encourages thinking in terms of victory or defeat.

Condensation Symbols in Political Subjects

In Chapter 3, we paid special attention to the language of politics. It is the imagery, ritual, and symbolism of political discussion that gives politics its meaning. We wish to return briefly to the subject of symbolism to highlight an additional striking feature. Political acts or actors are symbolic when they represent more than purely denotative (or specific) meanings. When images, acts, or words have the power to evoke widely shared and intensely held feelings, we call such evocations *condensation symbols*.

They differ from connotations in degree. A word has a connotation when it suggests not only a literal meaning but a sense of threat or reassurance as well. A condensation symbol takes this process one step further. It collects a wide variety of intense feelings and associations under one key word and, in doing so, becomes a powerful "shorthand" expression of a group's shared values and beliefs. "They condense into one symbolic event, sign, or act, patriotic pride, anxieties, remembrances of past glories or humiliations, [and] promises of future greatness."[21] For example, we cannot define an American president simply as the chief executive officer of the government, the bald eagle as just another bird, or the American flag as a colorful piece of cloth. All of these symbols evoke something more from the average citizen. Condensation symbols have their roots in the

Figure 9.3

Three Days in a Political Campaign

In 1981, New Jersey experienced one of its closest races ever for the Governorship. The campaign featured two political veterans making their first bids for the powerful position of state executive. The Republican, Tom Kean, had served as a key leader in the New Jersey Assembly. Democrat Jim Florio was a respected member of the House of Representatives. On November 5th, after 2,280,000 ballots had been counted, Kean emerged the winner with a paper thin 1158 vote margin. Here is a three-day schedule that was distributed to the press by the Florio staff near the end of this close contest. The range and number of groups addressed is a reminder of how tiring political campaigns can be, even in a relatively small state.

Wednesday, October 21

9:00 a.m. Guest Speaker: Meeting of the Middlesex/Somerset Assn. of Underwriters, Holiday Inn, Rt 1, N. Brunswick.

9:30 a.m. Guest Speaker: NJ Assn. for the Prevention and Treatment of Substance Abuse, Ramada Inn, E. Brunswick.

11:30 a.m. Guest Speaker: Mortgage Bankers Assn., Sheraton Inn, Freehold (meet employees, Q & A).

1:00 p.m. Guest Speaker: Membership Meeting of the Nassau Club, 6 Mercer St., Princeton.

3:00 p.m. Tentative: Channel 9 interview.

5:45 p.m. Guest Speaker: Middlesex County Board of Realtors, Pines Manor, Edison.

7:00 p.m. Guest Speaker: Mercer County Democrats Dinner Dance, Cedar Gardens, Hamilton Township.

8:00 p.m. Guest Speaker: Voters and Taxpayers of Lavallette regular meeting, Borough Hall, Rt. 35 and Washington Ave., Lavallette.

9:00 p.m. Guest Speaker: Builders League of South Jersey, Kenney's Suburban House, Cherry Hill.

[Continued]

Thursday, October 22

8:15 a.m. Black Leaders Breakfast, Atlantic City Casino.

9:00 a.m. Editorial Board: *Atlantic City Press.*

10:30 a.m. Guest Speaker: AFL-CIO Convention, Harrah's Casino.

11:30 a.m. Guest Speaker: NJ Health Officers Assn., Golden Nugget, Atlantic City.

12:00 p.m. Guest Speaker: CWA rally and Convention, Claridge House, Atlantic City.

1:00 p.m. Guest Speaker, NJ Convention of Senior Citizens, Beacon Manor, Pt. Pleasant.

3:00 p.m. Taping of "McLaughlin's Beat," Trenton.

4:00 p.m. Meeting with Editorial Board, *The Trentonian.*

6:30 p.m. Tentative: North Jersey Homebuilders Fundraiser, Forsgate Country Club, Jamesburg.

8:00 p.m. Guest Speaker: NJ Water Pollution Assn. Tri-Section Dinner Meeting, Forsgate Country Club, Jamesburg.

8:30 p.m. Guest Speaker: Manalapan Township Covered Bridge Senior Citizens Residence, Sheraton Gardens, Freehold.

8:45 p.m. Stop-in: Hudson County Democrat Dinner.

Friday, October 23

10:00 a.m. Guest Speaker: NJ Assn. of Children's Residential Facilities Fall Institute, Holiday Inn, N. Brunswick.

11:00 a.m. Guest Speaker: Steelworkers of America Convention, Ramada Inn, Exit 9, New Brunswick.

12:00 a.m. Guest Speaker: NJ Bell, 540 Broad St., Newark.

2:00 p.m. Guest Speaker: NJ Assn. of Colleges and Universities, Robeson Student Center, Rutgers Univ., Newark.

3:00 p.m. Campaigning with Cong. Claude Pepper, Irvington Senior Center, Springfield Ave., Irvington.

6:30 p.m. Tentative: Stop-in, Oil Heat Assn. Annual Banquet, Riviera Ballroom, 537 Nicholson Rd., Audubon.

7:30 p.m. Stop-in: Winslow Township Democrats Wine and Cheese Party.

8:00 p.m. Rally: honoring Florio, Machinists, Cherry Hill.

9:00 p.m. Stop-in: Burlington County Democratic Dinner, Merion Caterers, Cinnaminson.

10:00 p.m. Tentative: Guest Speaker: NJ Jaycees Model Legislature, Mt. Laurel Travel Lodge.

Used by permission of Rep. James. J. Florio.

unique circumstances of history and in events and challenges long remembered. Thus:

> Washington was a man of integrity (the cherry tree), determination (Valley Forge), and was democratic (refusal to be king). Lincoln was a man of patience (preserve the union), forgiveness (malice toward none), and a lover of freedom (Emancipation Proclamation).[22]

Condensation symbols such as these call up a broad range of associations that strongly influence our political views. The average citizen knows more about the personal attributes of politicians, for example, than about the issues that represent the substance of their work. The personal traits of leaders represent the easiest ways to place meaning on political acts. We don't think of Hitler, for example, as friendly or kind. As a condensation symbol, images of him are reverberations of the hated Third Reich: authoritarian, cruel, bigoted, and xenophopic. Conversely, a popular American president serves as a visible national symbol for a number of political values: free enterprise, toughness toward the Soviets, American military strength, and so on. A less favorable symbolic role was inherited by former Interior Secretary, James Watt. Watt was so disliked by environmentalists that it was often enough to display his picture or to mention his name to summarize complaints against the land use policies of the Reagan Administration.

It goes without saying that condensation symbols gloss over important distinctions and details. A Memorial Day tribute to troops killed in battle with music, flags, and soldiers would not be conducive to a discussion criticizing foreign policy decisions that caused the deaths being commemorated. The cross, the flag, the German swastika, and their verbal counterparts such as "socialist" or "free enterprise" are convenient but simplistic ways to reduce ideas to simple and sometimes unchallengable forms. When persuasion is reduced to such simple symbolic dimensions, it is hardly surprising that factual knowledge falls to very low levels. If policies are discussed only in terms of intensely held feelings of praise or blame, the quality of political dialogue itself is severely reduced. There is no shortage of critics who recognize the problem. Politics, notes Murray Edelman, is for most of us just a "spectator sport" that offers symbols that evoke feelings of fear or reassurance.[23] Presidents, we hope, will do things that we like. The leaders of other nations will be portrayed in the familiar images of friend or foe. The effect of such simplified persuasion is to encourage us to cling to the kinds of certainties found only in fairy tales. It is always easy to distinquish between good and evil; villains are always punished. Most of us do not want to exert the effort to combat stereotypical condensation symbols. There is a strange sort of comfort, for example, in continuing to view the Soviet Union as an "evil empire," rather than risking potential psychological discomfort in looking for merit in various aspects of Soviet life.

Political Issues and Status

A related but distinct feature of political persuasion is what Sociologist Joseph Gusfield calls "status politics." He notes that we tend to combine our attitudes towards specific issues with stereotyped attitudes about certain kinds of people. A topic becomes a status issue when a group collectively makes the judgment that where other people stand on a question demonstrates their superiority or inferiority. The "right" position indicates stronger morals and higher social prestige. The "wrong" side of an issue may be interpreted as a sign of moral weakness. A given issue is thus transformed into more than an expression of ideas; it becomes symbolic of a group's prestige and status. Gusfield cites two examples from the 1960s:

> In the election of 1960 Protestant-Catholic conflict was a major source of candidate loyalties. Were Protestants protecting the White House from papal domination? Were Catholics trying to en-hance Catholic doctrines by a Catholic President [John F. Kennedy]? Only the naive and the stupid will accept either of these suggestions. At stake, however, was the relative prestige of being Protestant in American life. The ability of a Catholic to break the traditional restriction in American politics does mean... the prestige of being Catholic is enhanced.... In a similar fashion the current school de-segregation struggle is symbolic rather than instrumental. Whether or not most negroes will actually be attending integrated schools in the near future is not the issue. Northern cities have developed little more than token integration. Public acceptance of the principle of integration, expressed as token integration, is an act of deference which raises the prestige of the Negro. Whether better educational conditions for Negroes will result is not the significant issue. It is that of equal rights.[24]

A more contemporary example is the recently defeated Equal Rights Amendment to the Constitution barring discrimination on the basis of sex. The Amendment was a source of constant public discussion through most of the 1970s. Although some changes in the status of women could have resulted from the approval of the Amendment by the necessary two-thirds of the states, what was most definitely at issue was the symbolic meaning of the proposal to bar sexual discrimination. Many supporters of the ERA saw it as an important declaration of the nation's commitment to feminism.[25]

The concept of status politics is a potent reminder that political

National Rally for Equal Rights

10,000 marchers walk toward the Capitol in Springfield, Illinois to demonstrate for the passage of the Equal Rights Amendment on May 16, 1976. Men and women from thirty states came to canvass legislative districts and to attend a rally.
Wide World Photos, Inc.

persuasion is not only about objective changes in policy; it also includes social recognition and legitimacy. Many issues remind us of our solidarity with certain in-groups. When decisions are made that enhance the prestige of groups with which we identify, our sense of self-worth and importance is also enhanced. There is a vivid parallel in the world of international sports competition. An American Olympic athlete's victory over a Russian opponent, for example, may be transformed from a relatively innocent sporting contest between two individuals to a misrepresentation of nationalistic glory. Millions of television viewers are constantly reminded of which countries hold the most medals, reducing the games to a bizarre and meaningless extention of political rivalries. Olympic competition in recent history is a sobering reminder that a sense of moral superiority can be created from the thinnest of pretexts.

Politics as "Mediated" Communication

Today, public knowledge of issues and advocates is undeniably shaped by the mass media, especially television. The role of the media in shaping political beliefs has both obvious and subtle aspects. In a simpler and more community-centered America, the average citizen's understanding of government grew from membership in a party and face to face contacts with local politicians. In many cities, the party's presence was (and in some instances, still is) made known by the neighborhood "ward healer" whose connections in city hall made it easy to get streets cleaned or potholes repaired. Between the Civil War and the advent of broadcasting in the 1920s, it was routine for the major parties and cultural organizations to hold large public gatherings to give the ordinary citizen a chance to hear the words of major political and social leaders. The popular temperance speaker, John B. Gough, for example, spoke to over nine million people in 9,600 separate addresses over the course of his career.[26] Major celebrities and leaders such as Teddy Roosevelt, Senator Robert LaFollette, and union leader Samuel Gompers were dependent on the network of theatres and lecture halls that tied even remote American towns to national issues.

There still are thousands of local office holders such as mayors and school board members who may be acquainted with individual residents. National leaders, however, are linked to Americans through the television reports of Dan Rather, Tom Brokaw and their colleagues. Television, rather than the party organization, now acts to bind the nation together. No institution including the political parties, the Congress or even the Presidency can match the ability of the three networks to convey attitudes and information to the nation. Within minutes of a crisis, citizens across the continent have access to the same information (or misinformation) about events such as the 1982 attempt on the life of Ronald Reagan or the 1986 explosion of the space shuttle "Challenger."

Television and other forms of rapid mass communication deliver political messages in a way that is fundamentally different from how listeners used to acquire information from "live" speakers. Notwithstanding the impression that television presents unfiltered reality, the fact that it and other mass media must exclude far more than can be included makes us all the recipients of "second hand" reports. The routine processes of newsgathering and reporting necessarily *mediate* between us and actual events. There is admittedly nothing new about this fact of life. Even President Lincoln was bound to deal with American public opinion that was shaped to a large extent by the nation's magazine and newspaper editors, many of whom hated him. What *is* unique about the idea of mediation is that it has intensified our interest in local politics while our links with local political contacts have withered. We no longer expect that political activism will flourish in our districts and neighborhoods. The political dialogue that does take place is carried on at a distance, some of it within the pages of newspapers, and much of it in the narrow confines of 30-second television commercials or video news headlines.[27]

Those who hold political offices usually cannot buy the extensive and direct access to the mass media that is common when companies buy advertising time. With the small exception of election campaigns for major office, politicians cannot afford the advertising budgets that guarantee corporations unmediated access to vast audiences. In simple terms, Proctor and Gamble has more time to sell its products on the major networks than all 435 members of the House of Representatives have to present their views. Political persuaders who want to communicate with the American public must typically reach them in the "free" context of a news story where they may be only one of many players. By attracting news reporters to a speech or press conference, they hope to earn a precious few seconds of free time in a nightly television newscast or several column inches of print in the daily press. With the rare exception of cable television's C-SPAN (which covers proceedings of the House and Senate), their messages are mediated. The "gatekeepers" of the mass media operate under severe time or space limitations which alter the original form and content of most political discourse.[28] A presidential candidate making a major policy statement in a campaign appearance, for example, may hope that enough attention is given to his or her views to influence public discussion on the issue. The network journalists following the candidate have their own priorities and limitations. Perhaps only 45 seconds of air time about the politician is available in a newscast. On a given day the media gatekeepers may also want to use visually interesting film, perhaps of the candidate's car as it was dented in a minor accident on the way to a campaign appearance. The journalist might decide to indulge in the ego-satisfying routine of appearing in an on-camera "stand upper" to summarize the activities of the day. The resulting report represents a mix of motivations that make it unlikely that viewers at home will see an unedited segment of anything as complex as a lengthy speech. The typical campaign news story features shots of the candidate going through the rituals of campaigning while the journalist on the scene does a "voice over" narrative telling us what the candidate *did*. Less frequently are we granted the opportunity to hear what the candidate actually *said*.[29]

Here, for example, is a transcript of a complete CBS report on a 1980 campaign visit of President Jimmy Carter to Philadelphia. The reporter, Lesley Stahl, tells us what Carter did, and suggests the political motivations behind his campaign visit; she neglects any mention of the campaigner's ideas.

> What did President Carter do today in Philadelphia? He posed, with as many different types of symbols as he could possibly find. There was a picture at the daycare center. And one during the game of bocci ball with the senior citizens. Click, another picture with a group of teenagers. And then he performed the ultimate media event—a walk through the Italian market. The point of all this, obviously, was to get on the local news broadcasts and in the morning newspapers. It appeared that the President's intention was not to say anything controversial.... Simply the intention was to be seen, as he was, and it was photographed, even right before his corned beef and cabbage lunch at an Irish restaurant with the popular Bill Green.... There were more symbols at the Zion (black) Baptist Church.... Over the past three days the President's campaign has followed a formula-travel into a must-win state, spending only a short time there but ensuring several days of media coverage... And today the President got a bonus, since the Philadelphia TV markets extend deeply into neighboring New Jersey—another must-win state.[30]

What Stahl missed was what print reporters such as UPI's Helen Thomas at least mentioned: that Carter on this specific occasion expressed concern over the fact that a split in the Democratic Party could lead to a Reagan victory; that American hostages were apparently no closer to being released by their Iranian captors, and that he felt the economic recession had "bottomed out."[31] Stahl's coverage is representative of modern political reporting because it tells consumers more about the *strategies* than the *substance* of politics. She was no doubt right to conclude that President Carter was using various types of audiences to increase his visibility and attractiveness in an important "must-win" state. Carter and his staff, however, must have felt some frustration on learning that virtually nothing of what he said to those audiences was reported to viewers of the CBS Evening News.[32]

To be sure, most of what we know about our world always has been communicated to us through intervening sources, even this book. While we expect a great deal from our politicians and those who report on their activities, it must also be remembered that millions of Americans are unwilling to match their high expectations of politicians with a willingness to pay attention to the political discourse available to them. Compared to other Western nations, for example, citizens in the United States vote in paltry numbers. A "good turnout" is about 50 percent of all eligible voters, compared to 70 to 80 percent in many European countries.[33] In addition, in spite of our advanced levels of education, Americans have relatively low levels of knowledge about issues and events. Many citizens lack even an elemental understanding of a candidate's positions on basic campaign issues.[34] The leaders of the mass media know that levels of political interest are low; they are therefore not likely to devote more time and space to news that may create bored viewers or subscribers. These constraints on modern journalism make it unlikely that detailed and complex ideas will be fully reported in the most popular news sources such as the three major television networks. Like many other kinds of persuaders, politicians are limited by the willingness of their audiences to listen.

"Expedient" and "Principled" Messages: A False Distinction

Finally, no overview of political persuasion would be complete without at least touching on the issue of ethics. If indeed we are "political creatures," for most of us it is not a feature that bears witness to the greatness of our species. We like to see evidence that a politician has demonstrated "political courage," but the more timeless image is of the relentless and frequently corrupt opportunist. Thomas Nast's turn of the century political cartoons (see Figure 9.4) still reflect this part of our folklore. In Nast's day as now, the politico is frequently a cynic, grossly over-inflated with a misplaced sense of self-importance and greed.

Some of the most potent figures in dramatic literature are characters caught in the classic bind between a sense of personal duty and the need to maintain a "public" face. Shakespeare used this dilemma in many plays; strong and decisive heroes such as Coriolanus are forced to weigh their private ideals against the need to say the "right" political things to satisfy potential allies. Of the honest Coriolanus who says what he thinks even when it is "impolitic," a friend observes that "His nature is too noble for the world." Because he has little interest in winning the support of others, he stands out as the non-political hero, a man who "would not flatter Neptune for his Trident."[35] In more contemporary dramas, Robert Redford's Bill McKay and Alan Alda's Senator in the film, The Seduction of Joe Tynan," are shown trying to survive in an alien world filled with people who lack the strength to stand by their own principles.

American attitudes toward politics are heavily shaped by images like these. We seem to be guided by the assumption that there are expedient or principled forms of political behavior, and that it is relatively easy to discern the differences. It is an item of faith that "public servants" are easily "bought off" by factions or special interests which effectively thwart what should be done to assure the greater public good. When examples contradict our expectations, we are easily surprised. For instance, a western Senator who urges the breakup of large oil companies is taking a position that would seem to

Figure 9.4

One of many Thomas Nast cartoons depicting corruption and
greed in New York City's political machine, Tammany Hall.

Used by permission of Oxford University Press.

involve considerable political risk. The narrow interests of the oil
industry in the West would probably favor fewer and larger
companies. Moreover, we would routinely conclude that campaign
funds had been dependent upon "big oil" interests. To account for the
failure to behave as we would have predicted, we might conclude that
the position resulted from conviction to principle rather than the
dictates of contributors. A midwestern Senator who supports a
Presidential boycott of the sale of wheat to the Soviet Union is in a
similar situation. Wheat farmers are aided when large surpluses of
their crops are sold to Eastern European countries. Since the support
of a boycott helps to drive down the value of constituents' crops, we
may conclude that the Senator did not make the expedient "political"
choice but rather chose the harder "principled" decision not to aid a

communist state. These are exceptions. We usually expect politicians to be smoother versions of the "Senator Claghorn" mentioned in Chapter 4.

We explore the issue here because no image more clearly characterizes the political persuader than that of the human weathervane blown by the winds of public opinion. As do many generalizations, this one falls apart when examined more closely. The reality is far more complex and much less simplistic. A problem with the examples of the Senators above making hard choices, for example, is that while they may *seem* to be acting in accordance to higher principles, they could also be judged as negligent of the people who elected them. Would they have been less noble if they had reflected the interests of their own constituents? Doesn't the very idea of representation include the "special interests" such as farmers, students, the elderly, or the oil industry? Democratic politics is a process of turning conflict into consensus; we should expect that the diversity of political opinions on any one question will reflect the diversity of opinion in society as a whole. It is easy to forget that democracies are based on the idea that pluralism is desirable, and that the "special interests" of citizens deserve representation. On many political issues there will be no public consensus, only a collection of splintered opinions and opposing coalitions.

Without doubt, political persuasion does occasionally deserve its poor reputation. There are clearly instances when public opinion is ignored because of the excessive power of special interest lobbies. It would be simplistic, however, to assume that every statement that defends a politician's known interests is somehow an indicator of weak-willed opportunism. Politicians make decisions for many thoughtful reasons. Some believe they must serve as a *representative* of those who elected them, sacrificing their own feelings to vote the way they perceive public opinion at home. Others function more as *trustees*, prepared to ignore public opinion in favor of their own determination of what is the best course of action.[36] Neither position is inherently superior. The first appears to be more "democratic," but the second, as then Senator John Kennedy noted, carries its own legitimate objectives:

> The voters selected us, in short, because they had confidence in our judgment and our ability to exercise that judgment from a position where we could determine what were their own best interests, as part of the nation's interests. This may mean that we must on occasion lead, inform, correct, and sometimes even ignore constituent opinion, if we are to exercise fully that judgment for which we were elected. But acting without selfish motive or private bias, those who follow the dictates of an intelligent conscience are not

aristocrats, demogogues, eccentrics or callous politicians insensitive to the feelings of the public.[37]

Any reader of contemporary political biographies is likely to be impressed by the sympathy individual politicians earn from even the most hardened observers. The same is true for most Americans, who usually express much more positive regard for *their* local Senators or Representatives than for the Congress as whole.[38] We think a good lesson of these findings is that we are too quick to dismiss political arguments and attitudes we disagree with as "expedient," and too comfortable with the easy judgment that those who think like we do are "principled."

Summary

In this chapter, we have illustrated the scope of American political persuasion by surveying a number of representative cases and issues. No brief space is adequate to describe the wealth of thought and research that has been directed to the processes involved in shaping public opinion. However, this chapter does offer some broad conclusions that the thoughtful student of persuasion should keep in mind. Among the more important observations reached here are a number that cut against the grain of everyday thought, specifically:

- The low repute in which most political rhetoric is held probably says as much about the competence of the public as the politician. Political appeals are a reflection of the society in which they are shaped.
- Unlike product advertising, political persuasion is concerned with portraying the positive and negative consequences that result (a) from the election of people with certain character traits, and (b) from the choice of policies intended to deal with social or economic problems.
- The processes of political communication can lead to deplorable decisions, such as occurred under Hitler in Germany's Third Reich. Those same basic processes placed at the disposal of decent leaders can remedy serious wrongs, such as the relatively recent actions against policies restricting the rights of women and minorities to vote.
- All of us have a considerable stake in political persuasion because it precedes (and warns us about) decisions that will alter our relationships with each other and with the state.
- In comparison to product advertising, political persuasion must overcome greater obstacles. Although the subject matter of politics can be vitally important, the abilities of advocates to communicate with constituents are restricted by news media filters and by public apathy.

Notes

[1] A portion of a radio report on the near-meltdown of the Three Mile Island nuclear power plant near Harrisburg, Pennsylvania, in Susan Stamberg, *Every Night at Five* (New York: Pantheon, 1982), 91-92. A discussion of news coverage of this crisis and others can be found in Dan Nimmo and James E. Combs, *Nightly Horrors: Crisis Coverage in Television and Network News* (Knoxville: University of Tennessee, 1985).

[2] Richard E. Neustadt, *Presidential Power: The Politics of Leadership* (New York: John Wiley and Sons, 1960), 33-57.

[3] Dan Rather and Mickey Herskowitz, *The Camera Never Blinks* (New York: Ballantine Books, 1978), 163.

[4] Helen Thomas, *Dateline: White House* (New York: Macmillan, 1975), 73-74.

[5] Robert MacNeil, *The Right Place at the Right Time* (Boston: Little, Brown, 1982), 228. For other accounts of Johnson as an interpersonal persuader, see Merle Miller, *Lyndon: An Oral Biography* (New York: Ballantine, 1980), Chaps. 2 and 4; and Kathleen J. Turner, *Lyndon Johnson's Dual War: Vietnam and the Press* (Chicago: University of Chicago Press, 1985), Chaps. 1, 2, and 3.

[6] A good overview of campaign persuasion is found in Judith Trent and Robert Friedenberg, *Political Campaign Communication* (New York: Praeger, 1983).

[7] Charles Peters, *How Washington Really Works* (Reading, MA: Addison Wesley, 1980), 48.

[8] Two other films which also deal with the issues of political opportunism and courage are Frank Capra's 1939 classic *Mr. Smith Goes to Washington* and Sidney Lumet's 1986 story of an amoral political consultant entitled *Power*. The increasing power of political consultants is documented in Larry J. Sabato, *The Rise of Political Consultants* (New York: Basic Books, 1981).

[9] The traditional American antipathy to politics is discussed in John H. Bunzel, *Anti-Politics in America* (New York: Vintage, 1970).

[10] Ann Firor Scott and Andrew M. Scott, *One Half the People* (New York: J.B. Lippincott, 1975), 9.

[11] Sherna Gluck, ed., *From Parlor to Prison* (New York: Vintage, 1976), 22.

[12] Scott and Scott, 39.

[13] William Safire, *Safire's Political Dictionary* (New York: Ballantine, 1978), 383-384.

[14] An interesting case study of legislative lobbying is T.R. Reid's *Congressional Odyssey: The Saga of a Senate Bill* (San Francisco: W.H. Freeman, 1980).

[15] Peters, 132.

[16] James David Barber, *The Presidential Character: Predicting Performance in the White House* (Englewood Cliffs, NJ: Prentice-Hall, 1972), 446.

[17] Ronald Reagan, Remarks and a Question and Answer Session with Farmers from the Landenberg, Pennsylvania Area, 14 May 1982, in *Public Papers of the Presidents of the United States, 1982*, Bk. I (Washington: U.S. Government Printing Office, 1983), 629.

[18] Quoted in Arthur Bernon Tourtellot, *The Presidents on the Presidency* (New York: Doubleday, 1964), 72.

[19]For a discussion of voter awareness of issues, see Thomas E. Patterson, *The Mass Media Election* (New York: Praeger, 1980), 153-169.

[20]Lyndon Johnson, Address to a Joint Session of Congress, Washington, D.C., 15 March 1965, in *Presidential Rhetoric (1961-1980)*, Second Edition, ed. Theodore Windt (Dubuque, IA: Kendall/Hunt, 1980), 67.

[21]Murray Edelman, *The Symbolic Uses of Politics* (Urbana, IL: University of Illinois, 1967), 6.

[22]Robert E. Denton, Jr. and Gary C. Woodward, *Political Communication in America* (New York: Praeger, 1985), 206.

[23]Edelman, 5.

[24]Joseph R. Gusfield, *Symbolic Crusade: Status Politics and the American Temperance Movement* (Urbana, IL: University of Illinois, 1963), 22.

[25]A persuasive speech suggesting that the Equal Rights Amendment would have made a big difference for women is Shirley Chisholm's, "For the Equal Rights Amendment," in *American Rhetoric from Roosevelt to Reagan*, ed. Halford Ross Ryan (Prospect Heights, IL: Waveland, 1983), 222-226.

[26]Kenneth G. Hance, Homer O. Hendrickson, and Edwin W. Schoenberger, "The Later National Period: 1860-1930," in *A History and Criticism of American Public Address, Vol. I*, ed. William Norwood Brigance (New York: Russell and Russell, 1960), 113.

[27]For interesting discussions of political information presented via television news, print reports, and television advertising, see Michael J. Robinson and Margaret A. Sheehan, *Over the Wire and on TV: CBS and UPI in Campaign 80* (New York: Russell Sage, 1980); and Thomas E. Patterson and Robert D. McClure, *The Unseeing Eye: The Myth of Television Power in National Politics* (New York: C.P. Putnam, 1976). The second study offers the surprising conclusion that political television commercials carry more useful information about candidates than many television news reports.

[28]See, for example, Dan Nimmo and James E. Combs, *Mediated Political Realities* (New York: Longman, 1983), 21-140; and Edward Jay Epstein, *News From Nowhere: Television and the News* (New York: Vintage, 1973), 3-238.

[29]For discussions of the many constraints on television news, see Robert MacNeil, *The People Machine: The Influence of Television on American Politics* (New York: Harper and Row, 1968), 38-55; and W. Lance Bennett, *News: The Politics of Illusion* (New York: Longman, 1983), 1-30.

[30]Quoted in Robinson and Sheehan, 5.

[31]Robinson and Sheehan, 6.

[32]On the subjects of politics and journalism, two conclusions are certain. Many reporters will talk about the "free ride" an administration received on many stories, and members of an administration will complain about the unfair reporting of the press. For an unusually thoughtful book illustrating the latter objection, see Jody Powell, *The Other Side of the Story* (New York: William Morrow, 1984). Powell was Carter's Press Secretary.

[33]Eugene H. Roseboom and Alfred E. Eckes, Jr., *A History of Presidential Elections*, Fourth Edition (New York: Macmillan, 1979), 336; David L. Paletz and Robert M. Entman, *Media Power Politics* (New York: Free Press, 1981), 234-241.

[34]For a theoretical presentation of this view, see Murray Edelman, *The Symbolic Uses of Politics* (Urbana, IL: University of Illinois, 1964), 1-43. Many

descriptive studies of the mass media and political information have been done. See Patterson, *The Mass Media Election*, 153-169; and Michael J. Robinson, "American Political Legitimacy in an Era of Electronic Journalism: Reflections on the Evening News," in *Television as a Social Force: New Approaches to T.V. Criticism* (New York: Praeger, 1975), 97-139.

[35]William Shakespeare, *Coriolanus*, ed. Reuben Brower (New York: Signet, 1966), 254-255.

[36]William J. Keefe and Morris S. Ogul, *The American Legislative Process: Congress and the States*, Second Edition (Englewood Cliffs, NJ: Prentice-Hall, 1968), 63-65.

[37]John F. Kennedy, *Profiles in Courage*, Memorial Edition (New York: Harper and Row, 1964), 36-37.

[38]Michael J. Robinson, "Three Faces of Congressional Media," in *Media Power Politics*, ed. Doris Graber (Washington, DC: Congressional Quarterly Press, 1984), 219.

Questions and Projects for Further Study

1. Identify and explain the meanings of two or three condensation symbols (words, people, or things) that have been prominent in the discussion of recent political issues. What makes the symbols potent as expressions of feelings within a group or movement?

2. An interesting way to experience firsthand the process of "mediation" is to attend a City Council Meeting, a session of the State Assembly, or an address given by a leading political leader. After observing one of these events, compare your overall impressions with the coverage provided by newspapers, radio, or television stations in your area. Did the mediation offer an accurate summary of what occurred or did it present a misleading picture?

3. Plan a group-viewing of the film, "The Candidate" (available on videocassette). After the film, compare your impressions. Specific questions to discuss might include:
   - Do you think the film is an accurate portrayal of the way modern election campaigns are run?
   - Who is responsible for the superficial nature of some political campaigns?
   - How did Bill MacKay convince so many voters to support him?
   - How would you like to see political campaigns change?
   - Which of the settings (political commercials, television news reports, rallies, and debates) offered the best opportunity for the public to assess the candidates?

4. The speeches of all modern Presidents are available in most libraries as part of a continuing series of volumes collectively titled *Public Papers of the Presidents of the United States*. Using one volume from a recent Presidency, find segments of speeches or remarks that illustrate the three subject areas of political persuasion.

5. Interview a local politician (council member, member of the State House or Senate) in person or by mail. Ask the politician to consider some of the persuasion approaches cited in the chapter. For example: What effect does he or she think lobbyists have on his/her own decision-making? Do members of the local mass media do an adequate job of presenting new ideas and proposals to interested constituents and voters? Does the politician see him/herself as primarily a "trustee" or "representative?" Would he or she agree with Edelman and the text authors about the general low level of political information in the general public?

6. In this chapter, we mention several social movements which have pushed for legislative action in civil rights, voter rights, abortion,

the Equal Rights Amendment, and so on. What major social issues are highly visible now? Do the activists in those movements share any of the tactics cited in the 1920 campaign to secure the vote for women? Are any of the current movements justifiably seen as raising "status issues?"

Additional Reading

Denton, Robert E., Jr.; and Gary C. Woodward. *Political Communication in America.* New York: Praeger, 1985.

Edelman, Murray. *The Symbolic Uses of Politics.* Urbana, IL: University of Illinois, 1963.

Gusfield, Joseph R. *Symbolic Crusade: Status Politics and the American Temperance Movement.* Urbana, IL: University of Illinois, 1963.

Nimmo, Dan; and James E. Combs. *Mediated Political Realities.* New York: Longman, 1983.

Paletz, David L.; and Robert M. Entman. *Media Power Politics.* New York: Free Press, 1981.

Sabato, Larry J. *The Rise of Political Consultants.* New York: Basic Books, 1981.

Stewart, Charles; Craig Smith; and Robert E. Denton, Jr. *Persuasion and Social Movements.* Prospect Heights, IL: Waveland Press, 1984.

Trent, Judith; and Robert Friedenberg. *Political Campaign Communication.* New York: Praeger, 1983.

PART 4

PRACTICAL APPLICATIONS

In previous chapters, we have explored persuasion from a variety of viewpoints. We have examined its origins in the western world, its symbolic nature, its theoretical roots in social, psychological, and philosophical studies, and its commercial and political uses. Up to this point, our primary goal has been to increase your understanding of how persuasion concepts and theories can account for changes in the attitudes of others. Persuasion is by nature a *practical* subject that marries theory to practice. Anyone committed to a full understanding of persuasion also needs the experience of applying general concepts to specific *applications*. Therefore, in the following three chapters our emphasis changes from *description* to *prescription* as we explore a number of practical suggestions ranging from how to gain news coverage for a social cause to the use of interpersonal strategies to increase sales. The task of successfully exercising influence over others is divided into chapters that include approaches for dealing with the largest mass media audiences as well as skills used by communicators engaged in direct face-to-face interaction. In Chapter 10, we begin with a look at the techniques employed by persuaders seeking to influence diverse audiences through many channels of communication including the mass media. Chapter 11 presents a complete sequence of steps and suggestions on how to organize and deliver a persuasive speech for a specific audience. Chapter 12 presents an overview of a number of techniques employed by individuals engaged in persuasion that is intensively focused on one or two other people.

10

Public and Mass Persuasion

 OVERVIEW

All this talk—this public talk—with which we are being inundated is not talk for the sake of talk. There is a reason for it—man has no other means as efficient as public communication for solving his problems, for creating and maintaining organizations, or for collectively making and implementing decisions.[1]

We experience the process of communication and persuasion in a wide variety of contexts ranging from sitting alone thinking to participating in a mass demonstration. There are three basic levels of persuasion: intrapersonal, interpersonal, and public. Although the essential processes of persuasion are alike at each level, there are noticeable differences in appeals, strategies, and tactics. Intrapersonal persuasion is communication with oneself. This form of communication provides cues about the self—our feelings, sensations, "who we are." Private cues are discerned from self-reflection and aid us in discovering our inner being and motives for our behavior. Interpersonal persuasion, the topic of Chapter 12, focuses on face-to-face interaction with others.

Public persuasion, the topic of this chapter, involves interactions of one with the larger society. Through public communication, we discuss issues, formulate and debate policy, campaign for public office, and implement societal reform and changes. As our society becomes more complex, individual and independent actions are no longer sufficient to guarantee success or survival. Other collectivities and groups impact us daily, and we join forces with others to insure that our views are heard and our needs are met.

Shearon Lowery and Melvin DeFleur argue that America has become a "mass society." For them, a mass society means more than a large number of citizens. It refers to "a distinctive pattern of social organization... a process of changing social organization that occurs when industrialization, urbanization, and modernization increasingly modify the social order."[2] Mass society emerges when:

1. social differentiation in society increases,
2. informal social control erodes as traditional norms and values decline,

3. use of formal control increases as a more impersonal society develops,
4. social conflicts increase because of social differences, and
5. open and easy communication becomes difficult.

Especially since WWII, Americans have increasingly identified their "interests" with the goals of formal organizations such as unions, interest groups, professional associations, and political alliances. Our sense of potential and social power is established through our contacts with formal organizations.

In this chapter, we are going to investigate the nature of public communication and persuasion. Although many of the concepts and examples presented thus far are of a public nature, there are two special cases that deserve a more thorough investigation: campaigns and social movements.

Public Communication and Persuasion

Public communication may be defined as "the conscious attempt of humans to change or modify the beliefs, attitudes, values, and behaviors of an audience in the public arena through symbolic manipulation."[3] Americans engage in more public communication and oratory today than ever before in our nation's history. Media technology and the communications industry have increased the quantity and the quality of public communication. They have also changed the form and content of public discourse.

Public communication possesses several characteristics that distinguish it from other forms of communication.[4] Although these distinctions have been identified in other chapters, it is useful to review them briefly again.

1. Public communication is simply more "public." The interactions are not private and intimacy is sacrificed. The communication settings become less relevant. Although Barbara Walters, a television journalist for ABC, frequently interviews celebrities within the seemingly comfortable security of their homes, their responses will be shared with millions of people—people who can directly impact the personalities' future popularity and income.

2. The audience is larger, more diverse, heterogeneous, and anonymous. This makes audience analysis more difficult. One message must suffice for many different people with varying backgrounds,

beliefs, and values. Adapting to a diverse audience becomes nearly impossible. Appeals are more general, less specific, and often devoid of commitment. In addition, language tends to be more restricted and less precise.

3. Media impacts the form and content of interactions. Presentation of message depends upon the medium used. Television is naturally better suited for movement, action, and drama than radio. Newspapers and magazines offer expanded space for written messages allowing for more examples, details, and argumentation. The use of mass media restricts audience feedback and thus the interpretation of the message is vulnerable to misunderstanding.

4. Public communication allows greater possible impact and potential change. People, groups, and opinions can be mobilized quickly and behavior can be converted immediately.

Public communication also provides several social functions including information, persuasion, entertainment, and culture dissemination. Public communication shares information needed to conduct business and to regulate social life. It has a persuasive function that provides opportunities for various viewpoints or ideas to be presented, discussed, and debated. The entertainment function encompasses literary and presentational communication art forms. Finally, public communication preserves and disseminates all the rituals and ceremonies of our culture. Films, speeches, lectures, television programs, and other similar events create a cultural fabric that brings together people, groups, and ideas. Through public communication, humans deal with their environment at large; a bewildering variety of daily events is given a cultural meaning.

Persuasive Campaigns

Herbert Simons defines persuasive campaigns as "organized, sustained attempts at influencing groups or masses of people through a series of messages."[5] This definition of persuasive campaigns emphasizes three key characteristics. First, campaigns are generally well organized events. There is an identifiable organizational structure with leaders, goals, and established routines. Campaigns most often have beginning and ending dates. The second major characteristic of a campaign is the audience size of the persuasive endeavor. Persuasive messages are designed to appeal to groups and large numbers of people. As already discussed, this factor influences greatly the form and content of messages. Finally, this definition of persuasive campaigns argues that there are multiple messages and attempts to alter the beliefs, attitudes, values, or behaviors of a segment of the general public. Single messages or persuasive attempts are only parts of a larger, systematic plan of persuasion.

Types of Persuasive Campaigns

Broadly speaking, there are four types of campaigns. Product or commercial advertising campaigns were the focus of Chapter 8. The purpose of such campaigns is to sell specific ideas, products, or services of identifiable commercial organizations.

Political campaigns were briefly discussed in the last chapter. Political campaigns do more than elect public officials.[6] They serve not only to reinforce voter attitudes or to convert voter preference but also to motivate specific action such as voting or helping in campaigns. By discussing issues, campaigns may stimulate awareness about vital national concerns, candidate positions, or vote position modification. Political campaigns help to legitimize our brand of democracy by facilitating new leadership with attendant social rules, laws, and regulations. Campaign-created, meta-political images and social-psychological associations provide the glue that holds our political system together. Political campaigns offer personal involvement in many forms including direct participation, self-reflection and definition, social interaction and discussion, and aesthetic experiences of public drama and group life. Political campaigns, then, communicate and influence, reinforce and convert, increase enthusiasm and inform, motivate as well as educate.

Although related to political campaigns, issue campaigns attempt to get audiences to support a certain course of action or belief independent of our normal official political structure, system, or procedures. We have already discussed lobbying in Chapter 9. In this chapter we will explore more "public" forms of issue campaigns taken up by social movements.

Finally, within recent years, corporate image and advocacy campaigns have increased in prominence and thus justify special consideration. The object of such campaigns is not apparent from the context of the message.[7] Corporate image advertising has grown in recent years because companies need to disseminate messages not accepted by various media as "advertising" or "public relations." Corporations have also noted the value of possessing their own image and public "goodwill." Thus, corporate advertising is more concerned with image than products and encompasses symbolic, financial, advocacy/issue, recruiting, and special opportunity messages. Today, corporations compete for public attitudes and/or behavior that will influence legislators, purchase of products and decisions about stocks. For example, Dow Chemical Company has generated a series of television ads that portray young college graduates excited about the opportunity to solve the farming crisis by working for Dow Chemical. To an older generation, however, Dow Chemical is remembered for its chemical warfare products used in Vietnam. Obviously, to attract bright young people, Dow must present an image of a good, humanitarian corporation. A more issue oriented campaign is that sponsored by the Tobacco Institute that presents "words to non-smokers" advocating freedom of choice and the lack of danger to health of secondary smoke. (See Figure 1, Chapter 4).

Campaign Implementation

The key to the execution of any successful campaign is systematic planning. The basic steps in developing a campaign are the same regardless of its size, scope, or focus. There are six basic considerations: situation analysis, objectives and/or positioning, strategies, budget, implementation, and evaluation.[8]

1. A careful *situation analysis* provides an assessment of the social environment, potential audiences or market, strengths and weaknesses of the product or idea. From an advertising perspective, the situation analysis includes investigations of the consumer, the product, and the competition. Research becomes vital to this phase of campaign planning. There are two basic ways to gather information: secondary and primary research. Secondary research is finding relevant information that is already produced and collected by others. The major source of secondary research is the local library. Such research can provide a general orientation and guide for campaign planning. Primary research is original research conducted to gather specific information. For example, although secondary research efforts may reveal a national trend toward consumption of healthful food and drink, a specific survey may be needed to isolate appeals and categories of food items to target.

In terms of the audience, there are three descriptive variables that should be investigated. Demographic characteristics are derived from statistical studies of the population. Such characteristics include age, sex, income, education, family size, and occupation. Geographic characteristics focus on differences among urban, suburban and rural areas of the country as well as regional differences. Finally, psychographic analysis attempts to describe markets based on lifestyle issues, activities, interests, and opinions. Thus, the primary purpose of the situation analysis step of campaign planning is to gather needed information that will become the basis for designing the persuasive message, strategies, and execution.

2. After research has been conducted and analyzed, *objectives* should be determined. Objectives are clear, specific, and measurable

statements of desired outcomes of the campaign. Clear objectives help reduce uncertainty, direct message formation, and provide standards for evaluation. Some objectives may be stated in terms of unit or dollar sales. Others may address specific behavioral activity by the audience. For example, the targeted audience of the campaign may be asked to purchase a product, call a number, return a reply card, seek more information, contribute to a cause, vote for a specific candidate, or attend an event. Sometimes the objectives focus on communication effects such as general awareness, message recall, product knowledge and preference, or issue position conviction. Campaign organizers must know what the campaign seeks to accomplish. Different objectives will influence how the campaign is developed.

3. If objectives are concerned with *what* needs to be done, then *strategies* are concerned with *how* to do it. Strategic areas of concern include message construction, media selection, tactics, publicity and promotions. The goal of the message strategy, according to Michael Rothschild, is "to develop a message or a series of messages that will be informative and persuasive in their compelling presentation of relevant issues to the target audience."[9] The key to most successful strategies is to isolate the appeals, promises, solutions, or benefits that will have the greatest impact upon the target audience. Good research provides the clues to message creation and tactic selection. (Message construction strategies are discussed in detail in Chapters 5, 6 and Chapter 11).

4. Whether conducting a commercial advertising campaign or a political campaign, *budget* impacts all other elements of campaign design and development. For some campaigns, budgets are of little concern, but for others funds may be limited. Today with the cost of media, labor, and material, the campaign budget becomes a vital consideration in the formation of a campaign.

5. Finally, the campaign can be *implemented and evaluated*. A systematic evaluation of the campaign not only reveals what worked and what did not work but also allows for the fine-tuning of various campaign elements in order to maximize effectiveness. Commercial advertising campaign evaluation is a form of research that attempts to determine what actually happened in the marketplace and why. There are many things to measure other than a win-lose situation. Elements of awareness (knowledge, recall, or recognition), attitude (perceptions, feelings, or preference), and behavior (purchase, vote, or support) are examples of areas to assess and evaluate. Many of the same research techniques used in analyzing the situation can be used in evaluating the persuasive campaign.

Figure 10.1

Campaign Implementation Overview

Stage	Components
1. Situation analysis	target audience product/issue/idea competition or opponent
2. Objectives	mission goals outcomes
3. Strategies	messages media presentation activities
4. Budget	labor material media talent production
5. Implementation	timing follow-up
6. Evaluation	what people say what people think what people do

Social Movements

There have been times in our nation's history when large groups of citizens mobilized to express anger, support, or ideas about a wide variety of issues and topics. Groups were organized by race, sex, age, social or political beliefs. Their actions ranged from advocacy to violent demonstrations. From the American Revolution to the Moral Majority, Americans have always joined together to exercise, and sometimes even stretch, the principles of democracy. Such social collective actions are called social movements and are a special form or type of persuasive campaign. Charles Stewart, Craig Smith, and Robert Denton argue that social movements are unique with special characteristics that distinguish them from other forms and functions of mass persuasion.[10]

Characteristics of Social Movements

Social movements must have a *minimal organization*. This means that there are identifiable leaders and proclaimed followers. Some movements are more organized than others. During the 1960s, the civil rights movement was well organized with Martin Luther King recognized as the major leader; the American Indian movement was less visible and much smaller in scope. It should be noted that there may be many organizations within the same basic movement. For example, within the prolife movement there are various religious and secular organizations that seek legislation limiting abortions.

Social movements are *uninstitutionalized collectivities* because they operate outside the established social order. This means that access to institutional channels of power, communication, and funding are not available. Thus, movement actions are often considered improper or extreme. The movement leader has little control over members. Persuasion is the sole means of accomplishing the various goals.

Movements *propose or oppose programs for change in societal norms, values, or both.* Innovative social movements are those that seek to replace or to reform existing norms or values with totally new ones. Examples of innovative movements include women's rights, black civil rights, or gay liberation movements. Revivalistic movements seek replacement or reform of existing norms or values with ones from an idealized past. The "Native American" and the "Back to Africa" movements are examples of revivalistic movements. Finally, resistance movements are those that seek to block changes in the existing norms or values. Often, such movements favor the status quo and arise in opposition to newly formed movements. Examples of resistance movements would be prochoice, pro-Vietnam, and anti black civil rights movements. Classification of movements is difficult because perceptions of members and audiences vary. A movement may seem just and moderate to some members but radical to many citizens.

Social movements are *countered by an established order*. The established order is more than just governmental officials. It includes various organizations such as universities, churches, businesses, regulatory bodies, and so on. The established order has many resources and avenues available to confront and to stall movement actions.

Movements must be *significantly large in scope*. Although a general characteristic, movements must be large enough in terms of geographic area, time, and participants to accomplish specified programs and tasks. The larger the movement, the greater the visibility and funding possibilities.

Martin Luther King was one of the Civil Rights movement's most successful advocates. Here, he addresses a crowd in Chicago's Soldier Field.

Wide World Photos, Inc.

Finally, *persuasion is the essence* of social movements. As Stewart, Smith, and Denton argue, "persuasion is a communication process by which a social movement seeks through the use of verbal and nonverbal symbols to affect the perceptions of audiences and thus to bring about desired changes in ways of thinking, feeling, and/or acting."[11] Violence associated with social movements is incidental and used primarily for symbolic purposes. Persuasion is the primary means for satisfying the major functions and requirements of social movements.

Persuasive Functions of Social Movements

Stewart, Smith and Denton identify five basic persuasive functions of social movements: transform perceptions of history, alter perceptions of society, prescribe courses of action, mobilize for action, and sustain the social movement.[12] Transforming perceptions of history include altering perceptions of the past, present, and future. Movements must challenge accepted ways of viewing historical events in order to emphasize the severity of a problem and the need for drastic action. While most Americans initially viewed our involvement in Vietnam as support for a free, democratic country against communist aggression, some Americans claimed that our actions were aggressive, intrusive, and providing aid for a dictator and his repressive government. The women's movement had to confront the established view that the woman's place was in the home caring for the children while the husband established a career and provided for the family.

There are several ways in which movements alter the perceptions of the present. For example, renaming or redefining an event or object provides an opportunity for people to view the circumstance differently. Within the prolife movement, language referring to the fetus as a baby and abortion as murder has a strong impact upon a listener. Movements create "god terms" and "devil terms" to create clear images of good and bad behavior or thought. For most Americans "god terms" include democracy, freedom, liberty, equality, and justice, to name only a few. "Devil terms" would be opposite notions such as communism, slavery, or prejudice. Another common way to alter perceptions of the present is to provide information that counters or demonstrates inconsistencies with the information provided by the established order.

Social movement leaders, like political candidates, must provide a utopian vision of the future that is full of hope and optimism. At the same time, the utopian future is tempered by bleak images if the goals of the movement are not met.

In transforming perceptions of society, movements must not only

Demonstrators of conflicting opinions concerning abortion show their signs in front of St. Patrick's Cathedral in New York on March 8, 1985.
Wide World Photos, Inc.

alter perceptions of the opposition but must also alter the current perceptions of the movement and its members. The opposition must be portrayed as bad with selfish motives and no redeeming value. The opposition are grand conspirators who have secretly committed a crime against the people. They are, according to the movement, the sole cause of the problem at hand. The opposition is subjected to name-calling, ridicule, and cruel associations. The movement is simply "at war" with the opposition.

Social movements must transform self-perceptions of members to believe in the righteousness of their cause and in their power to accomplish the goals of the movement. For example, the women's liberation movement conducted "consciousness-raising" groups to enhance self-concept, dignity, and worth. Through this transformation, women could recognize their potential and gain strength to compete in a "man's world." Blacks selected the word black to replace the word Negro which was selected by whites. "Black power" became the symbol for independence, power, and dignity.

In prescribing courses of action, social movements must first explain what should be done. Movements must not only develop a program of change with specific demands, actions, and solutions to problems, but they must also sell, defend, and justify the program to the people. In addition, movements must prescribe who ought to do the job. They provide rationales why their organization, leaders, and members are best to bring about the desired change. Finally, movements must articulate how the changes should be brought about. This may be one of the more critical persuasive tasks. Movement members differ in terms of intensity of identification, social abuse, and patience. Thus, the more radical factions or members may prefer ultimatums, confrontation, or terrorism to bring about the desired change. Others may prefer nonviolent resistance tactics such as sit-ins, boycotts, or strikes. Others may simply wish to petition the establishment for a fair hearing, preferring to work within the legislative structure to bring about the desired change.

The most difficult persuasive task for any movement leader is to inspire people to believe, join, and participate in the movement. Movements encounter much opposition, and available channels of communication are restricted. The movement's message must be disseminated continually in order to attract new members and to maintain old ones. Leaders must unify, organize, and energize a diverse membership while simultaneously pressuring the opposition.

Social movements often last for years; sustaining a movement is a major persuasive task. It is easier to start a movement than to maintain one. Leaders must justify setbacks and remain optimistic about accomplishing movement goals. For the movement to be successful, it must remain visible and viable. As a movement becomes older, these tasks become more difficult.

The Life Cycle of Social Movements

Although it is nearly impossible to divide movements into separate phases, there are recognizable patterns of development. Stewart, Smith, and Denton identify five stages of social movements: genesis, social unrest, enthusiastic mobilization, maintenance, and termination.[13] As a movement matures, the persuasive requirements evolve and change among the various stages.

In the genesis stage, primarily intellectuals articulate some imperfection in society through essays, editorials, songs, poems, pamphlets, lectures or books. They identify a problem and visualize a bleak future if the problem is not solved. Bob Dylan and others addressed the Vietnam war in folk songs nearly a year before the Gulf of Tonkin incident that escalated American involvement in the conflict. Betty Freidan's book entitled *The Feminine Mystique* initiated the women's movement by addressing status and the need for change. Such works provide public discussion about key issues. Sometimes a special event will trigger attention to an issue or cause. The Supreme Court Decision of 1973 allowing abortion in all the states provided the impetus for creating the prolife movement.

In the social unrest stage, leaders become agitators and the purpose and goals of the movement develop. Concerned citizens become active members. The movement produces its own literature and leaders accept all available forums for public discussion and debate. This phase of the movement is relatively short in comparison to the others.

The enthusiastic mobilization period of a social movement is exciting. The charismatic leader emerges and captures a great deal of attention for the movement and its issues. Membership expands to include sympathizers from both the general public and the establishment. All available channels and means of communication are utilized to advance the cause. The movement must now confront serious opposition and the strategies extend beyond legislative petition and discursive measures. Mass rallies and demonstrations are used to disseminate the movement's message and to pressure the opposition. The persuasive goal of the movement during this phase is to raise the consciousness level of the public and to force the establishment to comply with its demands.

It is difficult to maintain the energy and enthusiasm of the earlier stages. As defeats mount and goals are not immediately realized, the members become impatient and the public becomes bored. In the maintenance stage, persuasive tactics focus on legislative measures, membership retention, and fund raising. The leadership changes from agitators to statesmen. The primary channels of communication are newsletters, journals, and the occasional television talk show. Sweeping demands are compromised and the rhetoric is moderated. As noted earlier, movement visibility and viability are primary concerns.

In the termination stage, the social movement ceases to be a social movement. The movement may have accomplished its goal as did the anti-slavery movement of 1865 with the passage of the Thirteenth Amendment to the Constitution or it may be transformed into part of the establishment as was the Nazi movement in Germany. Some movements die while others become pressure groups such as the Native American Indian movement or the consumer rights movement. Few social movements are totally successful in their efforts. Some members become disaffected with the movement and drop out or join a splinter group while others simply become part of "the system."

Each stage requires specific persuasive skills, personalities, and tactics. In open societies, social movements are often the primary initiators to social change. Thus, although all social movements end, they do impact society in a variety of ways such as new laws, social awareness, or new social groups, to name only a few.

Summary

Public persuasion differs from interpersonal persuasion in size and scope. The larger the audience, the more elements of persuasion that are needed to alter beliefs, attitudes, and values. Collective action requires general understanding and agreement on goals and objectives. Mass persuasion requires numerous messages, numerous appeals, and numerous communication channels. Persuasive campaigns, therefore, are a highly organized and constructed series of messages. The messages are designed to appeal to groups and large numbers of people.

The systematic planning and execution of a campaign include the processes of analyzing the situation, developing objectives, strategies, and budget, and campaign implementation and evaluation. These processes are true for all types of campaigns: political, product advertising, issue, or corporate image and advocacy campaigns.

Although a form of public persuasion, social movements are unique collective phenomena that are more complex than campaigns. Persuasion is the essence of social movements that must transform perceptions of history, alter current norms of society, prescribe courses of action, mobilize for action, and sustain the movement. Across the various stages of a movement—genesis, social unrest, enthusiastic mobilization, maintenance, and termination—persuasion requirements evolve and change.

Social movements have played an important role in our society. They have stimulated argument and debate about human rights, war, and peace. They have provided the catalyst for social change and legislative action. Public persuasion is a vital part of a democratic society, influencing what we want, what we buy, what we think, and how we interact with others.

Notes

[1]Roderick Hart, Gustav Friedrick and William Brooks, *Public Communication* (New York: Harper & Row, 1975), 12.

[2]Shearon Lowery and Melvin DeFleur, *Milestones in Mass Communication Research* (New York: Longman, 1983), 10.

[3]Molefi Asante and Jerry Frye, *Contemporary Public Communication: Applications* (New York: Harper & Row, 1977), 13.

[4]The list is based upon those offered by Roderick Hart and Gustav Friedrick, *Public Communication* (New York:Harper & Row, 1975), 25-26.

[5]Herbert Simons, *Persuasion*, 2nd Edition (New York: Random House, 1986), 227.

[6]See Robert E. Denton, Jr. and Gary Woodward, *Political Communication in America* (New York: Praeger, 1985), 71-97.

[7]Simons, 78.

[8]There are numerous classifications of campaign planning and execution. The one used here is found in Michael Rothschild, *Advertising* (Lexington, MA: D.C. Heath and Co., 1987), 10-14.

[9]Rothschild, 180.

[10]See Charles Stewart, Craig Smith and Robert E. Denton, Jr., *Persuasion and Social Movements* (Prospect Heights, IL: Waveland Press, 1984).

[11]Stewart et al., 11.

[12]Stewart et al., see Chapter 5, 73-84.

[13]Stewart et al., see Chapter 3, 37-50.

Questions and Projects for Further Study

1. Select a product and find ads for the item in eight to ten different magazines. How are the ads similar? How do they differ?

2. Select an example of the following types of campaigns: commercial advertising, political, issue, and corporate image or advocacy. How are they similar? How do they differ?

3. Formulate a hypothetical product and develop a campaign according to the steps presented in the chapter.

4. According to the criteria presented in the chapter, which of the following is a social movement? Why?
   Survivalists
   Consumer rights
   Ecology
   American Indian
   Nazi
   Gray Panthers
   Tax reform

5. Select a social movement and demonstrate how the movement fulfills the persuasive functions identified in the chapter.

Additional Readings

Engel, James; Martin Warshaw; and Thomas Kinnear. *Promotional Strategy.* Homewood, IL: Richard Irwin, Inc., 1983.

Rothschild, Michael. *Advertising.* Lexington, MA: D.C. Heath, 1987.

Schultz, Don; Dennis Martin; and William Brown. *Strategic Advertising Campaigns.* Chicago, IL: Crain Books, 1984.

Stewart, Charles; Craig Smith; and Robert E. Denton, Jr. *Persuasion and Social Movements.* Prospect Heights, IL: Waveland Press, 1984.

Trent, Judith; and Robert Friedenberg. *Political Campaign Communication.* New York: Praeger, 1983.

Ineffective tools of persuasion

The Far Side. Copyright © 1987 Universal Press Syndicate.
Reprinted with permission. All rights reserved.

11

The Construction and Presentation of Persuasive Messages

 OVERVIEW

It is a great matter to know what to say...but how
to say it is a greater matter still.[1]

More than any other kind of communication, persuasion requires careful pre-planning. It may be possible to explain a non-controversial set of facts to an audience without much preparation, but persuasion requires more forethought. An American student attending college in England, for example, might feel comfortable "winging" an explanation of baseball rules to an interested English audience (although even such a simple presentation would benefit from planning). Imagine the increased burdens that student would face trying to prove that "On the whole, American newspapers are journalistically superior to their British counterparts." Since this second topic *in an English setting* calls for persuasion, the requirements are far greater. Such a claim would require tact as well as carefully rehearsed arguments fully supported by evidence.

Persuasive situations range from advertisements in the mass media to one-on-one encounters within a family. This chapter provides practical guidelines on preparing messages that fall in the middle of this continuum: persuasive speeches. Although persuasion clearly encompasses much more than speeches, speechmaking is still a common and representative form of communication. One recent study indicates that over half of a random sample of adults gave at least one speech in a two year period, with almost three-fourths of them giving four or more. The percentage rose dramatically for people with more years of education.[2] Even if you do not anticipate a career as a public communicator, a look at how persuasive messages are put together provides a useful opportunity to see how specific strategies of persuasion can produce concrete results. As we shall show, the process of constructing a persuasive message reveals a range of tactical questions that are otherwise overlooked. A thorough understanding of the process of persuasion must, at some point, move from theory to application.

Constructing a Persuasive Speech: Six Essential Steps

People often say that they are "writing a speech," but a speech on paper is only a guide for what really matters: the actual presentation to an audience. Just as the building produced by an architect is more than the blueprints, a speech is more than words. The communication which takes place between listeners and speakers at a particular point in time is the essence of the speech. What we actually write is a *plan* for that moment.

In the elementary but vital procedure described below, there is more thinking than writing. The suggested steps produce an *extemporaneous* sentence outline that serves as a flexible guide to every key idea, appeal, and phrase you want to use. This process avoids the tedious task of writing down every word, while it provides a sequence for locating the essential points that are right for you and your audience. The sentence outline provides built-in flexibility; for while the extemporaneous speech is planned, it allows enough freedom to adapt to unexpected situations and opportunities. As you read through these steps, it will also be apparent that this plan is a practical application of the "logic of good reasons" approach discussed in Chapter 5.

Know the Audience

Persuading an audience is similar to a journey over unfamiliar terrain. Your route has to be adjusted to fit the landscape of existing attitudes. As we indicated in Chapter 4, a fundamental requirement of communication is an awareness of *whom* you wish to influence. It is admittedly difficult to be precise about the attitudes, values, and interests of groups because people are too complex to be reduced to simple stereotypes. Since persuasion involves "adjusting ideas to people and people to ideas,"[3] thorough preparation starts with questions about the audience:

- How will they respond to your point of view?
- What do they know about you or your reputation?
- How interested are they in your topic?
- How much do they know about your topic?
- Has anything happened recently that would affect the audience's interest and attitudes?
- What position have opinion leaders in the audience taken on the topic?
- What feelings or values will you have to challenge when explaining and defending your position?
- Which audience values can be used as good reasons?

A skillful persuader can be successful even before a hostile audience. In 1983, Senator Edward Kennedy surprised his liberal supporters by accepting an invitation to address his political opponents at Liberty Baptist College.   Wide World Photos, Inc.

Your assessment of the audience through questions like these will point out what is possible in the speech. If you know that a respected member agrees with your position, for example, make reference to that fact during the speech. Conversely, if you know that many disagree, find areas of common agreement and document all assertions thoroughly.

Determine your Objectives

In 1931 the famous Irish author and socialist, George Bernard Shaw gave a radio speech that provoked strong criticism in the United States. Telephone lines linked England to the USA for the first time, and the British Broadcasting Corporation and CBS decided to share programming. One form of this international exchange featured Irish and British celebrities talking to American radio audiences. Shaw was clearly aware of his audience's negative attitudes toward Russia, but he plunged ahead in a calculated attempt to challenge his listeners to view the Great Depression as a sign of the failure of American capitalism.

> Hello America! Hello, all my friends in America! How are all you dear old boobs who have been telling one another for a month that I have gone dotty about Russia?... Russia has the laugh on us. She has us fooled, beaten, shamed, shown up, outpointed, and all but knocked out. We have lectured her from the heights of our modern superiority and now we are calling on the mountains to hide our blushes in her presence.... Our agriculture is ruined and our industries collapsing under the weight of our own productiveness because we have not found out how to distribute our wealth as well as produce it.[4]

Shaw's objective was to provoke his listeners, and he successfully angered so many that CBS felt compelled to give others time to respond on the air. It was classic Shaw; his best plays, speeches and essays were calculated to challenge comfortable ways of thinking. No doubt it is more typical for an advocate to work in less confrontational ways, but the playwright's audacity is an illustration that all persuaders must be clear about what they hope to achieve.

After determining the makeup of your audience, and their attitudes toward your topic, you are in a position to set realistic goals about what you can achieve. In some cases you may want an audience to *do* something: give money, volunteer time, pass on a message to others, or buy a product. In 1986, for example, there were a number of huge outdoor concerts on behalf of starving Africans, American farmers, victims of AIDS, and political prisoners. The audiences drawn by the entertainers heard many messages urging them to make financial contributions, to write letters, or to join organizations. In other cases, your goal may be to make listeners *think* differently about a topic: for example, to agree with the need for a new law or to accept or reject a person or idea. You have successfully found the objective for a speech when you know exactly what you want from your contact with the audience. Here are some representative cases:

Behavioral outcomes
- To get a jury member to vote for a "not guilty" verdict.
- To sign up volunteers or pledges for a campus organization.
- To have listeners vote for an all-Republican ticket.
- To make a sale.
- To discourage the purchase of products that your group is boycotting.
- To flood legislators with letters in support of a bill.
- To encourage changes in the eating, drinking or smoking habits of friends.

Attitude-centered outcomes
- To encourage an audience to appreciate the work of a controversial author, artist, or musician. ("The economist, John

Kenneth Galbraith, is one of America's most gifted writers.")
- To win supporters for a different philosophy. ("Everyone could benefit from the values held by vegetarians.")
- To encourage people to consider the merits of an unpopular position. ("The European idea of 'democratic socialism' has a lot of merit.")
- To convince an audience to lower or raise their opinion toward a figure in the present or the past. ("George Washington has been overrated as a president.")
- To redirect an audience's frustrations against one group toward another group. ("Tensions in the Middle-East are due less to the Palestinians than to the stubborn attitudes of major states in the region.")
- To remind people that the beliefs they already hold are worth keeping. ("Walt Disney was a great and innovative filmmaker.")
- To move listeners incrementally closer to accepting an attitude they still reject. ("Jimmy Carter was a good president.")

Some desired purposes may be impossible to achieve in one speech, such as a complete reversal of a group's opposition to a proposed law. Base your expectations on the fact that a single persuasive event will have limited impact. An American senator speaking to an all-white audience in a racially segregated country, for example, must know that he will not change fundamental attitudes. However, the senator may be satisfied if he contributes in a small way to internal and international pressure against a policy of racial segregation.[5] A solid statement of purpose is a guide to what is possible, given the specific circumstances you are likely to encounter. Even though you probably will not state them to your audience, write down your objectives and keep them in mind.

Determine your Thesis

To this point, your preparation has been largely concerned with thinking about the persuasive situation. Now that you have determined the nature of the audience, and have one or more objectives in mind, you are ready to draft the most important sentence of the speech. Write the thesis — the central idea, the primary point of view — that you want to communicate. It may take some time to arrive at a satisfactory thesis, but having done so, you have given yourself a guide that will enable you to construct everything else in the speech. The main parts of the message, the support you select, and even the introduction should follow the drafting of the thesis statement. *Think of this statement as the primary conclusion of the speech, the statement to which everything else in the speech is subordinate.* It should be the one idea listeners will be able to recall weeks later.

Inexperienced communicators are tempted to skip the thesis-writing stage and begin preparing the rest of the speech, or they may substitute a one- or two-word topic for a genuine thesis statement. Failure to enforce one central idea on your planning can result in wasted time and disorganization. Locating a general topic rather than a specific thesis falls short of providing the guidance necessary to construct the rest of the speech. For example, it is not enough to prepare a persuasive message centered on phrases such as "seat belt laws" or "the 55 mile-per-hour speed limit." Both topics are ripe for advocacy, but persuasive attempts on these issues should be constructed from more sharply defined declarative sentences. Consider the following thesis statements, all of which are far more explicit:

- Some airlines are risking lives by cutting corners on maintenance in order to save money.
- This state should pass a law that makes the wearing of seat belts mandatory.
- The 55 mile-per-hour speed limit on the nation's highways has made them safer and should be maintained.
- Cuba's Castro is not the evil villain most American presidents have made him out to be.
- The recording of albums onto audio tape cassettes amounts to theft and is morally wrong.
- The three television networks neglect the needs and interests of older Americans.
- Gerald Ford has been underrated as a president and world leader.
- Beer and wine advertising should be banned from all radio and television broadcasts.
- Television program producers should be required to indicate when a program is using "canned" laughter.
- Dollar for dollar, Ford products are more thoughtfully designed than those of General Motors.
- It was a mistake for the United States to withdraw from the United Nations organization, UNESCO.
- Pittsburgh, Pennsylvania is a terrific place to live and work.
- The Federal Government should end all of its subsidies to the national passenger railroad, Amtrak.
- The summer Olympic games should always be held in Greece.

Although no two people will develop identical speeches from the same thesis statement, the construction of a clear thesis remains essential to trigger the mental processes necessary for the next stage. A specific position must be defined before constructing the "good reasons" or main points that will be the framework for the body of the message.

Develop Main Points

The strongest persuasion combines a logical (well supported and well argued) structure with appeals appropriate to the audience. We are attracted to ideas that satisfy personal needs and build on attitudes we cherish. The basis of a 30-second television commercial for a "no-frills" airline may appeal to our desire to save money and to our admiration for a new company challenging the established giants. However, persuasion concerned with ideas and policies cannot take its appeals solely from the listener's self-interest. While advertising has limited time to be completely rational, we are less likely to accept lengthy messages unless convincing reasoning has been used. The best persuasive speaking requires evidence in the form of justifications which can be accepted by a diversity of people.[6] Aristotle stated the maxim that "it is not difficult to praise the Athenians to an Athenian audience,"[7] but it is a dangerous underestimation to assume that we can win over an audience with a few self-serving appeals.

After determining your thesis, the next step is to locate the "good reasons" which justify the thesis. As we noted in Chapter 5, reasons are "good" when they make sense to you and are likely to make sense to your audience as a defense for the thesis. One person's good reasons for a position may not be another's. One of the intriguing features of human communication is that reasonable people can disagree about what makes good sense. However, you should work to establish reasons that are consistent with what you believe and what you think an audience will accept. Here are two examples:

Thesis: The Summer Olympic games should always be held in Greece.

because...

    I. Greece was the original home of the games.

    II. Moving the games around to different countries has created enormous political problems and boycotts.

    III. Greece is still a good "neutral" site.

Thesis: The 55 mile-per-hour speed limit on the nation's highways has made them safer and should be maintained.

because...

    I. The lower speed limit saves lives.

    II. The lower speed limit saves fuel and money.

    III. Nearly all cars and trucks lack effective crash protection at the old, dangerous highway speed of 70 M.P.H.

    IV. 55 M.P.H. is increasingly appropriate for our aging and still incomplete national highway system.

In both of these preliminary outlines, the main points are worded as declarative sentences, making their relationship to the thesis clear and apparent. The insertion of "because" between the thesis and each of the main points is a useful test of this relationship since main points should make sense when bridged by this word. If a main point does not seem to follow, it may not be a good reason. Imagine, for instance, that a fifth main point is added to the above example:

Thesis: The 55 mile-per-hour speed limit on the nation's highways has made them safer and should be maintained.

because...

V. 55 M.P.H. is 15 M.P.H. less than the older maximum speed limit of 70 M.P.H.

"V" poses a problem. It fails to make sense when read after the thesis. Unlike the other points, a listener may agree with the fact that the current speed limit is 15 miles per hour less than the old and yet continue to disagree with the thesis. Good main points should advance your cause. It would seem far more difficult for a listener to accept any of the other points without at least moving closer to acceptance of the central idea of the message. The fact contained in "V" may be appropriate for the introduction, but it is not itself a good reason.

If you are satisfied at this stage that you have located major points that adequately defend your attitude, you are on your way to creating the superstructure of a persuasive message. When the main points are located, the preparation of the body of the speech involves filling in this framework with details that will make each main point clear.

Develop Clarification, Amplification, and Evidence for Main Points

The few sentences worked out so far are essential to the successful preparation of the speech, but general assertions by themselves lack the impact of specific evidence and examples. Many listeners will remember only two parts of your message long after you are done: your general point of view and your most interesting example or illustration.[8]

There are three ways to make ideas vivid and memorable: through clarification, amplification, and concrete evidence. These forms of support fill out the body of the speech, appearing as sub-points (A, B, C, and so on) under the main points already designated with Roman Numerals.

For example:

>   Thesis
>   I. Main point
>   A. Clarification, amplification, or evidence
>   1. Further explanation

Though we treat them as separate ways to develop ideas, some of the best pieces of support clarify, amplify, and prove all at once. Clarification makes complex or unfamiliar statements understandable; amplification dramatizes the familiar or ordinary, and evidence aims at proving what may be doubted.

Clarification and Understanding

Often we think that because a point has merely been *stated* that we have made it clear. Simply saying what you think does not guarantee that understanding will follow. Ideas must be sufficiently explained so their relevance and implications are instantly apparent. Examples, extended illustrations, comparisons, and analogies are the basic explanatory tools. Inexperienced communicators frequently overestimate the ability of a few sentences to clear away confusion; they forget that their own familiarity with a topic is not shared by the audience. A good teacher, for example, does not simply talk about a subject but *teaches* it—making the unfamiliar comprehensible. New words, technical relationships, and unfamiliar ideas all need explanation.

When is extensive clarification required? The best guide is your estimate of the audience's previous exposure to the topic. Some members of a group will always have greater knowledge than others, but in most settings you can determine whether what you are saying needs further clarification. The following comments from a speech urging curbs to help control the effects of acid rain point to the need for more details on a complex subject. The speaker notes that emissions from cars, power plants, and industries produce pollution that eventually falls to earth in rain. The difficulty for a lay audience is in understanding how the solutions will work.

> The clean air act is presently before the Congress and, when it acts, we hope it will pay heed to our proposals and require, at a minimum:
>
> • An emissions cap for sulfur dioxide from coal-fired power plants contributing to the acid rain problem;
>
> • A national coal washing program requiring coal with a sulfur content greater than three percent to be cleaned before burning;

- Installation, where feasible, of low nitrogen oxide burners on existing power plants to cut down on emissions.[9]

For a speech to people familiar with the problem, it would be a reasonable assumption that each of these briefly summarized recommendations could be understood. For most other audiences, this summary of legislative steps to reduce acid rain would require more explanation. The average listener may ask: What is the relationship between the sulfur content in coal and the production of acid rain? How is "coal washing" done? What is a "low nitrogen oxide burner," and "How would it cut down on sulfur dioxide?" *Audience members are unlikely to accept a new point of view if they do not understand it.* A good rule of thumb is to provide more clarification than you think you have to, but never "talk down" to the audience.

Amplification as Dramatization of the Familiar

A point needs amplification when it is so familiar or general that its full impact fails to register. Some assertions have become so familiar that they have lost their urgency. "Children today have to grow up faster," "Too many American families rely on television for entertainment," and "We can learn a great deal about industrial productivity from the Japanese" are claims that demand amplification. We may understand what each means, but they need to be dramatized in ways that can reestablish them as more than overworked generalities. Few statements are so novel or fresh that their mere utterance commands our attention. Listeners discover the significance of ideas in their application to specific situations. In a fascinating 1902 address to prisoners of a Chicago jail, the famous lawyer and social crusader Clarence Darrow sought to explain his belief that justice in the United States was class-conscious. It was a familiar charge; the old stereotypes about the failures of the criminal justice system had been made many times:

> When your case gets to court it will make little difference whether you are guilty or innocent, but it's better if you have a smart lawyer. And you cannot get a smart lawyer unless you have money. First and last it's a question of money.

These claims are easy enough to understand, but they are stale and vague. Darrow was too good a criminal lawyer to let them pass without dramatizing them. He usually followed up general claims with vivid amplifications that made their significance apparent:

> Let me illustrate: Take the poorest person in this room. If the community had provided a system of doing justice, the poorest person in this room would have as good a lawyer as the richest, would he not?

When you went into court you would have just as long a trial and just as fair a trial as the richest person in Chicago. Your case would not be tried in fifteen or twenty minutes, whereas it would take fifteen days to get through a rich man's case.

Then if you were rich and were beaten, your case would be taken to the Appellate Court. A poor man cannot take his case to the Appellate Court; he has not the price. And then to the Supreme Court. And if he were beaten there he might perhaps go to the United States Supreme Court. And he might die of old age before he got to jail. If you are poor, it's a quick job.[10]

Darrow's amplification of his point no doubt produced many nods of agreement from his prison audience. He used a general illustration that could fit the circumstances of many different cases, but the vividness of his details made the general point fresh again.

Consider the technique of amplification as applied to a different topic: the relationship between academics and athletics in college life. Countless persons have expressed opinions about the "professionalization" of college sports where scholarships go to athletes as payment for their services. In a recent speech on the problems associated with "big-time" campus sports, a university chancellor wondered if the recruitment of top athletes was becoming inconsistent with the academic mission of higher education.

Can athletics and academics continue their long and "comfortable" relationship, or should the professional nature of athletics be recognized and a divorce occur? The arguments for divorce are easy to muster. The dual role of student/athlete is incompatible in many individuals who are primarily athletes. Rules aimed at reconciling these two roles often result in recruitment violations, academic abuses, and differential treatment of minorities.

This point is most effectively made, however, when the speaker uses a comparison to marriage and divorce to point out the incompatabilities in the academic-athletics relationship:

It reminds me of the kind of relationship in which two very incompatible people are determined to go on with their marriage. They clearly define acceptable behavior. Their marriage becomes a charade of rigid role-playing. Soon one person disobeys those rules because the two people no longer (if they ever did) have a sense of shared values.... They have to be real and come to a common set of purposes. Sometimes it seems, then, that in the world of intercollegiate athletics we are trying to legislate incompatible forces. It is easy to argue for divorce.[11]

The primary benefit of explanations that dramatize points is that they strike chords of recognition in listeners. An assertion that takes on concrete form in an extended illustration has the advantage of allowing the listener to visualize the impact of an idea on real events. A detailed statement that dramatizes an idea is like painting an expression onto an empty face. We understand a person's feelings from the small details revealed in the way the eyes and the mouth are drawn, rather than in the universal features that make up the anatomy of every face.

Evidence and the Problem of Proof

Evidence is support—sometimes factual, sometimes informed opinion—for a controversial claim. It is designed to reduce doubts and reservations in a skeptical audience.[12] Since the qualities of credible sources of evidence were thoroughly discussed in Chapter 7, our focus here is on what evidence can and cannot do in overcoming audience resistance.

When people use the words "evidence" and "proof" they often make the mistake of assuming that they are talking about precise factual claims that cannot easily be deined. The word "proof" especially carries the connotation of undeniability and certainty. The suggestion that a persuader has "proof" sometimes carries the implication that a challenge of the "proven" claim would be futile. A 1983 speech on problems in American public school education uses statistics which seem to function as proof:

> The statistics are...chilling.... Among the most alarming: 13 percent of all seventeen-year-olds are functionally illiterate; among minority youngsters, the figure may be as high as 40 percent;... nearly 40 percent of seventeen-year-olds cannot draw inferences from written material; only 20 percent can write a persuasive essay; only a third can solve mathematics problems that require several steps...
>
>   . . . .
>
> American children go to school, on average, only 180 days a year, with another twenty days usually lost to absences, while children in Japan attend for 240 days. Our school day is about five hours long, while in many other countries it is eight hours long. And much of the American school day for the teacher is taken up with activities that have little to do with education—attendance, grading papers, maintaining discipline.[13]

With statistics and a comparison to a major economic competitor, the speaker provides what may be unchallengeable evidence for the claim that American education is not as strong and vigorous as it could be. If we accept the accuracy of the percentages and numbers, it would be difficult, if not impossible, to argue that the preparation of American public school students is now fully adequate. The proof clearly suggests the scope of unresolved problems.

Using evidence to reduce listener resistence is a reasonable goal, but it is also important to remember that overcoming objections is sometimes not simply a matter of providing irrefutable proof. Evidence is also used to support preferences and judgments as well as known (and seemingly undeniable) truths.

We noted in Chapter 5 that assertions that are *preferences* or *personal judgments* rather than *facts* can never be proved with certainty. Judgments have their roots in values; facts have their roots in observable events. Many judgmental claims are misinterpreted as claims that should have some basis in fact. It may be difficult to "prove," for example, that "Abortion is murder." Although the "is" has the effect of making the claim appear to be a matter of truth or falsity, it is actually a matter of judgment and value. "Murder" is the killing of one human being by another. But it remains unresolved within the medical, religious, or judicial worlds when a fetus becomes a human being. Is it in the first stages of cell division or when the fetus can survive without extraordinary medical care outside of the womb? The grammatically induced certainty of "Abortion *is* murder" must (and has) given way to a wide variety of conflicting interpretations made by reasonable people who have differences that cannot be settled by appeals to ostensibly self-evident "facts."

Does this mean that we cannot use evidence effectively to support a thesis that makes a judgment? Not at all, but we must use the term "proof" with care. We can "prove" beyond doubt that water freezes at 0 degrees Centigrade and that one of George Washington's most successful battles was fought on Christmas in 1776. But *certain truth* must give way to *reasonable judgment* when we use evidence to support issues where scientific or historical certainty is impossible. Should animals be subjected to severe pain as subjects in medical tests? Was Jimmy Carter a better president than Ronald Reagan? Should medical and other professional schools reserve places for minority students? Should women have combat roles in the armed forces? These questions have been the basis of passionate speeches reflecting different views; evidence has at times furthered the case for all sides. Such evidence can rarely produce ironclad proof because all of these questions involve values as well as certain facts. The qualities that make "good" presidents or combat-ready soldiers, for instance, are not defined by everyone in the same way.

A speech by a former chairman of the Federal Communications Commission to the National Association of Broadcasters includes statements of judgment as well as fact. In a 1961 address that sent shock waves through the industry and made "vast wasteland" a household phrase, Newton Minow challenged his audience of television network executives and broadcasters to do better than they were doing in serving the public interest requirements enforced the FCC. "When television is good," he noted, "nothing—not the theater, not the magazines or newspapers—nothing is better. But when television is bad, nothing is worse." He began with an amplification of his basic point:

> I invite you to sit down in front of your television set when your station goes on the air and stay there without a book, magazine, newspaper, profit and loss sheet or rating book to distract you.... I can assure you that you will observe a vast wasteland.
>
> You will see a procession of game shows, violence, audience participation shows, formula comedies about totally unbelievable families, blood and thunder, mayhem, violence, sadism, murder, western bad-men, western good men, private eyes, gangsters, more violence, and cartoons. And, endlessly, commercials—many screaming, cajoling, and offending.

Perhaps no government bureaucrat in the recent past ever gave a livelier and more critical persuasive speech. In the course of making his case against what he felt were the low standards of television, Minow resorted to several forms of evidence:

Testimony supporting a judgment

What do we mean by "the public interest?" Some say the public interest is merely what interests the public. I disagree.

So does your distinguished [N.A.B.] president.... In a recent speech he said, "Broadcasting to serve the public interest must have a soul and a conscience, a burning desire to excel, as well as to sell; the urge to build the character, citizenship, and intellectual stature of people..."

Statistics supporting a judgment

Is there no person in this room who claims that broadcasting can't do better?

A glance at next season's proposed programming can give us little heart. Of 73½ hours of prime evening time, the networks have tentatively scheduled 59 hours to categories of "action adventure," situation comedy, variety, quiz, and movies.

Examples supporting a judgment

Television in its young life has had many hours of greatness—its Victory at Sea, its Army-McCarthy hearings, its Peter Pan, its Kraft Theaters, its See it Nows, its Project 20, the World Series, its political conventions and campaigns...

Statistics supporting a fact

The best estimates indicate that during the hours of 5 to 6 p.m. 60 percent of your audience is composed of children under 12. And most young children today, believe it or not, spend as much time watching television as they do in the schoolroom...

Statistics supporting a judgment

There are estimates that today the average viewer spends about 200 minutes daily with television, while the average reader spends about 38 minutes with magazines and 40 minutes with newspapers. Television has grown up faster than a teenager, and now it is time to grow up.[14]

Minow's speech was unusual only in its adventurous attack on the audience. It was typical in the ways it used evidence to support a variety of factual and judgmental assertions. His effort serves as a useful illustration that evidence is often more than numbers and statistics; support for a claim must frequently include the use of materials that defend a reasonable—although not irrefutable—point of view.

Write the Introduction

After the main and supporting points of the speech have been outlined, the remaining task is the completion of the introduction. While the introduction is the first part of a speech, it is the last to be written. Just as it would be difficult to introduce a person you did not know, so it is awkward to write an introduction before the body of a message has been completed. At this stage, you know what attitudes or behaviors you want the intended audience to accept. Now you are in a position to build a "bridge" between the audience's existing attitudes and those you want them to hold at the end of the message. A good introduction prepares an audience to *accept* the main points that you will present, reducing resistance to your ideas and arguments.[15]

Consider the setting facing a University of Wisconsin student, Ken Lonnquist, who discovered through a pre-speech poll that virtually no one in his audience agreed with his thesis in favor of restricting abortions. What could he say in his opening remarks that might prepare the class to hear his thesis and good reasons? How might they be prepared to listen to his position? His approach was to identify his cause with the cause that divided pro-slavery and abolitionist citizens in the Civil War.

Now I have come here today, as you all know, to speak for life— human life and human rights. And there is something...reminiscent of, and haunted by, the days, the people, and the events of the 19th

Century. It is more than just a parallel between the treatment that was accorded abolitionist speakers and the treatment that is accorded anti-abortionist speakers today. It is deeper than that. It rests in the very heart of the issue—in the very heart of each moral struggle. You see, in the 1840s it was argued by pro-slavery forces that their rights as citizens of the United States were being subverted by abolitionists who were working to eradicate slavery. "The abolitionists," they argued, "are denying us our Constitutional right to hold property." They could not see that their rights of property could not supercede the rights of the black men and the black women to life, liberty, and the pursuit of happiness. They could not see because they did not regard black men or black women to be of human life. They were blinded by the prejudice of their age.

And today a similar logic has been evolved by the proponents of abortion...[16]

No single speech—even one that begins as eloquently as this—is going to reverse deeply held convictions completely, but a good introduction increases the likelihood that a persuader will get a hearing and may produce small changes in attitude toward the thesis. In this case, the alignment of the pro-life position with the anti-slavery position is a compelling way to encourage an audience to consider the ideas that follow.

An introduction can perform many functions. Each of the following is worth considering, although it is unlikely every introduction will need to achieve all of these objectives.

Gain Interest and Attention.   An old but valid communication axiom is to start with something that creates interest, because an audience cannot be motivated to accept an idea until it has been motivated to listen. Stories, relevant personal experiences, or vivid statistics are good ways to begin speeches. A detailed story or example is especially helpful because it may provide an accessible way into a topic. We never outgrow our interest in hearing abstract ideas explained in the actions of particular people. Here is the effective opening that describes the dangers of stereotyping people:

In the local newspaper of my community recently, there was a story about a man named Virgil Spears. He lived in a small town about 40 miles from my home. He had served five years in the Missouri State Penitentiary for passing bogus checks. When he returned to his family, Mr. Spears couldn't find a job. Everyone knew he was an ex-con and everyone knew that ex-cons aren't to be trusted. Finally in what was described as calm desperation, he walked into a local barbershop where he was well known, pulled a gun, and took all the money the barber had. Up to this point it had been a fairly routine robbery, but then something unusual happened. Mr. Spears didn't try to get away. He got into his car, drove slowly out of town, and waited for the highway patrol. When they caught him, he made only one request. He turned to the arresting patrolman and said: "Would you please ask that the court put my family on welfare just as soon as possible?"

To the people of Clarkston, Missouri, Virgil Spears wasn't to be trusted because he was an ex-con.[17]

The concrete images of this case gained the audience's interest while portraying the negative consequences of stereotyping.

Establish Goodwill. The greater the "gulf" that separates speaker and audience, the greater the need to say something that will establish a sense of goodwill between the two. A speaker may start by noting that differences should not overshadow common values and goals. One of the strengths of an open society is the belief that differences of opinion can be productive and can flourish without producing inviolate walls of hostility. For example, members of the United States Senate may oppose each other in speeches given from the floor, but many continue to be friends in less partisan settings, addressing even vehement opponents as "distinguished colleagues." This practice is not merely "good politics" but is part of a healthy framework for persuasion.

One common device for gaining goodwill is to refer to values the audience and speaker hold in common. Some way of expressing the fact that differences should not obscure similarities helps to put disagreements in perspective. Ronald Reagan used this approach in 1985 while addressing the Soviet people on radio. "Americans," he said, "will never forget the valor, the pain and at last the joy of victory that our people shared. I remember President Roosevelt's praise for the Russian people's heroism."[18] Another technique is to appeal to the audience's sense of fair play. Audiences can be complimented on their willingness to hear a position that is different from their own. This was the strategy of a *Playboy* editor at the beginning of a speech to Southern Baptists, few of whom could be counted on to share the "Playboy philosophy." He tactfully combined references to shared concerns with comments on the spirit of "openness" within the audience:

> I am sure we are all aware of the seeming incongruity of a repre-
> sentative of *Playboy* magazine speaking to an assemblage of repre-
> sentatives of the Southern Baptist Convention. I was intrigued by the
> invitation when it came last fall, though I was not surprised. I am
> grateful for your genuine and warm hospitality, and I am flattered
> (though again not surprised) by the implication that I would have
> something to say that could have meaning to you people. Both *Play-
> boy* and the Baptists have indeed been considering many of the
> same issues and ethical problems; and even if we have not arrived

at the same conclusions, I am impressed and gratified by your openness and willingness to listen to our views.[19]

Preview the Scope of the Message. Any human activity that requires work — and listening to a speech is hard mental work — needs to have its limits clearly defined. Just as runners pace themselves according to the distances that are set in advance, listeners must understand the length and scope of the topic in which they are about to invest their mental effort and attention. Lack of information about the length of the speech and the range of topics to be considered is as frustrating as not knowing the distance of a foot race until the finish line.

Your introduction should tell the audience what topics you will discuss, what topics will be excluded, and how long the presentation will take. The effect of an overview is to make the logical relationship between your thesis and your major contentions more apparent to a listener. By mentioning what will be *excluded*, for example, you can lay to rest misunderstandings about the scope of your speech and provide a better match between what an audience expects and what they will hear. In a speech attacking the National Rifle Association's persuasion tactics, for example, Raymond Rogers provided an initial indication of the framework of his remarks. He stated his thesis, referred to what he did *not* have time to talk about, and concluded with a summary of his main points:

> I would like to have a closer look at some of the arguments offered by the National Rifle Association in their ongoing opposition to handgun control legislation.
>
> I hasten to add the disclaimer that all of the arguments raised on all sides of the handgun control debate stand in need of improvement, but limitations of time and fully admitted personal bias dictate that today I will scrutinize only "The Rhetoric of the NRA."
>
> In the brief time available today, I would like to discuss several standard arguments of the NRA against handgun control by measuring them against some standard logical and rhetorical fallacies. Those fallacies are: (1) failure to define terms; (2) use of the "Big Lie"; (3) the fallacy of the "slippery slope"; (4) Bully Tactics; and (5) the fallacy of Improper Appeals to authority.[20]

This overview not only communicated the thesis and main points, but also signaled that the speaker was aware of the limits he imposed on his subject.

Define Key Terms. Successful communication sometimes depends on the way words or phrases are used. Some terms are misunderstood because they are technical; others cause confusion because ordinary usage may not coincide with the meaning intended by the speaker. In either case, definitions are useful. The meanings associated with special language can work for or against a position. The average listener, for example, thinks of "rhetoric" as trivial communication that is far less concrete than "reality." The exact and older meaning of the term defines rhetoric as a major discipline concerned with the formation and support of attitudes. Many other pivotal terms such as "legalized gambling," "brainwashing," "recreational drugs," "welfare rights," "law and order," "corporate monopolies," "mercy killing," "reverse discrimination," and "child abuse" are equally subject to misinterpretation. Each of us has a general idea of what these terms imply, but we are unlikely to define them in precisely the same way. Even very common terms can benefit from definitions that will prepare an audience to accept a new point of view. In the following example, an historian begins an address on the relationship between sports and television with just such a redefinition of two familiar words that imply two different worlds.

> Sport, I am convinced, is the best known yet least understood phenomenon in American society. Much of our misunderstanding and misconceptions about sports stems from our failure to make meaningful

"Perhaps, sir, your rhetoric was a little too harsh."

Drawing by Lorenz; © 1986 *The New Yorker Magazine, Inc.*

distinctions among the various components of the sports world....

One is sport. Sport is an extension of play involving two or more persons. Sport turns on games and contests which are highly organized, competitive, characterized by the established rules; but like play, sport has as its primary purpose fun for the participant.

Athletics, on the other hand, derives not from play at all, but from work. Athletics, as they have been referred to from the ancient Greeks on, refers to intensely competitive confrontation between specially trained performers whose primary objectives are (a) spectator entertainment and (b) victory. Although the game involved in sport and athletics may be the same, as, for example, basketball, the two activities are worlds apart in terms of purpose and attitude. ... I would simply call your attention to the obvious difference that we understand between intramural sport and intercollegiate athletics.

The speaker then uses the distinctive meanings of the two terms to state his thesis: "The telecommunications industry is interested in athletic contests, not sporting events."[21]

Finally, it may appear that opening remarks containing all four of the elements discussed above could consume much of the persuader's available time with an audience. If the receptivity of the persuadees has been increased, the time will have been well spent. The more unfamiliar an audience is with a topic or the more hostile they are toward your thesis, the greater the need to establish an appropriate foundation for the persuasive appeals.

Sample Persuasive Outline: A Case Study

A speech outline is only a guide, but the sample that follows illustrates how an effective outline looks, and how it helps to make an advocate's delivery orderly and convincing. Our example involves a controversial topic that is still the subject of debate, the attack on a Korean airliner by the Soviet Union.

The Topic

In 1983, 269 people lost their lives when a Soviet fighter pilot deliberately shot down Korean Air Lines Flight 007 after it crossed over Russian airspace in the North Pacific. The flight of KAL 007 had originated on September 31 in New York. The Boeing 747 was on its way to Seoul, South Korea after refueling in Alaska. It's flight path should have taken it safely over international waters off the Soviet coast, but instead took it 400 miles west over the Kamchatka Peninsula. Soviet fighters scrambled into the air as the plane passed over sensitive missile and submarine bases. After what Soviet authorities claimed were repeated attempts to order the aircraft to return under escort to a military base, the plane was shot down with heat-seeking missiles, killing all of those on board.

The flight of KAL 007 remains an issue not simply because of understandable outrage over the attack on a civilian airliner by a military fighter, but because people in the United States and other Western nations have expressed suspicion that the plane was on a spy mission. Tom Wicker of the New York Times, and others have publicly wondered if KAL 007 was used in conjunction with an American military intelligence flight that took place at approximately the same time with a similar plane.[22] American intelligence planes had routinely taken such flights, although they had always been careful to remain in international airspace. On this tragic night, a U.S. reconnaissance plane came within 400 miles of the doomed airliner, but reportedly made no contact with it.

Since the Korean airliner has not been recovered, we may never be certain of what happened. Did the airliner's navigation system fail? Did the pilot make an error in programming the complex computer that sets the plane's direction? Did the Soviet military make a terrible miscalculation in assuming it had caught an American reconnaissance plane spying on its military base on Sakhalin Island? Was this yet another incident in the intelligence gathering activities of the two great superpowers? Many Americans recalled that an American spy plane had been shot down and captured over the Soviet Union in 1960. When the United States initially denied the story, the pilot, Francis Gary Powers, was prominently displayed on Russian television. As inexcusable and barbaric as the Soviet Union's act had been, was the United States partially responsible for tempting the secretive Soviets to murder innocent civilians on a defenseless airliner?

Prominent magazines such as The Nation and Newsweek have implied that there may have been a conspiracy between Korean Airlines and American intelligence. Perhaps the airplane was on a spy mission, or was used to test Soviet defenses. Americans could be expected to condemn the Soviets but also to have suspicions about our government's involvement. The speech summarized below attempts to take away such doubts. As you read it over note that it is not a word-for-word manuscript. Although for the sake of clarity we have included more explanation within the outline than you might need (especially if you are very familiar with your topic), all outlines should be constructed on the assumption that you will embellish and further explain many of your points.

The Jetliner Outline

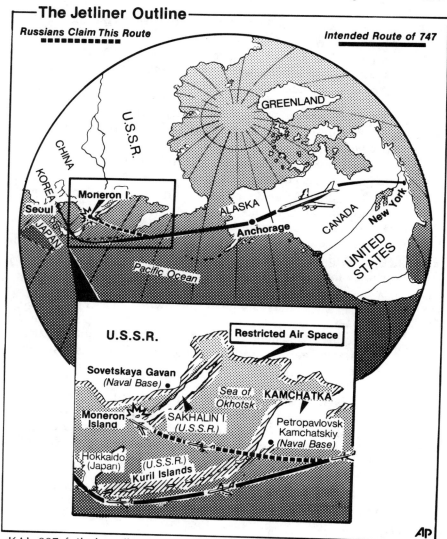

KAL 007 failed to fly its intended route around Soviet airspace. Instead, it was shot down after crossing Sakhalin Island in the U.S.S.R.
Wide World Photos, Inc.

The Outline

Was KAL Flight 007 on a Spy Mission for the United States?

Introduction

A. KAL 007: a summary of what occurred on Sept. 1 1983.

B. A personal note: when I first heard of the crisis I felt that there was some likely American involvement.

   1. An American U-2 was shot down in Russia in 1960.
   2. An American intelligence plane was shot down over Soviet Armenia in 1958.

C. The circumstances surrounding American interests in the region and the flight of the airliner make conspiracy theories attractive.

   1. When it comes to tragedies like this, the least satisfying explanation is one based on simple mistakes.

      a. A mistake or accident makes the consideration of conspiracies impossible.
      b. Human error on the part of the pilots deprives us of a satisfactory explanation for such a newsworthy event.

   2. Conspiracy theories keep this event alive as a political topic rather than the "conspiracy of circumstance" that it really was.

      a. In a world that has been filled with James Bond films, Communist "witch hunts" in Hollywood, and *National Inquirer* "accounts" of visitors from other planets, it is easy to see that bizarre conspiracies have their attractions.
      b. One of our most respected historians, Richard Hofstadter, has noted that for a minority of Americans tragic events can only make sense when explained as conspiracies. To paraphrase him: Bad things never just happen, they are always caused by some gigantic and demonic force.[23]

D. But in this case our government's protestations of non-involvement are probably valid.

   1. The Soviets may have felt "provoked," but the truth is probably that they shot down an innocent plane on a routine flight.
   2. The most convincing accounts of why the airliner took its course come from people who understand how a plane is navigated and set automatically on its course.

THESIS: Even though we may never know for sure, it was probably navigation error and bad luck that lead KAL 007 over Soviet territory.

Body

I. There is convincing evidence that the pilots had correctly programmed their computer for a path that would take them around the Soviet Union, but failed to engage the computer to the autopilot.

    A. According to Murray Sayle, a prize-winning Australian journalist and experienced navigator, there are two primary forms of internal navigation: (1) *inhertial* (computer based) and (2) *magnetic* (based on the earths magnetic field.)

        1. Direction is effected by which one is used.

    B. For the first part of the flight from Alaska KAL was to fly on magnetic heading of 246 degrees to a particular mountain landmark.

    C. Prior to approaching Soviet airspace they were supposed to turn a knob one "click" to set the auto pilot on an *inhertial* navigation course that would change their course slightly over safe international waters.

    D. According to the Russian's own radar, the plane was eventually shot down still on the *magnetic* heading of 246 degrees.

        1. Evidently, the pilots forgot to reset the autopilot for the new and proper heading.

        2. As Sayles notes, the reset is just one "click" away on the same knob, much like changing the volume setting on a radio. "The pilot, having turned the rotary switch on the control panel to set the autopilot on a heading mode of 246 degrees magnetic toward Cairn Mountain, could have failed to recouple the autopilot to the INS. There is a good deal of circumstantial evidence that this is exactly what did happen."[24]

    E. The Airline Pilots Association notes that this "scenario" fits with the known facts.[25]

II. Navigational errors of this type are not common, but do occur from time to time.

    A. Four Soviet air flights have recently experienced navigation problems involving deviations as great as 400 kilometers.[26]

    B. There are about 12 gross errors a year on the North Atlantic.

    C. Since 1975 five serious cases of navigational error have been caused by leaving the autopilot in the magnetic heading mode.[27]

III. As luck would have it, ground guidance and radar over the North Pacific is sparse; thereby leaving flights in this area with very little opportunity for correction from ground-based controllers.

A. Although there are guide radio beams available to pilots in the Alaskan sector, one was not working, and a second was probably ignored.

B. Further, over that part of the ocean pilots are responsible for reporting their own positions.

C. What radar was available tended to belong to military rather than civilian aircraft controllers.

IV. According to Korean Airlines, a warning indicator on the co-pilot's side which indicates the use of magnetic heading navigation was not functioning. It stayed on all of the time, thereby depriving the crew of the knowledge they were flying by magnetic heading rather than the Inhertial Navigation System.

A. As the investigation of the International Civil Aviation Organization confirms, the "heading flag" light was reported as defective by the crew that flew the plane from New York to Alaska.

B. As Murray Sayle notes, it was "a fault in the very instrument that could have warned the co-pilot that he was flying in magnetic heading."[28]

CONCLUSION: restate thesis and major points indicated with Roman numerals.

Delivery of an Outline Speech: A Few Suggestions

Two habits usually fatal to good delivery are the tendencies of speakers either to read their remarks to an audience or to memorize everything they intend to say. Both are awkward and unnatural ways to communicate with others because preoccupation with either our memory or our reading of a text almost insures dull communication. Practice the speech orally, but don't memorize it. Memorization and reading "short-circuit" the thought processes that give feeling to our words. Only a skilled professional actor can make a printed speech text seem spontaneous. "Because variety has an almost constantly positive effect upon listener reactions," notes Jeffrey Auer, "the reading aloud from a manuscript, which is almost inherently more static, is understandably less effective than lively, direct, and extemporaneous delivery."[29]

An outline contains all of the essential points that should be raised in the speech but avoids the problem of the speaker who is *reading to* but not *communicating with* an audience. Because an outline can be read at a glance, the actual explanation of points can be made by direct eye contact with the audience. Use the outline as a set of talking points. It provides all of the landmarks that are necessary to "talk your way through the speech" in an oral style that is closer to everyday conversation than to oral reading. As Otis Walter and Robert Scott have noted, we tend to be more expressive in voice and gesture if we *think about our ideas as we say them:*

> Good delivery makes the meaning and spirit the speaker intends to express as intense as possible... *What is needed, in James Winans'* memorable phrase, is "the full realization of the content of your words as you utter them..." The speaker can attain the best effect by not attending to delivery itself, but to the meaning and spirit of what is being said.
>
> . . . .
>
> Good delivery, springing from a re-creation of the thought and mood, has the variety in voice that holds attention, and it has, as well, the mark of individuality. When you feel something strongly, your gestures will suit the meaning and spirit of what you are saying...[30]

Several additional suggestions:

1. Feel free to cut out or add items to the outline. The actual circumstances of delivery (running out of time, unanticipated comments made by a previous speaker) may force you to vary your speech from its original form. The outline can easily accommodate change.

2. Use a systematic pattern of indenting so that key points can be easily located along the left-hand margin. If you lose your place, for example, you can always restate the main points of the speech by searching them out on the left margin. Note that, for this reason, main points in the introduction are identified with capital letters rather than Roman Numerals. Roman Numerals are reserved for major contentions in the body of the speech that will be repeated several times.

3. Avoid writing a conclusion that introduces new ideas that have not been developed in the body. The real conclusion of the speech is the thesis. An extended conclusion may involve a review of all main points, and perhaps a closing story or illustration.

4. Remember that oral communication is more idiomatic than formal written prose. Don't be overly concerned about pauses, the urge to rephrase an idea, or the desire to make another attempt to clarify a point. These are natural features of all oral communication. It is more *unnatural* to read to someone in a way that makes their presence seem marginal rather than central to your reason for speaking.

Strategic Considerations

To this point, we have described a general method for translating a persuasive intent into an actual message. We conclude this chapter with a brief review of several strategic considerations which can affect how ideas and topics are introduced to the audience.

When to Reveal the Thesis

Ideally, you should state the thesis in the introduction to give direction to the remarks that follow. Most speechmakers have been taught to explain the key idea of a message clearly in the first few moments. But, as Gary Cronkhite notes, a persuader may be completely open at the outset of a message, only to find that "his hostile audience refuses to listen to the rest of his speech."

> Henry Grady, for example, after waiting for General Sherman to finish his speech, and after waiting for the audience to stop singing "Marching Through Georgia," might have clearly stated his thesis that the northerners must forget the Civil War and help rebuild the South. He might have done that, but he would probably have ended up spending his next paycheck from the Atlanta *Constitution* on tar solvent. Instead, he chose a second type of introduction designed to emphasize the interests he and his listeners had in common...[31]

If your audience's hostility to the thesis is known to be very strong, you might withhold it until you have established a basis of support and evidence. The option to withhold the thesis until the end is an "inductive" method of development because the thesis is the conclusion that logically follows from everything you have said prior to it. A delay in stating an attitude may avoid an early rejection of your message before you have established the reasoned basis for it. In his famous "Funeral Oration," for example, Marc Antony begins by "praising" Brutus, one of the assassins of Caesar, as an "honorable man." He does so because Brutus has just given his speech in which he has convinced the crowd that Caesar deserved to die. As Shakespeare writes his part, Antony begins with the famous lines that give no hint as to the eventual conclusion he wants his audience to reach:

> Friends, Romans, countrymen, lend me your ears;
> I come to bury Caesar, not to praise him.

Only later in the speech is it evident that he has actually come to bury Brutus and to praise Caesar. Antony concludes that Brutus is the true villain. This attitude gradually emerges from the signs of Caesar's goodness that Antony weaves into his observations, almost, it seems, as an afterthought. Finally, the repeated phrase that Brutus was an "honorable" man takes on a calculated irony that is not lost on the audience.

> When that the poor have cried, Caesar hath wept:
> Ambition should be made of sterner stuff;
> Yet Brutus says he was ambitious;
> and Brutus is an honorable man.[32]

The pattern of Antony's speech is similar to television advertisements which withhold the "tagline" or "pitch" for the product until after they have established an entertaining context.

Whether to Recognize Opposing Views

When we think of a "persuader" or a "passionate advocate" we usually assume that the ideas to be presented will be "one-sided." Few persuaders, whether they are consumer advocates testifying in a Congressional hearing or people selling cars will give equal time to ideas or attitudes they oppose. Frequently, successful persuasion requires commitment to one side of a case because the communicator's conviction must be apparent. The ringing certainty of "Give me liberty or give me death" would not be as profound if Patrick Henry and other revolutionary propagandists had recognized that the British in colonial America had some legitimate complaints against the local inhabitants. Part of what makes a persuader credible is the evident passion he or she has for a cause.

Yet audiences do not live only in the persuader's world. In many cases, their awareness about a topic includes significant information about the other side of a controversial question. They have been subject to counterpersuasion—persuasion intended to weaken the impact of opposing advocates—and will be subject to it again. In the case of heavily advertised products such as beer and automobiles, for example, counterpersuasion frequently occurs within a matter of hours or even minutes. The newspaper reader or news viewer is similarly subjected to thousands of persuasive claims that may be retained and recalled on a vast range of social and political issues.[33] Thus, while a persuader must make a strong case for one side of an issue, it may be necessary to deal with some of the counterarguments a listener has retained and may recall as a topic is discussed.[34] Even if members of an audience lack knowledge of counterarguments, it may be beneficial to present some of "what the other side thinks" in order to control the way opposing ideas are raised. This interesting strategy is called "inoculation":

> [J]ust as we develop the resistance to disease of a person raised in a germ-free environment by pre-exposing him to a weakened form of a virus so as to stimulate, without overcoming, his defenses, so also

we can develop the resistance to persuasion of a person raised in an "ideologically clean" environment by pre-exposing him to weakened forms of counterarguments or to some other belief-threatening material strong enough to stimulate, but not so strong as to overcome, his defense against belief.[35]

Many experimental studies measuring how attitudes are affected by single and both-sides persuasion have been done.[36] For example, a classic study conducted by Carl Hovland and his associates found that a two-sided presentation may not be as effective for an audience that already agrees with your point of view as for an audience that is initially opposed.

> (1) Presenting the arguments on both sides of an issue was found to be more effective than giving only the arguments supporting the point being made, in the case of individuals *initially opposed* to the point of view being presented.
>
> (2) For men who were *already convinced* of the point of view being presented, however, the inclusion of arguments on both sides was less effective, for the group as a whole, than presenting only the arguments favoring the general position being advocated.[37]

Individuals hostile to a speaker's thesis were evidently impressed by the recognition and awareness given the other side of a question. This was especially evident in "better educated" listeners.[38]

Overall, we think three guidelines are useful. First, in this age of "objective" journalism and "objective" science, it may seem fair and natural to deal with both sides of an issue. However, extensive attempts at "balance" within a persuasive speech may weaken your impact on the audience. We expect persuaders to be partisans for their causes. There are usually many others who will carry the burden of presenting opposing views on your topic. The demands for strong advocacy are to some extent at odds with the requirements of "balanced presentation." As a persuader, you should see yourself as a person with deep convictions rather than neutral observations. Second, it is never enough to prepare a message by knowing only your side. The best way to know what to anticipate from a hostile audience is to know their grounds for disagreement. At a minimum, refer briefly to some objections, but don't be ashamed to spend most of your time as a forceful advocate for your own ideas. Third, remember that any time you spend dealing with the "cons" in opposition to your "pro" position may produce the unintended effect of planting the seeds for objections that otherwise might not exist.

Finally, the consideration of the subject of one-sided arguments raises an important ethical issue that has plagued persuaders for centuries: should an advocate deliberately ignore information that goes against his point of view? We think he can. Although it is wrong to distort information to fit a belief, we do not think there is an inherent ethical problem in focusing on only one side of an issue *if a speaker's belief is genuine.* Passionate advocacy is preferable to timid neutrality. Even if a speaker knows that there is a good case to be made for a different point of view, we think it is ethical to concentrate on making the best possible case for one side. An open society functions better when there are many competing voices on issues rather than single voices trying to represent all sides.

Where to Place the "Best" Arguments

Assuming that an audience will hear a number of points, is there a place in a speech or in a sequence of speeches that produces the greatest impact? There are no clear answers, although many researchers have seen a slight advantage to starting with your strongest point.

> If no other consideration is involved, one might as well put the strongest and longest argument first, but the evidence for no significant difference is strong enough that climax versus anticlimax should not be an overriding principle governing arrangement.[39]

The most extensive work on placement of arguments was done in the late 1950s by psychologist Carl Hovland and his colleagues at Yale. He attempted to assess differences in order of presentation in two ways: within the sequence of claims made by a single speaker and in the sequence of pro and con messages made by different communicators. In summarizing these studies, Hovland noted that "when two sides of an issue are presented successively by different communicators, the side presented first does not necessarily have the advantage."[40] But he also noted that there are situations when the *first* arguments heard were more effective than the last. This "primacy effect" rarely makes a potent difference in the way people accept ideas, but it can work (a) when "contradictory information is presented in a single communication," (b) when needs relevant to the listeners are aroused and then satisfied by information supporting the thesis; (c) when a pro-con order of presentation is planned: your position first, followed by a recognition of some opposing ideas; and (d) when listeners have a relatively weak desire to understand what has been said. In these cases, Hovland and his researchers noted that the ideas which come first have a slight edge in the ability to gain acceptance over ideas that come last.[41]

Several factors could account for these results. There is the old cliche about the importance of "first impressions." In addition, the willingness to listen may decrease with time as the acceptance of ideas is replaced by boredom or inattention. The most powerful explanation, however, may be that inoculation can take hold quickly. Once we are prepared to accept an idea, everything that follows — especially contradictory ideas — will meet with greater resistance. After we have acquired an attitude, we are usually anxious to avoid the mental confusion that results from hearing further ideas and arguments.

How to Use Persuasive Language

When Richard Nixon was running for the Presidency in 1960, he frequently campaigned with his wife Pat at his side. A favorite story among reporters was that Nixon was fond of a political cliche that he later realized carried an unintended meaning. "America," he liked to say, "cannot stand pat." After receiving icy stares from his wife, the story goes, he decided to talk about how "America cannot stand still."[42] Nixon's problem is a fitting reminder that the language of persuasion needs to be carefully considered. We may get so involved in the structure of the outlined speech that we overlook the importance of key terms. A finished speech outline is like a finished but unpainted car. The basics are in place, but how we react to it depends to a great extent on the exterior color that is applied. Just as paint color can make a car acceptable or unacceptable in our eyes, so can the semantics of the speech make a difference in our attitudes toward an idea. Several questions are important to consider before preparing a final draft of the delivery outline. Have you used evocative phrases or words that help shape the point of view you want your audience to accept? Is there a better way to convey a feeling or attitude? Are there specific words or phrases that should be emphasized or repeated to the audience? While one of the virtues of an outlined speech is its extemporaneous and flexible nature, it would be a mistake to overlook the most attractive key terms to express your points. Look closely at adjectives, nouns, and verbs that make up the major headings, and phrase them in ways that contribute forcefully to your appeals and arguments.

Here are two main points of a rough-draft outline for a speech arguing that employers should not use lie detectors to assess the honesty and performance of employees:

I. Lie detectors are unreliable, and
II. Lie detectors violate our personal liberties.

While these ideas may be well chosen, their wording could be greatly improved. First, a speech that is arguing against these devices should not use the inexact and misleading phrase "lie detector." Although the term is a common one, its use works against a main point of the speech (that these machines do *not* detect lies). A less "loaded" term is "polygraph." Second, you could intensify the impact of the main points with more vivid and specific language. Consider, for example, the nouns, adjectives and verbs added to these points to increase their impact:

I. Polygraphs are *supposed* to detect "lies," but the *outdated machine* is itself a *notorious liar.*

II. The *forced* use of the polygraph *destroys* our *rights* to *privacy,* our *freedom,* and our *honor.*

Although the ideas in the original and revised drafts are essentially the same, the wording of the second attempt is more compelling. A fallible machine is a more obvious threat to our liberties. Every persuader should take care to describe through evocative language the ideas built through reasoned argument.

Summary

In this chapter, we have reviewed a sequence of six steps for organizing and preparing persuasive speeches: (1) Know the audience, (2) Determine your objectives, (3) Determine your thesis, (4) Develop main points, (5) Develop clarification, amplification, and evidence, and (6) Write the introduction. We have made two basic claims in suggesting this approach. The first is that it is important to think of a speech as more than a written copy of what you intend to say. Preparing to persuade an audience is as much a process of thinking about the event as it is about writing words on paper. Everything done before the speech should make the contact between you and your listeners as successful and satisfying as possible. The single most important consequence of this conslusion is that no speech is completed when it is written—only when it is delivered. The outline contains the basic ideas needed to keep you on track; it should not get in the way of the spontaneous and flexible communication expected when we meet others face-to-face. Our second claim is that the preparation of a speech requires careful attention to detail: how to defend and to explain points, how to introduce controversial ideas, and what kind of language will evoke the right response. Obviously, there are no simple answers on how to fill in the right details for a specific occasion. Even so, the specific steps offered here break down the process of preparing a speech into clear and manageable stages. The speaker who follows them may be surprised to discover that the problem is no longer "What can I do with this topic?" but "Will they give me enough time to include all that I want to?"

Notes

[1]Cicero, quoted in Harold Croft, *A Guide to Public Speaking,* Labour Party Publication (Leicester, England: Leicester Printers, n.d.), 34.

[2]Kathleen Kendall, "Do Real People Ever Give Speeches?" *Spectra* (December, 1985), 10. See also, Kathleen Kendall, "Do Real People Ever Give Speeches?" *Central States Speech Journal* (Fall, 1974), 233-235.

[3]Donald C. Bryant, "Rhetoric: It's Function and Scope," *Quarterly Journal of Speech* (December, 1953), 401.

[4]Shaw quoted in Erik Barnouw, *A Tower of Babel: A History of Broadcasting in the United States to 1933* (New York: Oxford, 1966), 249.

[5]For a description of this encounter, see Harriet J. Rudolph, "Robert F. Kennedy at Stellenbosch," *Communication Quarterly* (Summer, 1983), 205.211.

[6]See Karl R. Wallace, "The Substance of Rhetoric: Good Reasons," *Quarterly Journal of Speech* (October, 1963), 239-249; and Walter R. Fisher, "Toward a Logic of Good Reasons," *Quarterly Journal of Speech* (December, 1978), 376-384.

[7]Aristotle, *The Rhetoric,* in *The Basic Works of Aristotle,* ed. Richard McKeon (New York: Random House, 1941) 1356.

[8]It is very difficult to design experimental studies that permit broad generalizations about how we retain information from persuasive messages, but there is significant research showing that "major ideas are better comprehended and retained than details." See Wayne N. Thompson, *Quantitative Research in Public Address and Communication* (New York: Random House, 1967), 63-64. Experienced persuaders and teachers also know that a well-chosen example will sometimes stay with an audience longer than other kinds of details, such as clarifications or definitions. An example sometimes has the power to symbolize a complex point of view in a relatively simple form. For a theoretical discussion of this point, see Kenneth Burke's discussion of "synecdoche" in *A Grammar of Motives* (New York: Prentice-Hall, 1954), 507-508.

[9]Robert F. Flacke, "Acid Rain: Controlling the Problem," *Vital Speeches,* 1 November 1982, 49-50.

[10]Clarence Darrow, "Address to the Prisoners in Cook County Jail," in *The Rhetoric of No,* Second Edition, ed. Ray Fabrizio, Edith Karas, and Ruth Menmuir (New York: Holt, Rinehart and Winston, 1974), 140.

[11]Barbara S. Uehling, "Academics and Athletics," *Vital Speeches,* 1 June 1983, 506-507.

[12]As we noted in Chapter 7, audiences do not always respond to the presence of strong evidence as a basis for accepting claims, but we believe that ethical persuasion requires reasoning from available evidence. For more discussion of research in this area, see Michael Burgoon and Erwin P. Bettinghaus, "Persuasive Message Strategies," in *Persuasion: New Directions in Theory and Research,* ed. Michael E. Roloff and Gerald R. Miller (Beverly Hills: Sage Publications, 1980), 146-148.

[13]W. Ann Reynolds, "What is Right with Our Public Schools?" in *Representative American Speeches: 1983-1984,* ed. Owen Peterson (New York: H.W. Wilson, 1984), 16-17.

[14]Newton Minow, "The Vast Wasteland," in Glen E. Mills, *Reason in Controversy* (Boston: Allyn and Bacon, 1964), 271-282.

[15]There is surprisingly little research on how audiences respond to various tactics for introducing controversial topics to audiences. For a dated, but useful, survey of research on introductions, see Gary Cronkhite, *Persuasion: Speech and Behavioral Change* (New York: Bobbs-Merrill, 1969), 192-195.

[16]Ken Lonnquist, "Ghosts," in *Contemporary American Speeches*, Fourth Edition, ed. Wil A. Linkugel, R.R. Allen, and Richard Johannesen (Dubuque, IA: Kendall-Hunt, 1978), 178.

[17]Sally Webb, "On Mousetraps," in *Contemporary American Speeches*, ed. Will A. Linkugel, R.R. Allen, and Richard Johannesen (Belmont, CA: Wadsworth, 1965), 216.

[18]"Transcript of President Reagan's Address Broadcast to the Soviet Union," *The New York Times*, 10 November 1985, A18.

[19]Anson Mount, "The Playboy Philosophy—Pro," in Linkugel et al., *Contemporary American Speeches*, Fourth Edition, 182.

[20]Raymond S. Rodgers, "The Rhetoric of the NRA," *Vital Speeches*, 1 October 1983, 759.

[21]Larry R. Gerlach, "Sport as Part of Our Society," in *Representative American Speeches, 1983-1984*, 106-107.

[22]Tom Wicker, "A Disintegrating Story," *The New York Times*, September 3, 1985, A21. Another *New York Times* reporter has written a well-documented study that convincingly argues that the plane was not on a spy mission. See Seymour M. Hersh, *The Target is Destroyed* (New York: Random House, 1986).

[23]Richard Hofstadter, *The Paranoid Style in American Politics* (New York: Vintage, 1967), 29-31.

[24]Murray Sayle, "KE007: A Conspiracy of Circumstance," *The New York Review of Books*, 25 April 1985, 46.

[25]Thomas Maertens, "Tragedy of Errors," *Foreign Service* (September, 1985), 31.

[26]Thomas Maertens, "KAL 007—Key Questions and Answers," undated mimeograph.

[27]Sayle, 47.

[28]Sayle, 48.

[29]J. Jeffrey Auer, "The Persuasive Speaker and His Audience," in *The Rhetoric of Our Times*, ed. J. Jeffrey Auer (New York: Appleton-Century-Crofts, 1969), 272.

[30]Otis M. Walter and Robert L. Scott, *Thinking and Speaking*, Fifth Edition (New York: Macmillan, 1984), 292-293. (Our emphasis.)

[31]Cronkhite, 192-193.

[32]Marc Antony's Funeral Oration," in *The Dolphin Book of Speeches*, ed. George W. Hibbitt (New York: Dolphin, 1965), 10-11.

[33]Estimates that reveal our constant exposure to persuasive messages are fascinating. In *How to Talk Back to Your Television Set* [(New York: Bantam, 1970), 11], former FCC Commissioner Nicholas Johnson estimates that the average 65-year-old, American male will have spent the equivalent of *nine full years of his life* in front of a television set. In *Processing the News* [(New York: Longman, 1984), 1], Doris Graber notes that available news sources on just one

day present a wealth of material that would tax even the most committed news junkie: "between 50 to 100 pages of newsprint...25 to 50 stories served up at dinner and bedtime by national and local television newscasts, plus assorted bulletins on radio throughout the day, not to mention news magazines and journals...."

[34]For an interesting discussion of strategies for increasing resistance to persuasion, see Gerald R. Miller and Michael Burgoon, *New Techniques of Persuasion* (New York: Harper and Row, 1973), 18-44.

[35]Arthur R. Cohen, *Attitude Change and Social Influence* (New York: Basic Books, 1964), 122.

[36]For a review of recent research, see Raymond S. Ross, *Understanding Persuasion*, Second Edition (Englewood Cliffs, NJ: Prentice-Hall, 1985), 147-149.

[37]Carl Hovland, Arthur A. Lumsdaine, and Fred D. Sheffield, "The Effects of Presenting 'One Side' Versus 'Both Sides' in Changing Opinions on a Controversial Subject," in *Experiments in Persuasion*, ed. Ralph L. Rosnow and Edward J. Robinson (New York: Academic Press, 1967), 224-225.

[38]Hovland, Lumsdaine, and Sheffield, 225.

[39]Thompson, 70.

[40]Carl I. Hovland, ed. *The Order of Presentation in Persuasion* (New Haven: Yale, 1957), 130.

[41]Hovland, *Order of Presentation*, 132-138.

[42]William Safire, *Before the Fall* (New York: Doubleday, 1975), 530.

Questions and Projects for Further Study

1. In discussing "one-sided" versus "two-sided" presentations, the authors note that there is no inherent ethical problem in focusing on only one side of an issue. Agree or disagree with the authors citing real or hypothetical examples to support your point of view.

2. As an exercise in generating "good reasons" for an assertion, (1) write a thesis statement that presents an attitude that a partner *disagrees* with, and (2) identify two or three good reasons in support of the thesis. These are steps 3 and 4 in the six-step sequence for writing a persuasive speech. Working alone, write down the strongest case that you.can, for example:

   Thesis: Women should have to register for the draft just like men.
   I. If women want true equal rights, they should have equal obligations, including military service.
   II. Women today could handle most of the combat positions that men occupy.
   III. As the space program has shown, women may actually have physical skills (such as making precise manual adjustments) that are slightly better than those of men.

   Ask your "hostile" colleague questions about the "bare bones" logical structure you have developed. Your questions may include the following: Does this seem like a strong argument? If not, where are the flaws? Do you accept any of the good reasons? If so, does your acceptance of a good reason make you feel uncomfortable about rejecting the thesis? Is there a major objection that the outline overlooks? Is there any good reason I could cite that would change your attitude toward the thesis?

3. Locate and analyze the evidence used (or missing) in the arguments of a newspaper columnist. Some good examples of nationally syndicated writers include Ellen Goodman, Mike Royko, Jimmy Breslin, James Reston, James Kilpatrick, William Buckley, and David Broder. Identify the *kinds of evidence* the writer employs using the categories developed in this chapter, and the *types of sources* cited by the columnist using the categories developed in Chapter 7.

4. Amplification is an important type of development in almost any message. Write vivid hypothetical examples (of one or two paragraphs) to amplify three of the following overly familiar contentions:

   Enormous medical costs can ruin a family.

Higher education today is still a matter of privilege rather than right.

Today's children are tomorrow's adults.

Foreign travel is the best form of education.

Americans watch too much television.

5. Considering our comments on "good" and "bad" delivery, analyze and evaluate a persuasive presentation (i.e., at a campus forum, in Congress over cable television's C-SPAN, in church, or in a persuasion class). Some questions to consider: What kind of notes is the speaker using? Are the notes a help or a hindrance in promoting successful communication with the audience? If the speaker were to ask you, what could you suggest to improve his or her delivery?

6. Good examples of contemporary speeches can be found in the weekly periodical *Vital Speeches* and the yearly compilation *Representative American Speeches.* Using one of these sources, locate a persuasive speech that contains an especially effective introduction. Explain why you think the introduction was successful in preparing the audience to listen to the speaker's ideas.

Additional Reading

Auer, J. Jeffrey. "The Persuasive Speaker and His Audience." In *The Rhetoric of Our Times.* Ed. J. Jeffrey Auer, 255-276. New York: Appleton-Century-Crofts, 1969.

Burgoon, Michael; and Erwin P. Bettinghaus. "Persuasive Message Strategies." In *Persuasion: New Directions in Theory and Research,* 141-169. Beverly Hills: Sage Publications, 1980.

Clark, Ruth Ann. *Persuasive Messages.* New York: Harper and Row, 1984.

Cohen, Arthur R. *Attitude Change and Social Influence.* New York: Basic Books, 1964.

Hovland, Carl I., ed. *The Order of Presentation in Persuasion.* New Haven: Yale, 1957.

Ilardo, Joseph A. *Speaking Persuasively.* New York: Macmillan, 1981.

Miller, Gerald R.; and Michael Burgoon. *New Techniques of Persuasion.* New York: Harper and Row, 1973.

Rosnow, Ralph L.; and Edward J. Robinson, eds. *Experiments in Persuasion.* New York: Academic Press, 1967.

Wallace, Karl R. "The Substance of Rhetoric: Good Reasons." *Quarterly Journal of Speech* 49 (1963): 239-249.

Walter, Otis M.; and Robert L. Scott. *Thinking and Speaking,* Fifth Edition. New York: Macmillan, 1984.

12

Interpersonal Persuasion

 OVERVIEW

We have the capacity for controlling and choosing among alternative patterns of communication behaviors. By understanding the interactive, on-going, process nature of interpersonal communication, it becomes possible to alter elements within the process with more predictable results.[1]

In Chapter 10, three levels of persuasion were identified: intra-personal, interpersonal, and public. We spend a great deal of time interacting face-to-face with others. Much of this interaction, whether among family, friends, or strangers, is purposeful and persuasive. It may be as simple as requesting someone to bring you a book, as important as asking someone to hire you, or as emotional as asking someone to marry you. Within the interpersonal context, persuasive efforts may be characterized as:[2]

1. *dynamic:* participants are both sending and receiving signals continually and simultaneously.
2. *interactive:* there is mutual influence and interdependence between the participants. Each person is constantly aware of the other and assumes the roles of both sender and receiver which involves constant adaptation and adjustment.
3. *proactive:* it involves the total person. Beliefs, attitudes, values, social background and previous transactions all influence the nature of the interaction.
4. *contextual:* environmental and situational factors influence the interaction.
5. *intense:* content of the interactions is most often personal, intimate, and revealing thus producing the risks of rejection, withdrawal, exposure, and even weakness.

In this chapter, we are going to investigate interpersonal persuasion in the arenas of interviewing, sales, and conflict. These areas maximize the persuasive potential as outlined above.

Interpersonal Persuasion

Nearly all the various theories, strategies, and tactics of persuasion are applicable to any level or context of human communication. They may differ, however, in terms of degree and effectiveness. The forms of dyadic (two-person) communication range from the most social (intimate) to the most formal (interview) to the most stressful (interrogation). Within these areas, persuasive strategies and tactics may range from subtle to overt, from rational to psychological, and from verbal to nonverbal.

Dan Rothwell and James Costigan recognize three distinct levels of interpersonal communication: instrumental, manipulative, and expressive.[3] Persuasion plays a role on each level. The *instrumental* level of interpersonal communication is directive in nature. The communication is primarily one-way. It is on this level that much business is conducted. The superior, or boss, conveys information, establishes goals, and assigns tasks. The communication is task oriented requiring little or no sustained interaction. The question of compliance is not an issue. Discussion focuses on methods of task completion. Thus, on the instrumental level most of the persuasive activities rely upon the elements of power, credibility, authority, information, rational argument and negotiation. The *manipulative* level attempts to seduce favors, action, or consensus with other individuals. Persuasive activities, while incorporating those of the instrumental level, also include more subtle and psychological appeals. From the receiver's standpoint, the motives of the persuader may be hidden. For example, in a business setting individuals may lobby for project support, extra help, or pay raises. Cooperation with others results in more efficient task performance and thus job security. Such a perspective implies that many of our actions are self-motivated rather than other-motivated. On the *expressive* level, individuals share their thoughts, ideas, and feelings through more creative and artistic forms of communication. Through novels, poems, paintings, and music, authors express concerns, articulate issues, and rally support. However, a great deal of literary and artistic work espouses a social critique, perspective, or ideology; rarely is art today purely esthetic.

There are two basic dimensions of the interpersonal communication process that reveal persuasive elements. The first deals with the cognitive or rational processes. Within the interaction, there are planned, inherent persuasive strategies to be executed. Elements of these strategies include language choice, attitudes, logic, and credibility. Most interactions are purposeful; the parties have a goal or business to accomplish. During the encounter, information, opinion, and action will be exchanged. Information shared may be incomplete, inaccurate, or biased. Opinions expressed may be unwarranted based upon the information presented. The actions or behavior desired may reveal the persuader's motives.

To illustrate the cognitive or rational dimension of the interpersonal communication process, suppose you wanted to buy a new car. In order to do so, you must first sell your old car. Within the sales pitch, how much information do you share—mileage, motor size, oil usage, miles per gallon, prior accidents, etc.? What type of opinions will you offer about the car's condition, treatment, value, etc.? Will you attempt to sell the car by placing an ad in the paper or offer it to your friends or acquaintances? As the example reveals, on the rational level there are many decisions one must make that influence the degree of persuasiveness of the message.

The second dimension of interpersonal communication with persuasive potential involves the relational processes. Relational processes include the human needs for inclusion, control and affection.[4] The inclusion issue addresses the degree of acceptance of individuals by one another. If one feels unaccepted, it is natural to attempt to create identification and to relate to another person. In any interaction, the element of control may rotate or may be dominated by a single individual. Control can be relevant to items discussed or might include behavior manipulation. The affection issue includes how people feel about other individuals. There are obvious factors of persuasion that emerge from this dimension. We know that it is easier to persuade someone if they know us, trust us, and like us.

To continue with the car example above, if you were going to sell the car to a stranger, the first part of the interaction would be to establish trust and identification. You must persuade the person that you are honest and have nothing to hide; the potential buyer must convince you that funds are available to purchase the car. You would also, for the sake of inclusion, emphasize similarities and commonalities such as mutual friends or experiences shared by you and the potential buyer.

With this overview in mind, it is useful to investigate interpersonal persuasion more fully in the contexts of interviewing, sales, and conflict.

The Interview

It is possible to argue that nearly all dyadic communication is a form of interviewing. Even in social conversation with another person there is the rotation of roles and the exchange of information that provides the basis for future transactions and behavior. However, here we are referring to a more formal, prescribed form of dyadic communication.

Charles Stewart and William Cash define interviewing as "a process of dyadic communication with a predetermined and serious purpose designed to interchange behavior and usually involving the asking and answering of questions."[5] The key concepts of this definition lie in the words "predetermined and serious purpose." Thus, according to Stewart and Cash, an interview is a formal communication transaction where one or both of the parties have specific behavioral objectives to accomplish (i.e., altering a belief, attitude, or action). Even "mini-interviews" — those that seek to elicit the opinions of colleagues, etc. — may mask a persuasive intent. The questioner may appear to have an "open mind" but may, in reality, have no intention of accepting the interviewee's position.

In an interview situation, there are the dual roles of interviewer and interviewee. These roles, however, are interchangeable. In fact, a really good interview is one where the participants freely rotate between the roles. Without such an exchange, participants sacrifice power, control, and personal motives. This perspective recognizes that each participant in an interview has a purpose and thus needs to prepare for the encounter. The rest of the discussion is directed to the roles of both the interviewer and the interviewee.

There are many types of interviews: informational, persuasive, employment, appraisal, or counseling, to name only a few. The differences distinguishing each type are the general purposes and contexts of the interviews. Most interviews employ strategies and tactics found in other persuasive contexts, such as public speaking and advertising. Before entering an interview you should analyze thoroughly all the elements. What should be accomplished, what can be expected, how can you best present yourself? Many of the suggestions provided in this book relating to other persuasive topics can be used in your analysis (see Chapter 11, in particular).

Minimally, you should analyze the persuadee, situation and topic, and then carefully develop appropriate strategies and tactics. In terms of the persuadee, you should reflect upon the person's values and background in order to gain insight into possible motivation. The goal is to understand better how the receiver will perceive the situation. You will then be better able to develop strong arguments and appeals. Attention to the situation of the interview is also important. When and where the interview takes place will impact such persuasive elements as attention, control, and length of interview. Finally, you should spend as much time preparing the content of the interview as you would a public presentation. You should structure your argument carefully by identifying key appeals and by supporting your ideas with examples and evidence.

Stewart and Cash suggest a basic structure to follow for a

persuasive interview.[6] In the opening, it is important to develop rapport with the other party. The goal is to establish an open climate where there can be free exchange of dialogue and information. Feelings of trust and mutual goodwill between the participants are important. A brief explanation of the purpose and nature of the interview will provide a foundation for the interchange to follow.

In the body of the interview, Stewart and Cash recommend preparing a clear and concise statement of the need or problem being confronted. This should be followed by a point-by-point development of the reasons and causes for the problem or need. As with a public or written presentation, specific information and evidence should be provided to support arguments. Throughout this portion of the interview, it is useful to obtain agreement periodically from the interviewee to the problem, causes, and information presented. Finally, you should present solutions and evaluate each one by providing advantages and disadvantages. Obviously the goal is to get agreement on the best or preferred solution.

In the closing portion of the interview, it is important to summarize what has been discussed and to review agreements reached. At this point, you should obtain a final agreement and commitment from the interviewee to the solution and course of action. Finally, it is a good idea to arrange for a follow-up interview. This is useful to establish rapport once again and to check the status of commitment expressed throughout the interview.

This brief overview of interviewing indicates the importance of persuasion in other forms of communication. The key element in all communication is planning and preparation.

Sales

James Engel argues that selling is a "special form of interpersonal communication."[7] The fact is that we are all salespeople advocating a specific position, idea, service, or product. Regardless of occupation, anyone who is successful is an effective salesperson. As with interviewing, the basic appeals, strategies and tactics of persuasion are essential to successful sales.

The key concern in sales (and all persuasive situations) is the potential customer. Spencer Johnson and Larry Wilson, authors of the popular The One Minute Sales Person, state that one must not forget that "behind every sale is a person," and the sole purpose of selling anything is "to help people get the good feelings they want about what they bought and about themselves."[8] They describe the "wonderful paradox" of selling where "you will have more fun and enjoy more financial success when you stop trying to get what *you* want and start helping other people get what *they* want."[9] This perspective defines salespeople as problem solvers attempting to meet other people's needs, wants, and desires.

An interesting approach to sales is provided by Theodore Levitt in *The Marketing Imagination.*[10] He argues that expectations are what people buy—not things. These expectations encompass aspects of trust, service, and satisfaction. The "act" of buying changes the buyer. Although the active, intense aspects of the purchase end for the seller, the process just begins for the buyer.

As Figure 12.1 shows, before the sale the seller has high expectations and real hope of completing the sale, whereas the buyer may be unaware of the product or impending sale or may have a vague or general interest in the product. Levitt argues that the most intense stage of the sale for the seller is convincing the prospect to buy. During this stage, the buyer is testing arguments and confirming desire. The culmination of the sale reduces tension for the seller but increases tension for the buyer. Upon the sale, the seller has met the prime objective and can begin to focus on the next sales opportunity. The personal relationship has virtually ended for the seller. The buyer, however, seeks commitment and affirmation of expectations and promises made. For Levitt, relationship selling means understanding the process from the viewpoint of the buyer and consciously spending time after the sale to confirm and reassure the buyer that the "right" decision was made.

In sales, therefore, the goal is to meet a need of the buyer. This is done in two ways. First, the product or service must be couched in human motivational terms. Edwin Greif provides eight classifications of buyer motivations: profit and thrift, safety and protection, ease and convenience, pride and prestige, sex and romance, love and affection, adventure and excitement, and performance and durability.[11] Thus, whatever the product or service, the task is to rationalize the purchase based upon one of the motives listed. The second way to address the needs of buyers is to discuss product benefits. Each product feature has a corresponding benefit. For example, if a car has a larger engine that generates more power, the benefits to be discussed are greater passing safety, less strain from driving, longer-lasting engine, less repair costs, etc. In short, benefits sell products, not features.

Finally, the steps and preparation for a sales presentation are very similar to other persuasive endeavors.

1. *Pre-approach:* The buyer becomes familiar with product features and benefits, and the seller learns about target customers. Sales questions and statements for an automobile would probably include topics such as specific features, buyer

Figure 12.1

Characteristics of Relationship Management

A. Stages and Objects of the Sale

Stage of Sale	Seller	Buyer
1. Before	Real hope	Vague need
2. Romance	Hot & heavy	Testing & hopeful
3. Sale	Fantasy—bed	Fantasy—board
4. After	Looks elsewhere for next sale	"You don't care."
5. Long after	Indifferent	"Can't this be made better?"
6. Next sale	"How about a new one?"	"Really?"

B. When the First Sale is Made

The Seller	The Buyer
Objective achieved	Judgment postponed, applies test of time
Selling stops	Shopping continues
Focus goes elsewhere	Focus on purchase, wants affirmation of expectations
Tension released	Tension increased
Relationship reduced or ended	Relationship intensified, commitment made

C. Things Affecting Relationships

Good Things	Bad Things
Initiate positive phone calls	Make only callbacks
Make recommendations	Make justifications
Candor in language	Accommodative language
Use phone	Use correspondence
Show appreciation	Wait for misunderstandings
Make service suggestions	Wait for service requests
Use "we" problem-solving language	Use "owe-us" legal language
Get to problems	Only respond to problems
Use jargon/shorthand	Use long-winded communications
Personality problems aired	Personality problems hidden
Talk of "our future together"	Talk about making good on the past
Routinize responses	Fire drill/emergency responsiveness
Accept responsiblity	Shift blame
Plan the future	Rehash the past

It is useful to remember that motives, emotions, and attitudes differ between buyers and sellers throughout a transaction.

budget, buyer auto usage, and exploration of buyer motives for purchasing a new car.

2. *Approach:* In this step, the seller designs sale messages based upon customer type and needs. The assumption here is that varied arguments and benefit emphases are needed for different customers who have expressed particular needs, desires or problems. If a middle-aged business executive was buying a car, the salesperson would emphasize such factors as auto luxury, comfort, status, design, and style. If the buyer was seeking a second family car, the salesperson would probably emphasize cost, reliability, gas mileage, and quality.

3. *Presentation:* This step refers to the face-to-face interaction with the buyer. The presentation should have an appropriate introduction that builds rapport and uncovers customer needs, a body that argues product benefits, and a conclusion that addresses objections and closes the sale. This is the most spontaneous and reactive phase of the sales pitch. The presentation phase is critical to the success of any salesperson.

4. *Follow-up:* Depending upon the size of purchase, this phase refers to showing appreciation and providing reassurance or confirmation of the buyer's decision. Here the salesperson acknowledges the wisdom of the selection, the value of the product, and projects a vision of customer enjoyment and satisfaction.

We would be remiss if we did not highlight some of the problematic areas of sales in relation to traditional persuasive theory. Especially in a democratic society, persuasion is based upon the concept of informed choice. Despite the phrase *caveat emptor* (let the buyer beware), the ethical burden is upon the persuader to ensure that products are fairly presented. There are also other issues to consider. Does the seller really *believe* in the product? Are the products offered to solve real needs or transparent needs? Does the buyer really need the product or service? These are a sampling of issues that sellers should address. In terms of persuasion, there is little difference between the selling of ideas and the selling of products. Both are important to our society and utilize the same "tools" of persuasion.

Conflict

There is a fine line between conflict and persuasion. Resistance to persuasion can lead to open conflict just as open conflict can lead to attempts to persuade. The seeds of conflict are always present in human communication. Persuasion often assumes that there will be winners and losers, elements of compromise and acquiescence, and some degree of conflict. Conflict is not an external reality but a mutually shared or agreed upon attitude and resulting behavior. In other words, participants have actually "agreed" to disagree. They have consciously labeled their differences as *conflict*. For example, even among nations, there is not war until someone in authority labels or declares certain acts as war. It is through communication that we engage in conflict and sometimes resolve it.

There are several different kinds of conflict.[12] Pseudoconflicts are those where people believe their differing goals cannot be simultaneously achieved. For example, being confronted with a choice between joining friends for pizza and writing a paper is not really a conflict. One could write the paper first and join friends later, leave friends early to write the paper, or exercise countless other options. Pseudoconflicts are sometimes a result of misunderstanding or interpretation. If parents intervened to dictate that you could join your friends when the paper was finished, would that mean when it was outlined, written, or typed? In such instances, solutions to the conflicts seldom require major compromise and provide "win-win" opportunities for the individuals. Content conflicts are the most common type of conflict involving disagreement over facts, definitions, goals, or interpretation of information. More interaction between the parties is critical in solving content conflicts. More interaction often results in mutual understanding and the realization that the differences are not as great as originally perceived. Ego conflicts can become the most harmful. Such conflicts are based upon the personalities of the participants. In a sense, each side gets pleasure out of disagreeing with the other side. Participants view themselves as equals in power, knowledge and expertise. The participants feel compelled to advocate and defend specific views or arguments. More interaction alone will have little impact upon solving ego conflicts. Value conflicts are the most difficult to solve and, depending upon the values in conflict, can be the most intense or violent.

It would be a mistake to view all conflict as bad. Conflict can establish social interactional boundaries, reduce tensions, clarify roles, objectives, or differences, and can provide the basis for negotiation and continued interaction. Gerald Miller finds conflict desirable because conflict can engender creativity as well as produce some form of human relationship or contact.[13] Conflict, according to Saul Alinski, is an essential element of life. He asserts, "Life is conflict and in conflict you're alive."[14]

In terms of your own persuasive efforts, there are specific communication styles or behaviors that encourage conflict and thus should be avoided. The use of value statements makes an audience defensive rather than open to your arguments. Therefore, avoid labeling actions of the receiver as bad, silly, crazy, etc. Second, avoid presenting "all or nothing at all" distinctions or alternatives. It is best to make suggestions and offer solutions without implicit threats if rejected. Third, avoid name calling and personal attacks. Although you may be angry, you want to keep the lines of communication open as well as the minds of people who have not firmly committed to one action. Insulting friends or acquaintances will surely lose allies. Fourth, avoid speaking in broad generalities. Always provide specific facts and examples to support arguments. Finally, avoid emotional verbal and nonverbal communications. Emotional outbursts dilute arguments by redirecting attention to the outbursts rather than the arguments. Aggression, hostility, tension, or rivalry seldom help in accomplishing long-term goals and objectives.

There are numerous suggestions for managing conflict. They generally revolve around good practices of persuasion and human communication. For example, it is important to accept the other party as a person. This recognizes that they have feelings and pressures as well as you do. This also helps us to look for commonalities rather than differences. Therein lies the basis for compromise. Indeed we want to keep our focus on the problem descriptive and not judgmental, making sure that our words match reality. As good persuaders we should check frequently for validity to confirm that we are being understood and eliciting the right interpretation. Finally, by projecting a positive attitude, persuadees will more likely grant a fair hearing.

Solving a conflict is not unlike solving any other communication problem. First, you must analyze the conflict. Second, assess the causes of conflict. Third, develop possible solutions and courses of action. Fourth, select the best solution. Fifth, implement the course of action or solution.

From this brief overview, we can characterize conflict as inevitable. Depending upon the style of communication chosen, conflict can be either harmful or beneficial. It may increase or decrease and will sometimes be irresolvable.

Summary

If you read this book in the order presented, there is very little "new" information shared relevant to interpersonal persuasion. Basic theories and concepts of persuasion are equally valid in the interpersonal context. The foundation for all persuasion is preparation and a thorough understanding of the audience—whether it is an audience of one or of millions.

Informally, we engage in interpersonal persuasion daily and much more frequently than we recognize. We investigated the more formal forms of interpersonal persuasion in the discussion of interviews and sales. These forms of interpersonal persuasion are more similar than different. They rely upon the principles identified and discussed throughout the book.

Conflict often results from prolonged, intense efforts of interpersonal persuasion. Conflict is often viewed as a negative concept. Frequently, a negative reaction results not from the contention but from the quality of the communication exchanged. The most important aspect to remember about conflict is that it must be managed. If we apply the knowledge we have gained about how to communicate effectively, we should be able to conduct our participation in interpersonal exchanges, including conflict, successfully.

Notes

¹Bobby Patton and Kim Giffin, *Interpersonal Communication* (New York: Harper & Row, 1974), 45.

²Every book on interpersonal communication provides such characteristics with very little variation of concepts. See David Mortensen, *Communication: The Study of Human Interaction* (New York: McGraw-Hill, 1972), 13-21.

³Dan Rothwell and James Costigan, *Interpersonal Communication* (Columbus, OH: Charles Merrill Publishing Co., 1975), 20-23.

⁴William Schultz, "The Postulate of Interpersonal Needs," in *Messages*, ed. Jean Civikly (New York: Random House, 1977), 174-84.

⁵Charles Stewart and William Cash, *Interviewing* (Dubuque, IA: Wm. C. Brown, 1974), 174-84.

⁶Ibid, 129-33.

⁷James Engel et al., *Promotional Strategy* (Homewood, IL: Richard Irwin, 1983), 407.

⁸Spencer Johnson and Larry Wilson, *The One Minute Sales Person* (New York: William Morrow & Co., 1984), 17 and 25.

⁹Ibid, 21.

¹⁰Theodore Levitt, *The Marketing Imagination* (New York: The Free Press, 1983), 111-26.

¹¹Edwin Greif, *Personal Salesmanship* (Reston, VA: Reston Publishing Co., 1974), 32.

¹²Kathleen Verder and Rudolph Verder, *Inter-act* (Belmont, CA: Wadsworth, 1977), 150-54.

¹³Gerald Miller, "Introduction: Conflict Resolution Through Communication," in *Conflict Resolution Through Communication*, ed. Fred Jandt (New York: Harper & Row, 1973), 3.

¹⁴Sual Alinski, *Rules for Radicals* (New York: Vintage Books, 1969), vii.

Questions and Projects for Further Study

1. You have a 1984 Pontiac Firebird automobile you wish to sell. Develop the sales appeals and arguments for persuading a friend, a stranger, a middle-aged man or a woman to purchase the car. How do the appeals differ and why?

2. You are the manager of a department at a large clothing store. Prepare questions for a job interview, a work appraisal interview for a "problem" employee, and an employee termination interview. How do these interviews differ in strategies and appeals?

3. From your own experience, provide an example of a pseudoconflict, a content conflict, and an ego-conflict.

4. You have been working in a clothing store for one year. Prepare arguments you would use in asking for a raise.

5. Discuss the ethical issues, dimensions, and implications of:
   a. attempts of selling a $50 Bible to a family of six with an income of $10,000 a year;
   b. attempts to sell a used car that had been in a major accident and recently repaired.

Additional Reading

Frost, Joyce; and William Wilmot. *Interpersonal Conflict.* Dubuque, IA: W.C. Brown, 1978.

Giffin, Kim; and Robert Patton, eds. *Basic Readings in Interpersonal Communication.* New York: Harper & Row, 1971.

Jandt, Fred. *Conflict Resolution Through Communication.* New York: Harper & Row, 1973.

Knapp, Mark; and Gerald Miller, eds. *Handbook of Interpersonal Communication.* Beverly Hills: Sage, 1985.

Miller, Gerald, ed. *Explorations in Interpersonal Communication.* Beverly Hills: Sage, 1976.

Miller, Gerald; and Herbert Simons. *Perspectives on Communication in Social Conflict.* Englewood Cliffs, NJ: Prentice-Hall, 1974.

Index